FROM
NOTHING
TO NEARLY
EVERYTHING

FROM
NOTHING
TO NEARLY
EVERYTHING

LINA BUTTICE-JANOVITZ

TATE PUBLISHING
AND ENTERPRISES, LLC

Published by Tate Publishing & Enterprises, LLC
127 E. Trade Center Terrace | Mustang, Oklahoma 73064 USA
1.888.361.9473 | www.tatepublishing.com

Tate Publishing is committed to excellence in the publishing industry. The company reflects the philosophy established by the founders, based on Psalm 68:11,
"The Lord gave the word and great was the company of those who published it."

Published in the United States of America

ISBN: 978-1-63122-064-7
1. Biography & Autobiography / General
2. Biography & Autobiography / Personal Memoirs
14.02.20

DEDICATION

I dedicate this memoir to the two most influential men in my life—Uncle Peppino Fantauzzo, who was there for me in my young years, and my late husband who then fulfilled my life.

ACKNOWLEDGMENTS

I am very grateful to three people, James Lannoo and Dina and Leo Horowitz for their valuable time in helping me bring my memoir to completion.

Since English is my second language and is not flawless, James Lannoo, a former English teacher, was particularly helpful in editing the first draft of my manuscript.

Dina Horowitz, my best friend, encouraged me to pursue my sudden idea of writing my personal history. She then spent numberless hours editing my memoir and made many valuable suggestions, comments, and recommendations in order to enhance my narrative. Because I valued Dina's command of the English language and her deep intuition into literature, any recommendations she made I appreciatively implemented. The manuscript was also enhanced by the additional editing of her husband, Leo.

CONTENTS

PREFACE

Following the death of my husband on July 17, 2009, like in a storm, I was assailed by intense despair; I had lost the man who had changed my entire life. However, as the months went by, I began looking for something overpowering in order to keep my mind engaged for the desolation and loneliness were very devastating.

Indifferently, I started leafing through and reading here and there on the former First Lady Barbara Bush's memoir when suddenly it came to my mind that, with so much personal experience, maybe I could write mine, but that was just a thought. Then in a phone call with my friend Dina Horowitz, I told her about the idea of writing my personal history. She liked that and encouraged me to go ahead because putting down the experiences of my life, it would keep me fully engaged and consequently would help with the healing of my great loss.

Afterward, I decided to write my biography, but this was a huge project for the fact that I never kept any diary. In addition, I was now living in a foreign country where not many people really knew me. Anyhow, my memories were the only possession I had, and therefore, the following pages have been assembled on my best recollections.

INTRODUCTION

My name is Lina Janovitz, née Carmelina Butticé. I was born on Christmas day in 1931, and I have an incredible personal story, which up till now I have never discussed with anyone, especially the experience of my early years. Each chapter of this book contains a vivid description of periods in my life with captivating events that took place in unpredictable circumstances, and in the darkest periods, a gleam of hope was suddenly on the horizon.

As an underprivileged child, I was orphaned by both parents and left destitute. My possibilities to succeed in life were grim, and I understood that at a very early age. Nevertheless, I was determined to improve my situation, and so with a strong willpower, I overcame the many obstacles that I encountered along the way. It was not an easy path as the hardship seemed to be endless. In the end, with great satisfaction, I climbed the ladder, and my biography provides real astonishing evidence.

I think that reading this memoir can be boring for those who had a comfortable childhood. Others may be drawn to it by curiosity. But for those who find themselves, more or less, in the same circumstances, perhaps it can be inspirational.

Sicily - Casteltermini is my home town

MY BACKGROUND

Casteltermini—the town of my birth. It sits above a hilltop in the Sicilian province of Agrigento and is located about seventy kilometers southeast of Palermo. During the eighteenth and nineteenth century, the town encountered a major economic expansion due to the nearby location of extensive mineral deposits of rock salt and sulfur, which were mined by companies such as Cozzo-Dizi—employing over one thousand people—Italkali and Montecatini, as well as the factory of San Giuseppe that produced pastas. The town, which had a small theater, was populated by rich and poor alike, where craftsman as well as laborers together created a population that reached nearly twenty thousand in the years before my birth. Unfortunately, because of a number of mining disasters, the mines closed, and the town's economy began to be adversely effected, which in turn caused the population to decline. The current population is below nine thousand people.

The town itself, typical of sixteenth century feudal Italy, was steeped heavily in Christianity and was home to at least eight churches. Among the more notable of the eight churches were the Church of San Giuseppe, built in the architectural style of Sicilian Baroque, and the Church Madre that housed paintings and sculptures of famous artists and whose eighteenth-century façade made it stand out from all the other structures. In addition to the churches arrayed across the town was a large central square, Piazza Duomo, which not only commemorated fallen soldiers of the past wars with a monument but a place where Christianity and Sicily's ancient Moorish history intermingled. Here, many festivals were held, highlighted by parades with costumes and orchestras that brought the usually quiet town to life, attracting religious pilgrims and tourists. Besides the Christmas and Easter celebrations, there was the Sacra Della Croce Taratata festival, reenacting the confrontation of Christians and Muslims who had arrived in Sicily in the eleventh century. Another festival was Saint Calogero, which celebrated the ardent monk who came to Sicily from Caledonia to convert the Sicilian population to Christianity, and afterward, he became a venerated Sicilian saint because of the many miracles that the citizens received from him. The town's tradition was the barefooted pilgrimage to the church where San Calogero resided. This celebration always occurred at the end of August. It was very interesting to watch the believers, who had made the pledge to the Saint, walking from their homes to the sanctuary, elegantly dressed and carrying the shoes in their hands. Piazza Duomo was, most of all, a place for enjoying daily life. Here the townspeople could leisurely take a stroll or spend a pleasant time at the coffee house. This is the town I remember as I left for US in 1964.

FAMILY ROOTS

My father was Gaetano Butticé, the oldest son of Vincenzo Butticé and Carmelina Rizzo. Vincenzo Butticé grew up in a high-middle class family, which was well known and respected in town. They owned many properties, including a gunpowder factory that, in the old days, was a very lucrative business. However, once Vincenzo's parents died, my grandfather and some of his brothers lost everything due to their bad vices; they were gamblers and womanizers. Carmelina Rizzo, who was from an aristocratic family of Cammarata (Sicily), died very young, leaving six children—my father Gaetano, Caterina, Arcangela, Peppina,

Giuseppe, and Rosina. Later, my grandfather married Raimonda, the lady who was taking care of his children, and together they had a daughter, Marietta.

What I am writing now is what I was told by some of my relatives in my later teens. Once I had the opportunity to know all of them better, my grandfather, Vincenzo Butticé, was already dead. My grandfather was a very difficult and insensible man who commanded with an iron fist. His entire family was terrified of him and couldn't do anything about it. From childhood, the relationship between my father and his father was always troubled and became worse when my father refused to study. Later, my father started a small business, dealing with bicycles for rent. At that time, automobiles were rare, if any in town, so that trade was satisfactory. When my father wanted to marry my mother, my grandfather became furious because he considered the Butticé's family socially higher than the Fantauzzo's family. With or without his consent, my father married my mother, and I don't know if grandfather went to the wedding of his first son, probably not. For Grandfather, nobody was good enough to marry his children. Aunts Caterina and Peppina were fearful of their father's behavior and remained single because of him. Aunt Arcangela married Ferdinando Martorana; I don't know how her father approved it. Uncle Giuseppe, who became medical doctor, went to northern Italy to be far away from his father. Aunt Marietta married Enzo Ricotta when her father was already dead. I remember Aunt Caterina with affection for she was one of the best and caring aunts toward me and my brother.

My mother was Giuseppina Fantauzzo, the youngest daughter of Giovanni Fantauzzo and Rosina Caltagirone, and she grew up in a low working-class family. When her father died at a very young age, her mother remained a widow with six children—Vincenza, Silvestro, Vincenzo, Sigismondo, Peppino, and my mother. There was no inheritance, so the boys soon started to work to help their mother. In time, with hard work and great sacrifices, life improved for everybody. As matter of fact, some of them became prosperous business men.

In a very special and warm way, I want to give a brief description of Uncle Peppino. This wonderful man was my mother youngest brother, an individual of an incredible goodness, kindness, and sensibility. When I think of him, even now, my eyes fill with tears of emotion for he was the most caring and generous man I ever knew. He was like a real father to me. I thank God that he sent him during my young years. Peppino was married to Angelina Palumbo, and they had four children, Giovanni, Rosetta, Gino, and Lina. Giovanni, the oldest son, had the characteristics of his father, and up until now, I receive greetings from him on every holiday. Rosetta, the oldest daughter, was my favorite cousin and like a sister to me. Gino and Lina, both younger than me, were warm and kind individuals.

MY EARLY YEARS

My father died in May of 1936 at the age of forty-two after a long illness, leaving my mother, my brother Vincenzo, and me destitute. I remember him vaguely, so I cannot describe what kind of father he would have been. My mother was in her thirties when my father passed away. I imagine what she went through during that difficult period, what devastation and despair! After my father's death, my mother was compelled to look for work, but in Casteltermini, it was impossible to find a job with no skills, and especially for a woman. She had a cousin living in Palermo who offered her a job as a housekeeper, but that was just to take care of herself. There was no place for me and my brother in her home. The only one who could have helped us was my paternal grandfather, Vincenzo Butticé, but that was unrealistic because he was a cold and strange human being.

Soon, my mother had to make a fast and painful decision, so with a broken heart, she placed me in the Boccone del Povero orphanage in Casteltermini, and then through her cousin and her brother Peppino interventions, she found an institution for my brother in Palermo. It was a sad situation; the reality of the circumstances was terrible, and there was no other choice other than the fact that we all had to be separated, which turned out to be a separation for life. I remember when my mother brought me to the orphanage; her tears could not stop, especially when she was saying good-bye. I too cried a lot when she left me alone there. After a few days in the orphanage, my mother left for Palermo, taking Vincenzo with her. Now was my brother's turn to be separated from my mother. Fortunately, he was placed at the Salesians of Don Bosco in Palermo.

The Boccone del Povero orphanage in Casteltermini was one of the many institutions of the Missionary Servants. Its founder, the blessed Giacomo Cusmano, was a medical doctor, and years later, he became a priest and dedicated his life to helping people in need. He opened hospitals and nursing homes and worked with the neglected, the needy, and the orphans. He was a great man and became the "doctor of the poor" for his generosity and selflessness. The purpose of the organization was, and currently, is great, except when the nuns fail to execute their duty as "servants of the needy," which is the oath they make when ordained.

The Salesians of Don Bosco is a Catholic religious organization, very well known throughout the world for helping troubled youths. Its founder, St. John Bosco, was a priest who dedicated his life to instilling good behavior and giving an education accordingly to the boys' capability. The boys were orphans, from poor or rich families in need of a good upbringing. It was an excellent and prestigious institution, just appropriate for my rebellious brother. But he did not want to stay there. He felt like he was in prison, although this was a much better place than my orphanage. Anyway, he didn't have any other choice but to stay.

After waiting for days, weeks, months, and years in the orphanage, the hope to be reunited with my mother was completely gone.

Because of the distance—I was in Casteltermini, and she lived in Palermo—my mother came to visit me only a few times, and all the good-byes were filled with sadness. I remember once, my uncle came to pick me up, and we went to Palermo together by motorcycle. I was so excited and very happy because three things were happening: first, I was going to see my mother and spend a day with her; second, I was going out of the institution without the nuns; and third, I was traveling on my uncle's motorcycle, and sitting on the back was really something out of the ordinary.

It was February of 1939 when my mother returned to Casteltermini very sick, and Uncle Peppino (her brother) took care of her. I remember when she came to see me in the orphanage for the last time; she was inconsolable. A nun asked her what was wrong, and she brokenheartedly replied, "My little girl will be left with no parents" (la mia bambina rimarrá senza genitori). That was very painful! Then on April 28, my cousin Nino Castania came to the orphanage to take me to see my mother. Unfortunately, when I arrived at her bedside and called "Mamma," she didn't answer me as she was slipping away. On the morning of April 29, 1939, at the sound of the church's bells and counting how many tones there were, I suddenly said to a nun with an alarming voice, "My mother died!" At that time in my hometown, when somebody died, the church's bells gave an indication in the number of tones if it was a man or a woman who had passed away. This time, it was my mother. Afterward, the word *Mamma* vanished from my vocabulary, but the great loss left a thorn in my heart forever. As a matter of fact, until now, when I hear the popular Italian song "Mamma Son Tanto Felice" (Mom, I am so happy), it brings melancholic tears to my eyes.

My mother died of ovarian cancer at the age of thirty-eight and less than three years since the death of my father. I was seven and a half years old, and my brother was almost fourteen. I did not go to her funeral, but I was told that the entire town was at her memorial and my uncle Peppino provided for everything, including her burial in his family chapel that he had built years earlier. At that time, besides having four small children to take care of, Uncle Peppino had a struggling business, and he was also looking after his mother Rosina who was blind. Earlier, I remember telling the nuns that when my mother gets well, I will ask her to bring me a roasted chicken. That, for me, was a big thing, and subsequently, on the day of my mother's death, the nuns gave me a piece of roasted chicken.

THE ORPHANAGE

I want to start by giving a brief description of the place first. The orphanage was sustained by the town's people contributions, embroidery made by the girls, and some other income coming from different sources. The residences included twenty girls, eight elders, five nuns, and one gardener. The girls were from all backgrounds and ranged in age from two to twenty. The nuns, including the mother superior, were on rotation from other institutions. They stayed three to four years in one place, then new ones came. This change was sometimes good, sometimes bad. Sometimes, we had nice and kind nuns; other times, the nuns were not qualified to be in the position they held. Everything inside the place ran on schedules and with strict discipline.

Life began at 6 a.m. At the ringing of the bell, everyone was on their feet, made the bed, rushed to the lavatory (there was one toilet only for the girls), dressed up, and got ready for church. The nuns took care of the little children.

Every morning, a priest came to celebrate the Mass. So every day, we went to church, received the communion, and recited the prayers. Naturally, to get the communion, we had to be free of any sins; otherwise, we had to wait until the coming Friday to confess ours wrongdoings to the priest.

For breakfast, we had a meager meal consisting of a piece of bread with seasonal fruits, such as pears, or figs, or oranges or orange salad with olive oil and salt, and frankly speaking, I liked these lean breakfasts. After the war, we received powdered milk. For lunch, on weekdays, we had minestrone with a piece of bread. Every day, the minestrone varied according to the ingredients used. The food did not have any taste. Lunch was really bad. Anyway, after lunch, we had thirty minutes of free time. At 6 p.m., we recited the rosary while we were still working, and afterward, we went to have supper, which consisted of vegetable soup or a few olives or a piece of cheese, and a piece of bread. The dinner was okay too, and I liked it. Then we had some free time. On Sundays and holidays, the food was better, and we had more recreation time.

The daily activities depended on the season of the year, day of the week, and time of the day. There were several tasks to be performed, and the assignments were given according to the age and the capability of the girls, and some of the tasks were rotated weekly.

Our education included elementary school only. The teachers were the nuns or volunteers from outside, or when there were no educators available for that scholastic year, the girls were sent to the town's public schools. The public schools had a much better educational system, and the girls had to take part in the annual gymnastic exhibitions held in the town main square. For us, it was great to be exposed to a different environment. At the end of the scholastic year, for the first, third, and fifth grades, the girls were sent to the public schools for the examinations.

The Embroidery - A nun was in charge of teaching the girls and directing the embroidery projects. The town's people were bringing some dowry work to be made. In those days, the embroidery was in great fashion, and it was also producing some money for the orphanage. In due course, the embroidery was one of my main tasks because I had become one of the best. How did I reach this point? I was about eleven or twelve years, and I did not like the other assignments, so the only way out was learning the embroidery fast and proficiently. No child was left free to play, except the very young, age two to six. The girls were learning the elements of the embroidery at a very early age, and everyone had to stay at the same assigned seat in an absolutely silent room. Naturally, there were exceptions to the rules.

The Cleaning - During winter time was a hard job. With no gloves, putting our hands into the basin full of icy water to wash the mop was really painful, but we did it because that was one of the assigned tasks.

The Laundry - In those days, there were no machines to do the job, so the laundry was done by hand with no gloves. During winter time, the laundry was the hardest task of all, and it was reserved for those girls considered to be robust and strong. A day before, all the items that had to be washed were put in big cement containers for soaking, and the next morning, the water in the containers was icy cold. I cannot describe how terrible it was to wash by hand. Then we put the laundry in the garden to dry, and this was not fun either. I remember the sensation of those cold and strong winds while we were hanging the laundry to dry on the clothes lines! Thank God that the winter season was short! Then most of the ironing we did was for the nuns' clothes.

The Kitchen Work - This included helping the nun who was in charge of the cooking. Our work was usually washing pots and pans. The food for the nuns was very well prepared and was cooked separately from that of the girls. Anyway, this was one of my favorite tasks because I was able to steal and enjoy some of their food. In the afternoon, I had plenty of free time to do whatever I wanted. For me, spending time in the garden was the best place to be. There were many fruit trees such as figs and peaches. Some of the trees were tall, and I enjoyed climbing up to the top.

Part of the garden was at the orphanage building level, and the rest was in an ascending hill. It was fun to run up and down the hill. I remember once, I got tired from running, so when I reached the end of the alley, I sat on a big stone without looking at the top of it. I suddenly felt a pinch in my behind. I had just killed a lizard. For a few days, it was very uncomfortable to sit down, but I never said anything to anyone because I was ashamed.

The Upkeep of the Chapel - It was our job to maintain a spotless altar with fresh linen, polished brass candelabras, and flower vases properly kept. In addition, we had to make sure that the perpetual lantern didn't run out of oil, and there were enough wafers (ostia) and wine for the celebration of the mass. If there was a shortage, we made the wafers from scratch and then cut them with the appropriate shapes—the big for the Holy Mass and the small for the Communions. Anyway, for one girl, there was plenty of work to be done, including the setup of the altar for the religious ceremony.

The Church Choir - To be part of the choir, the girls naturally had to have good voices; otherwise, they were disqualified. Close to the religious holidays, there were the evening rehearsals in the church, and I was part of it.

The Theater - About twice a year, the orphanage entertained the town's people, and the purpose of it was to get more contributions. The performance was held either at the town's theater or at the orphanage, and because the orphanage was not equipped with a stage, a platform had to be built. The entertainment consisted of a dramatic play, which was always based on religious subjects. A comedy always ended the program so as to cheer up the audience. The performers were the orphans, and to pretend to be adults, we were dressed as grown-up people with special costumes, hairdos, and makeup. At that time, I was one of the tallest girls, so I always got one of the main parts to play. To learn the part by heart, it was tough due to the fact that we had to study it on our free time. Only the rehearsal went on a scheduled time. When the day arrived to go on the stage to perform in public, I was scared; my legs were trembling, but then I was encouraged by the clapping and whistling of the audience. Anyway, the great satisfaction was at the end when the spectators gave a prolonged applause. How strange and amusing it was when I looked at myself in the mirror and saw a completely different person. It was like living on another planet, and that gave me a pleasant feeling.

The Day Nursery - Working parents brought their infants to the orphanage to have peace of mind. This task was okay for us girls and lucrative for the orphanage. Sometimes, I was assigned to take care of the children, and my job was to let them play, eat, sing, and sleep.

The Religion - In the Catholic Church, in order to receive First Communion and afterward confirmation, it was necessary that we study the catechism to learn in a systematic way the Christian religion, starting from the New Testament to the present time. This education was given once a week during school hours. I remember the big influence that it had on me when the nuns were telling us stories of the life of some saints who faced the martyrdom for their faith. For example, long ago, there were girls from noble and rich families who refused to marry noble pagan men. As a consequence of their rejection, they were sent to prison and tortured because they were denounced for being Christians. Such was the case of St. Lucy from Syracuse, Sicily, whose eyes were extracted with the fork for refusing to marry a pagan noble-man, and he, for revenge, denounced her for being a Christian. For many other saints, the descriptions were so vivid that they became very interesting and beautiful at the same time to the point that I was ready to die for the faith. Young people are very vulnerable when an indoctrination is inculcated in their minds at an early age; although, I don't think the nuns tried to indoctrinate us to that point. Moreover, talking about death and eternal life was at times very discouraging. In fact, I was thinking why I had to study and work hard if I have to die. Realistically speaking, yes, it is true that we all have to die, and because we don't know when, it is essential that we do the best and keep going.

The Evening Free Time - During the summer months, we had the task of watering the flowers in the garden. We filled buckets of water from a basin and sprinkled the plants. It often took all our free time, and that was not pleasant because after we finished the job, it was time to go to bed. Winter time was different. A few of us girls often went to see the storyteller lady who was one of the orphanage's old folks residing on the second floor. There, we sat on the floor around her to listen intensely. She was really terrific! Sometimes, she could not finish the long story, so we went back the following evening to hear the conclusion. Listening to the storyteller was fantastic because it permitted us to live in an imaginary world.

The Frigid Temperature - During the winter season, the cold temperature was unbearable, and there was no place to go to warm up. In those days, many buildings, including the orphanage, had no heat. I remember a few occasions (I think I was about seven or eight years old) when I went to bed with my shoes on because it was too painful to remove them for the fact that the wounds on my toes were adhering to the inside lining of the shoes. It was at night that, during my deep sleep, the nuns took my shoes off, but they never asked me why I went to bed in that way; they understood. Only in the morning did I notice my bare feet and saw some blood on my bed linen. For many years, the extreme cold temperature was one of my biggest problems, and every year, I got the chilblains on my toes and fingers. I also remember when the big skylight in the center of the orphanage building was covered with heavy snow; the entire area was dark and very depressing.

Christmas Time - The orphans had a better time and good food too because the meals had just been prepared for the holidays. On Christmas Eve, we played bingo until 11 p.m., and it was especially fun when we were winning something. Then we went to church for the midnight mass. Afterward, we went to bed, and the next day we could sleep as long as we wanted. On Christmas morning, the nuns gave us a "Cuddureddu," which is a classic Sicilian cookie filled with figs.

Easter Time - From Thursday to Easter Sunday, every day, there was a religious event, including visits to the various churches in town. On Good Friday, we enjoyed the tasty "pasta con le sarde," consisting of pasta, sardines, fennel, and toasted bread crumbs. On Easter Sunday, the nuns gave us a canilleri, also a classic Sicilian sweet consisting of sweet dough with a colored hardboiled egg in the middle. This was the one and only egg we had for the year.

Family Visitation Day - It was in the afternoon on every Sunday and holiday. When the families arrived to see their children, the nun in charge for their meetings called the names of the girls to come to the receiving room. The visitation's day was a sad occasion for me. I never got a visit on Sunday, and although young, I understood why. I had no parents; both were dead. The only time I heard my name called was on holidays when my uncle Peppino Fantauzzo or some of his children came to see me, and it was then that I received some money to buy whatever I wanted. As soon as my relatives were gone, I was always compelled to hide the money in some secure place where nobody could find and steal it. That's what happened with my golden earrings. They were from my godmother at my christening. I was about eight or nine years old. It was evening, and we were already in bed when a strong storm suddenly erupted, and the lightning and thunders were so loud that I was frightened. One of the girls told me that gold attracted the lightning, so being naive, I took the earrings off and put them under the pillow. The next day, they were gone, and I never found them.

Going Outside The Orphanage - Going out was normally for religious or funeral processions, occasionally for some pleasant events, and we were always accompanied by the nuns. Personally, I didn't like to go out and many times I detested it, but I had no other choice because that was an order. Sometimes, the nuns gave us girls a warning not to look at the men directly in the eyes because it was too dangerous.

The Fascist Period - Depending on the health of the child, every summer, the school children were sent to camps by the sea or to the mountains for four weeks. It would have been wonderful for me to go out of the orphanage for a while, but unfortunately, I never went because of the problem I had with my eyes. For years, I was suffering with an inflammation. Just a minimal draft and my eyes became very red in no time. This problem lasted until I reached my teens. After that, it resolved itself. At the end of each scholastic year, the school children, aged eight to fourteen, dressed in fascist uniforms, performed the gymnastics in the town's main square, Piazza Duomo. The girls, called piccole italiane, wore black skirts and white blouses, while the boys, called balilla, wore their special uniforms. It was a great event, and I enjoyed very much being able to participate because it took place outside the orphanage. The celebration of the Fascist Epiphany, which occurred on January 6, for us orphans, was another big event of the year. The nuns took us to the town's theater where a box had been reserved just for us. The festivities started with long speeches on fascism and Mussolini and concluded with the distribution of gifts to the students. It was wonderful when they called our names and we went on the stage of the theater to receive the gift. One year, I got a doll, and that was the first and last doll I ever received in my childhood.

The War Years (1940 to 1943) - They were lean. Food was scanty. Everything was rationed, and I was very hungry. In the orphanage, the food given to us was awful; many times a week, for lunch, we had minestrone with beans, which was making me sick. I could not swallow, and when I tried, I felt like vomiting. As punishment, the nuns took the small portion of bread away from me. Three of us girls decided to steal food. We knew how to get to the pantry while all the nuns were with mother superior on the second floor, so we just needed to choose the best time for action, synchronize our movements, and decide what each of us would do. Once ready, we started executing our plans, which happened as often as we needed. Therefore, by stealing, we were able to get enough bread, cheese, olive, and so forth. The chickens were kept in the garden, and we also started stealing eggs and drinking them on the spot. The raw eggs, still warm, were very tasty, and until now, when I eat soft boiled eggs, I remember those stolen eggs in the orphanage. After obtaining our necessities, we confessed our sins to the priest. Two or three times, a girl caught a small pigeon in the garden, which she killed, cleaned, and prepared it for cooking. In order to cook the pigeon, we went to the garden and down the alley until we reached the high wall, which kept the outsiders out. We found the right location where we built a fireplace with stones. Afterward, in an empty food can, we put the cleaned pigeon with a little water and salt, cooked it, and ate it. For us, the pigeon was delicious. There were times when we could smell the cooking of gourmet food coming from the window of the girls' lavatory on the third floor. With great curiosity, we watched outside the small window where we could see some German soldiers eating the good-smelling food in their station.

They could not see us, but the sight of their food was enough to make our mouths water. How wonderful it would have been to consume the same food.

During this period of war, we had two refuge places to go at the sound of the alarm for the bombardments. During daytime, we ran to the garden shelter, and at night, we ran to the girls' refectory and slept on the floor. The town was never hit, but we heard the noisy attacks in the surrounding area. One day, the mother superior called me for questioning. She wanted to know if it was true that I had seen a nun and the municipal secretary, who had a cottage next to orphanage's garden, embrace and kiss each other. I didn't know what she was talking about. I was too innocent to understand the meaning of that comprised posture and was also very surprised when she told me that I had started the rumors. For sure, it hadn't been me. Some of the girls had made the story up, or maybe it was factual, but I never found out. The institution had actual orphans and also children of prostitutes who had some knowledge of the outside-world life.

Toward the end of the war, the orphanage got infested with lice, bedbugs, and scabies. It was a dreadful situation. Everyone's scalp and clothing was full of lice. The beds were full of bedbugs, and many girls got scabies also. There were limited treatments for all these bugs, so it took a long time to eradicate them. Scabies was the worst. I remember the girls screaming because of the pain when the nuns were washing and treating them. Thank God that I was spared of the scabies, but not of the lice.

On July 19, 1943, we heard the noise of the American armored trucks going through Casteltermini Main Street. Some people were jubilant, and others were sad. A few fascists were still in town, but the German soldiers were all gone. It was not easy for the trucks to go through this mountainous town because many bridges had been destroyed. The allies had to use whatever was accessible to go through the cities and towns of Sicily. After the invasion of Sicily, the Americans started to send a lot of goods to the island, and what I remember most was the yellow cheese and the powdered milk.

Today, it seems ridiculous to think that the girls felt unhappy when the bombardments were over. First of all, we were too young to understand what was going on in Europe, and second, from that day on, we had to obey the strict regulations of the orphanage. For us girls, the period of the bombardment was exciting and seemed to provide us vacations.

* * *

In 1944, my grandfather, Vincenzo Butticé, passed away, and the nuns asked me if I wanted to see his dead body. At the news of his death, I didn't have any emotion. It was as if a stranger had passed away, and frankly, I didn't care at all. Grandfather had never come to visit me in the orphanage; as a matter of fact, for him, my brother and I didn't exist. The nuns learned of his death because the Butticé's family had invited the girls of the orphanage to attend the man's funeral. Speaking of funerals, in those days, if the family of the deceased had money, they invited the orphanage to attend the funeral. In this case, accompanied by the nuns, the orphans went to the house where the deceased lay. Prayers were recited at his bedside, and then a procession accompanied the coffin with the body to the church for the religious ceremony. After that, in procession, the orphans accompanied the coffin to the cemetery for the burial.

* * *

At some point, Mother Superior called to inform me that there was a couple by the name Cusmano who wanted to adopt me. Both husband and wife were professors, teaching at one of the universities in Palermo. One of the professors was from Casteltermini, and by chance, I had met a member of his family living in town. They knew everything about me, and they had no children and were very interested in adopting me. I took a few days to think it over. Although my situation was very miserable, my future was unknown, and I didn't have anything to lose. I could not decide because the idea of losing my family's name was terrifying. At that time, I didn't know why I felt so terrified, and later, I thought that I was stupid for not accepting the adoption. Anyway, no one tried to convince me, and so I refused the offer. Many years later, I found out that the Cusmanos were my father's second cousins.

It happened that a girl next to my bed was very ill. She could not stop coughing, had high fever, and was spitting blood. I couldn't sleep, so I was getting up and tried to help her by holding the basin for the spitting. This lasted for several days until the nuns took her to the hospital in Agrigento where they made the diagnosis that she had tuberculosis. Afterward, I don't know what happened to her for I never saw her again. Sometime later, the nun who was sleeping in our dormitory but separated from us by a curtain got sick. She had also contracted tuberculosis. We could not help her because it was prohibited for the girls to enter the place where the nuns slept or ate. Therefore, this was a way for us to conclude that God was protecting us!

When I was almost fifteen years of age, I was sent to the hospital in Agrigento for a month. The nuns were concerned and thought that there was something seriously wrong with my health because I hadn't reached puberty yet. In the hospital, they didn't find anything wrong with me; it was just a question of time. I liked being at the hospital. I had good food, felt free, and being under the tutelage of the Sisters of Charity (those nuns with big white hats). I was treated very well. In a certain way, I was sad when I returned to the orphanage.

In Casteltermini lived Cavalier Lo Bue, who did a lot for the orphanage. He invited the girls more than once a year at his villa on the outskirts of the town. The invitation was always accompanied by a good and rich banquet, and afterward, the orphans were left free to stroll all over the wonderful place. The villa had a palace with beautiful architecture and gardens with a great variety of plants from all over the world. Many times, we saw his wife, but I don't recall much about her because it was the cavalier who had contact with us orphans. He was a very warm and kind man. He knew my uncle Peppino and always asked if he had come to see me.

In Casteltermini was also the Count Castiglia's family (comprised of the count, countess, and their three daughters), who invited the girls of the orphanage at their villa for a pleasant afternoon every year during the wine harvest. The orphans were given a banquet with delicious food and plenty of grapes and, afterward, freedom to walk in the gardens. For us, it was definitely a special afternoon. The main residence of the Castiglia's family was in Palermo, and their summer villa was on the outskirts of Casteltermini.

*   *   *

Agata Arena was our new teacher after the war. She was in her middle twenties, a real gifted young lady. She was good looking, fabulous in everything she touched, and came from a small Sicilian town by the name Valquarnera. Soon after the arrival, she took over the management of the embroidery projects and of the theatrical entertainment in which she also played a part. In addition, she directed the church choral group, played the piano, and sang.

Since he had some expertise, my cousin Giovanni (Uncle Peppino's son) came to the orphanage to help with the setup of the stage for the entertainment. Two or three times a year, the Catholic Association of Casteltermini carried out shows at the town's theater, and my cousin, who was a member of the association, also played a part. In the old days, with no television, the theater was a big event for the town's people.

Being both involved in the preparation of the stage, soon, Agata and Giovanni started to like each other a lot. In fact, many times, Agata got romantic serenades sang by Giovanni, who was accompanied by his guitarist friend. A few times, Agata called me to listen to the serenade played under the window of the orphanage building. It was amusing. Unfortunately, nothing happened between Agata and my cousin because he was engaged to a girl from Casteltermini. Although his engagement was not official, for some reason, he could not break it. Agata had fallen in love, but seeing that there was no hope for a future with Giovanni, she resigned and left the orphanage. Afterward, we kept in touch by mail. She stayed at the orphanage over three years, and those were the best years for me because Agata and I had become very good friends. In all the years I spent at the orphanage, I never made real friends, I just trusted a few girls because on many occasions, we helped each other.

* * *

In 1946, I had a bad dream. The last time I saw my brother was in 1942. At that time, he had escaped from the Salesians of Don Bosco in Palermo, had enrolled in the army, and before going to the war, he came to see me in the orphanage to say good-bye. Afterward, I had no idea where he was or what he was doing until now, when for the first time in my life, I dreamed of my mother. It was like an apparition. In tears, she was telling me, "Your brother is in serious trouble." It was so real that I woke up shaken and was sure that something terrible had happened to him. The next day, I asked a nun a favor to contact my uncle Peppino because I needed to talk to him. In no time, my uncle came, confirmed my bad dream, and told me that Vincenzino got in serious trouble and was in prison in Northern Italy. Soon after, I started corresponding with my brother, and unfortunately, all the letters that I received from him were censored with blackouts. Anyway, a new chapter started for my brother and also for my uncle Peppino who was involved in helping him.

I remember a big scandal that erupted in the orphanage. The storage room containing straw, wood, and carbon was a fun place for the girls to play, like jumping up and down and hiding in the straw. It happened that the gardener who had access to the storage room through an extra door in his living place started molesting the girls sexually, and I too was touched in that way. The scandal became public, and some of the girls' relatives reported the incident to the police who became involved in the investigation. The nuns were shocked when they learned of the scandalous episode through the police. Regarding the gardener, I don't remember what happened to him, except that a new man replaced him.

Another vivid recollection of one specific incident involved a cruel mother superior. First of all, this superior treated us like we were in a reformatory, disregarding the fact that the children were there by misfortune. I don't remember the reason why a girl named Lia was punished and locked in a dark room where everybody knew that the place was infested with mice. Lia's loud screams were chilling, then they suddenly stopped, and it was like something bad had happened to her. Nobody could enter the dark room because the mother superior had the door key. In many circumstances, I remained neutral, but not in this case; I was very concerned about Lia. I went to the gardener and asked him to go to the police to report what was happening in the orphanage. In no time, a high rank police officer came and started interviewing the girls one by one. Lia, who was very shy, was out of the darkroom and had already recuperated from the shock. The mother superior denied to the police what had just happened; but in front of her and under interrogation, I told the police the truth regarding this last episode and also some of the previous bad occurrences. At a certain point, the mother superior became enraged and started scolding me saying, "One day God will be your judge." Soon after the incident, the mother superior was transferred to another institution, and we got a new one.

SAYING GOOD-BYE TO THE ORPHANAGE

For years, I didn't know there was a better life outside the institution because I had never had the opportunity of knowing it. As a matter of fact, each time my uncle Peppino came to see me, I never complained to him of anything. Without a doubt, I was a good girl. However, growing up, I started to understand my circumstances better, and in the last few years, I had done a lot of thinking. I remember those times when, going to the garden, I felt like a caged bird that wanted to fly far away. The escape was easy, but the dilemma was where to go to. While in the garden, I also recall how many times I wished to go to America when looking at the flying machines high in the sky. I didn't know why, but then, my big desire was to go to another world. Who knew that many years later, my dream would be realized. In fact, I am writing my memoir here in America. I still cannot believe that!

The latest scandalous episodes in the orphanage troubled me a lot and encouraged me to sort things out in order to leave the place. So after a considerable time of reflection, I arrived at the conclusion that once out, I knew how to support myself with the embroidery and some help from Uncle Peppino to start with. I was fully aware of my lonesome existence in the world. At my age, I was more than mature enough to comprehend the difficulties that I would have to face once I was outside the institution. I had neither parents nor close family members waiting for me with open arms. I, alone, had to confront whatever came along my way.

I was over eighteen years of age. In the spring of 1950, I went to the mother superior and told her that I wanted to have a talk with my uncle Peppino, and I also told her my reason. Present at the meeting was a nun who suggested that I should instead consider becoming a nun because nobody in my family wanted me in their homes. I knew that from the beginning of my internment in the orphanage. In fact, that was why I was there in the first place. Through the nuns' mouths I had also learned that, more than once, my aunt Angelina (Uncle Peppino's wife) had told them that the best thing for me was to become a nun. I thought what a big burden I would be for the relatives. Therefore, the idea of becoming nun was the best solution for them all. Anyway, I ignored the advice of the sister and insisted that I wanted to see my uncle. In my heart, I knew that I could count on him.

Without delay, Uncle Peppino came to see me. I imagined that he had already perceived something regarding my request for when I told him that I wanted to leave the orphanage, he was not surprised at all. Anyway he said to me, "Don't worry. Just give me a few days to make some arrangements, and I will be back." Though the nuns were surprised by my uncle's willingness, they still continued to tell me that I would regret leaving the orphanage. They were really concerned about me, but I was not paying any more attention to them. I had already decided and was happy to get out of the institution. Before leaving, the sisters gave me plenty of advice for my good. With sincerity, I have to say that during my years in the orphanage, with the exception of some bad apples, the nuns had been very good to me.

One week later, Uncle Peppino came to pick me up, and I left the orphanage with nothing except what I was wearing. Once out the orphanage, the arrangements for me were made. During the day, I would stay at Uncle Peppino's place, which was a small apartment where his four children were still living, and at night, I would go to Aunt Vincenzina's place.

Vincenzina was my mother and Uncle Peppino's oldest sister. At the beginning, she refused to take me in, but after she was convinced by her sons and Uncle Peppino, she reluctantly agreed to let me sleep at her apartment. Regarding this aunt, when her husband died, she was very young and was left with four boys aged two to eight and with no means of support. She was a dressmaker, so with sacrifices, she was able to support her family and also strongly managed the upbringing of her sons with a strong hand. She was like a military general. And although she was living alone, her sons all successfully married; she didn't feel like starting with me all over again because she had, had enough with her four boys.

MY NEW UNFAMILIAR WORLD

LEAVING THE ORPHANAGE

On the same day, Uncle Peppino first took me to Aunt Vincenzina. Her welcome was distant, and I was not surprised with her indifference toward me because in all the years I was in the orphanage, she never came to see me. We were practically strangers to each other. Later on, I met her sons—Salvatore, Giovanni, Nino, and Giuseppe. They were much older than me and friendlier than their mother. Then Uncle Peppino took me to his home where I met his wife and their children—Giovanni, Rosetta, Gino, and Lina. Aunt Angelina was not enthusiastic about her husband's arrangements. She wanted me to stay in the orphanage, and as mentioned before, become a nun, so her welcome was also cold. Lastly, I went to the Buttices' home to meet my father's family. There were my step-grandmother, four aunts, one uncle, and some of the cousins.

In meeting the relatives, my inner reaction was mixed with sadness and loneliness. In a few words, it was an experience filled with dejection. Although I didn't expect a better welcome, still their coldness hurt me tremendously, but I kept calm and politely kissed everybody.

Because I didn't have anything to wear, the following day, cousin Lina took me to a store where I bought the basic outfits with the money that Uncle Peppino had given me for the purchases. Subsequently, Uncle Peppino wrote to his brother Silvestro, who was living in America, concerning my needy situation, and afterward, my American uncle started sending me money and packages full of beautiful clothes. Uncle Silvestro had two daughters, Rosa and Rosalia. Rosalia's clothing size was precisely my size so that whatever I was getting from them, required no alterations at all. They just looked like they were tailored for me. I was so happy.

When living in a small town, it is normal for everyone to know one another and also to know what is going on in the inner city, except when it concerned my existence. Not knowing what had happened to me as a child, some of the folks thought that I had died a long time ago. Believe me that was not pleasant for me to hear. Now that I came into existence, the town's people started to know me as Peppino Fantauzzo's and/or the Buttice's niece because both families were well known.

* * *

The start of my new life was very difficult. With the relatives, I was related by blood only, so in reality, I was like a stranger coming into their home. While all my cousins had grown up in a warm family circle, I had grown up in environment that had been cold and indifferent. My behavior was also different from that of my cousins as my upbringing with the nuns had been different too. I was shy, reserved, and answered only questions I was asked. I was like an alien from another planet because the reality was that nobody knew me, so everybody and everything was new to me. I really started from square one like a child, except the infant doesn't know what is happening to him. I tried to ignore whatever unpleasantness I was hearing about me. I controlled myself and always pretended that everything was fine with a smile. It was hard to swallow, but I had to because for the moment, I needed them, thinking that in time everything will change. Also I didn't want to create any problem, which would have been much worse for me. Anyhow, with all the unpleasantness and in addition to having no one to talk to, as strange as it appears, at the same time, I was not profoundly demoralized because, due to my optimistic nature and strong willpower, I had a certain confidence in my future.

Uncle Peppino made sure that his children would behave kindly toward me and would also include me in every family leisure activity. For him, I was another daughter. Every Sunday, Uncle Peppino distributed some money to his children, and he always included me—although later, I was earning some of my own. This action was not agreeable to one of his children who, one time with arrogance, took the money from my hands. Though this bad action hurt my feelings, I didn't say a word because the incident would have upset her father, and I didn't want to cause any trouble.

Little by little, my life started to improve. I became more open, started to have better relationships with the relatives, and also became close to some of the cousins. In the evening, I joined a walking group consisting of cousins and friends. Together, we were strolling on the town's main street, which, at that time, was known as Pecoraro to San Giuseppe. We were never concerned about the weather. We went out with or without an umbrella, except on stormy days. During the summer, the same group often took long walks on the outskirts of the town where we enjoyed singing some Sicilian songs loudly. How wonderful it was to feel free. Many times, on Sundays after lunch, my cousin Gino, one of Uncle Peppino's sons, would take his fiancée, his sister, and me for a ride to Agrigento where we would spend the rest of the afternoon. Because Gino was always in a hurry to go away and to come back home, once, driving at high speed, the car had a flat tire and almost flew from the curved road down the cliff. The curve was on a mountainous, narrow, and steep road, and it was a miracle that nothing happened to all of us, including the car, but it was a dreadful experience! On several occasions, Uncle Peppino took his youngest daughter and me to the circus in Palermo or in Agrigento, and every time, I had a lot of fun. Besides the show itself, what I liked most was my uncle's gesture in my regards.

Of the many religious festivities, Christmas was the biggest holiday of all for this was the special occasion when all the families were getting together and enjoying each other amid the warm atmosphere with cheers and traditions. As an orphan, this holiday was the saddest period of the year for me because, while everybody seemed to be happy in their family circle, I always felt an emptiness in my heart and lonely more than never. The Easter holiday was interesting because, among the events, on Good Friday, there was the characteristic procession consisting of a man carrying the cross to the town's calvary, followed by the townspeople and the orchestra playing somber music. On Sunday, other traditions were taking place in Piazza Duomo, and also, there were the traditional family reunions.

From the first day outside the orphanage, I didn't like my living arrangements, the days at Uncle Peppino's place, and the nights at Aunt Vincenzina's home. But for the time being, I didn't have any other choice other than being thankful. I recognized that I was a burden to them all, and especially to Aunt Angelina. At her place, however, I was busy doing some embroidery for her daughters.

A few months after leaving the orphanage, I had a talk with Uncle Peppino. I told him that I wanted to earn some money with the embroidery, knowing that I was very good with that trade. Uncle Peppino suggested that I become a dressmaker because in those days, they were making good money. Subsequently, he found a place for me to go to learn the sewing, and I went. However, I soon understood that to become a dressmaker, it would have required three to four years of apprenticeship, and that was a long time for me. The long apprenticeship was profitable for the dressmakers and tailors because the apprentices were helping their business for free. Three months later, I left the place.

I had a heart-to-heart talk with my uncle again. I was very serious and determined when I told him that I would like to have a place where I could start my embroidery business. It was laughable to talk about business as I didn't know its real meaning and, most of all, had no money to begin with. However, I was more than sure that Uncle Peppino would help me for he was a very caring man who understood me completely. In those days, to have an embroidered dowry was an indication that the girl's family was well off economically. As a matter of fact, a week before the wedding, with a great satisfaction, the bride's family displayed the dowry to their relatives and friends.

THE EMBROIDERY BUSINESS

Uncle Peppino rented a small apartment, which consisted of one large room, lavatory, and no kitchen. He also paid the rent for three months and bought some furniture for the apartment. Afterward, Uncle Peppino took me to the apartment and, with his usual paternal smile, gave me the key, some money, and said, "Are you happy now to have your own place?" Of course I was happy, though I didn't know how to thank him. Anyway, he then wished me good luck and told me not to worry about paying him back and he also expected me to go to his place every day to eat. I could not believe how fortunate I was to have had an uncle like him. What a wonderful man!

I was about nineteen years of age. I didn't have any certificate for the business, but it was okay; no one asked me for one. I knew that I was an excellent hand embroiderer (*ricamatrice*) with years of experience. It sounds strange for my young age, but it was the reality for I started to work in that line of work when I was less than eleven years old.

With my uncle's money, I bought an embroidery round hoop and a long floor standing frame. These tools were used to stretch the material to work with, and they were indispensable for the job. I also bought an armoire and a few catalogs with embroidery designs. I had never done any embroidery preliminary work, but I quickly learned by myself, and soon after, I applied it. Each design had different type of embroidery stitches and special thread to be used. My favorite was the cross-stitches, but my clientele never asked for that.

I got my customers by word of mouth through some of my relatives, and in no time, I had plenty of work. My business was based on embroidered dowry. This was the work that the townspeople wanted. It consisted of bed linens, pillowcases, nightgowns, table linens, bath towels, curtains, cushions, and occasionally, some monogram pieces. The type of embroidery stitches varied, and it all depended on the type of material, such as cotton, linen, silk, damask, and others. It also depended on the design that the clients were selecting for a particular job. Many times, the clients brought their own designs, and other times, I provided it.

The work required a lot of patience, precision, and much time. I was spending many hours a day, and sometimes, seven days a week. The end results were satisfying, and I was glad to earn some money. I remember the first time I got paid, what thrilling feeling I had! The clients were very pleased, and I was getting more and more customers to the point that I had to apologize for refusing some of their work.

Winter time was difficult for it was very cold and my place had no heat, and as a matter of fact, for the embroidering, I had to wear woolen gloves with its fingers cut off. Because the town is located at a high level in the mountains, Casteltermini's winter season was terribly cold but with little snow. I remember one time when the town got a lot of snow, and afterward, the temperature drastically dropped. The town remained completely paralyzed for two full weeks because it didn't have any equipment to remove the snow, which then became ice. From the balcony, it was beautiful to look at the snow. For us, it was a novelty, but it was not a fun situation because we didn't have the proper boots to wear in order to go out of the house. What a great relief when the weather finally started to warm up and everything began to normalize again.

Every evening throughout wintertime, I went to Uncle Peppino's and sometimes to the Butticé aunts because their homes had a big brazier in the middle of a large room to keep the place warm. Sitting around the stove, everybody enjoyed playing cards. Sometimes, I joined them in the games; other times, I brought my embroidery work there. During the evenings spent at Uncle Peppino's place, I was working on an embroidery project for my cousin Lina, my uncle's youngest daughter. There was a type of embroidery design that didn't require the frame to hold the material. It just needed specific material, thread, a needle, and a thimble. I did some nice handiwork for my cousin. This was the least I could do for them and also make Aunt Angelina happy.

I had to move three times during the course of my embroidery business. Each time I had to change apartments, my cousin Giovanni, Uncle Peppino's son, took care of the move for free. He was incredible, and he always did the transfer with a smile and jokes. My last small apartment on via Rome, a part of the main street, was almost across the street from my uncle's residence. Because of the good location and big balcony, some of my friends and cousins often came to my place to have a chat with me and to show themselves on the balcony to look at the passersby. Through their stay at my place, I continued working, and they didn't mind for they knew that I didn't have any time to waste. Sometimes, my friends just came to me to unburden themselves.

I was getting many clients, and it was in this way that I met many interesting people and also made some good friends. To make easy and extra money, during the summer school vacations, I was teaching embroidery to a few young girls. They were full of life, pleasant, and made me feel good. A lady by the name Ninetta Cuffaro brought her two young daughters, Maria and Crocetta, to my place to learn the embroidery. Her family was in the transportation business. They owned many buses and serviced many parts of Sicily. Ninetta and I soon started developing a good friendship. She invited me to her house for lunch or dinner, and many times, her family took me to some excursions, movies, and so forth. One specific trip, which for me was fabulous, was for "La Sagra del Mandorlo in Fiore," the festival of the blooming almond trees in Agrigento.

With great surprise, one time, the young Countess Flavia came to my place to have some embroidered monograms done. When I met her, I felt very excited and at the same time honored to have her at my place. Her introduction was wonderful, and that made me feel comfortable. I had seen her at one of her father's banquets held for the girls of the orphanage at the count's villa on the outskirts of Casteltermini. I think she knew about me through my uncle Peppino.

During the carnival season, clients from the high society club of Casteltermini came to my place a few times to have some shawls embroidered. They were bringing the already-designed silk stoles and golden thread for me to do the job. Every time the work was done, I got paid nicely, and each time, they invited me to the carnival ball held at their club. I didn't know how to dance nor did I have anybody to accompany me there, so I told them about my situation, and the invitation remained the same. The first time they invited me to the ball, I was twenty, and I cannot describe how excited and honored I felt at the same time. For the ball, I bought whatever I needed to make me look nice, and the evening of the ball, I went to my uncle's place to wait to be picked up. While waiting, I heard one of my cousins saying to her mother, "Do you think anybody will show up to take her to the ball?" There was so much sarcasm in her voice; I understood what she meant. I was nobody, just a young girl with nothing. She didn't know that I heard her remark, and as usual, I pretended that I heard nothing, but it did hurt my feelings a lot. A few minutes later, a person from the club arrived to pick me up, and afterward, I gave my cousin a nice smile and left for the ball proudly. Throughout the embroidery period, the persons that I met liked my individuality, which for my age was unusual in a small town like Casteltermini.

I had no business experience, so I was making decisions on my own without having any idea how much my work was worth. Consequently, I charged the clients very little money for the embroidery. Of course, people were happy not just for my good work but because they knew that my labor was inexpensive. Then there was also the problem that certain customers were not paying me at all, and when I told my aunt Peppina, one of my father's sisters, of my trouble, she became enraged that people were taking advantage of me. Because my aunt knew many people in town, she went to the clients to collect the hard-earned money personally. It was very nice of her for doing that for me.

* * *

At that time, television didn't exist, so the cinemas were the only places to go for enjoyment. The films in town were shown at the theater in winter and at the park during summertime. If there was a good love story, which was my favorite subject, I went to see the movie with my cousins Memma and Lina Martorana. One time, while we were at the park watching the film, somebody approached us and told my cousins that their father had, had a heart attack. At the shocking news, we left the place and hurried to the Martorana's home where we found Ferdinando already dead.

In the summer, I also liked getting some rides from my cousin Enzo on the Lambretta, the Italian motor scooter. He often came to my place to pick me up, and together, we went to the Butticé-Martorana's country house for the weekend. The cottage was at a higher level than that of the town of Casteltermini, with plenty of fruit trees, a vineyard, and so forth. It was a real nice place for breathing fresh air, spending time with my father's relatives, as well as eating the delicious cooking prepared by my aunts.

From time to time, I received anonymous love letters, which I thought were impertinent. At first, I didn't have any idea who was sending them, but soon, I realized that those individuals were the young men strolling under my balcony and looking up to catch my eyes. I didn't like any of them. In fact, many times, I closed the balcony on their faces. The letters were incredibly amusing and ridiculous too. Occasionally, I read them to some of my close relatives who got some good laughs.

With having many relatives, there were many family events to attend, such as engagements, weddings, christenings, funerals, and so forth, and I went to each of them. However, I had become part of only Uncle Peppino Fantauzzo's and Butticé-Martorana's families.

In my town, in the old days, girls and boys were prohibited from being seen together without a chaperone, so communicating with each other was through eye contact as they strolled on Main Street, in church, or on a balcony, and in addition, there were the secret love letters exchanged. The official engagement periods were long and costly for both families, especially for the girl's family, but that was the only way boys and girls in love could see each other openly and of course, always escorted by somebody. Occasionally, I too accompanied my cousin Rosetta when she went out with her fiancé.

I remember the weddings of Uncle Peppino's four children, which three of them took place in Casteltermini. Cousin Rosetta married Agostino Giudice, and the festivities in town lasted for three full days. Cousin Giovanni married Carmelina Di Liberto, and a few years later, cousin Gino married Rosetta Renna, and both weddings were celebrated with big fanfares. Cousin Lina married Enzo Arnone, and the ceremony was held in Palermo.

I also recall when my cousin Franco Martorana was engaged to Adalgisa Ferlita. Her family invited the fiancé's family and me to spend a few days in Santo Stefano Quisquina, her home-town. I never expected that kind of treatment from them. They were strangers to me, but they were very kind toward me. I also attended their wedding, which took place in Santo Stefano Quisquina with a lot of partying that lasted for two days.

Every week, salesmen were coming to town to sell merchan-dise for dowries. Once, a salesman came to my place and showed me, among other articles, some bath towels that I instantly liked very much. They were so beautiful that I could not decline the bargain, so, to get the towels, I signed twelve invoices to be paid on monthly basis. As soon as a few of my relatives came to know of my purchase, they started to gossip because they thought that those towels were too luxurious for my position. I didn't care about the talk. What I bought made me feel good, and after so many years, I still have three of those towels left.

* * *

During the four years since I left the orphanage, my life had improved a lot. The relation with some of my relatives had become warm, and I had also made many good friends. With my embroidery earnings, though small, I was able to dress elegantly like my cousins, pay the rent and the utilities of the apartment, and was always left with some money to spend as per my wishes. Regarding food, first of all, my uncle Peppino insisted that I went to his place to eat; second, the food was too expensive for me to buy; and third, I didn't have a kitchen in the apartment.

I remember the times when I was too busy with my clients and had no time to show up at Uncle Peppino's home for lunch. Before sitting down at the table to eat, my uncle came to my apartment to find out why I was not at his place. He wanted to know if there was anything wrong going on. His concern in my regard was really incredible, especially in view of the fact that he didn't have any free time because he was working from 6 a.m. to 8 p.m. in his business with a short break at noon for lunch.

Though economically I was *not* independent because I needed my uncle's help to survive, how strange it was that I never had the awareness of being a poor person when in reality I was. Maybe I didn't realize it due to the fact that in the orphanage, I had experienced hard times and lack of freedom. I thank God that in those days, I felt the way I did as it made my life tolerable. Settling down in Casteltermini with a marriage was not my dream. I wanted to get out of the town and didn't know why. In my innermost being, there was something far away waiting for me, and my desire was always to go to America.

UNCLE SALVATORE BUTTICÉ

He was my grandfather's brother. Around 1954, when he was dying, all the relatives, except me, were at his bedside because he was going to have his will done. One of my cousins present, Franco Martorana, and a priest by the name Mondello asked the dying man to remember his niece Lina. He was leaving me nothing; in fact, he ignored my brother completely. Anyway, from this uncle, I inherited a small piece of land.

More than two years had passed since Uncle Salvatore's death, and though I was the owner, I didn't know anything about what was going on with the land or where it was located. The only thing I knew was that there were inheritance taxes and other expenses for the maintenance of the lot to be paid. Consequently, there was nothing left for me. The person in charge of the property was a cousin of mine, and one day, taken by curiosity, I asked him for some details without knowing the bad effect that my simple request would cause. My cousin and his entire family became furious and very irritated. They told me that I was too impudent to ask for specifics and said to me, "You only trust your uncle Peppino Fantauzzo." Politely, I replied to them that with Uncle Peppino, I had never had any conflict of interest. I couldn't believe that their reaction and behavior toward me would be so negative even though I had the right to know what was going on with my property. Anyhow, a few months later, I decided to sell the land and put the money in the bank where, at least, I would receive some interest. So that was the end of my owning the land, which at that time was worth something.

Some years later, my uncle Peppino was having problems with the payment of some of the bills for his business, and he asked me if I was willing to lend him a certain sum of the money and he would give me the same bank interest. I was very happy that he had come to me. I immediately said yes because there was no need of thinking twice. For him, I would have done anything. I went to the bank and withdrew the cash he needed. When I gave him the sum of money, he insisted that we both sign the papers with the interest included. He was meticulous, and he wanted to make sure that if something should happen to him, I would be covered.

*　*　*

In 1955, for the first time, uncle Silvestro Fantauzzo, one of my mother's brothers living in St. Louis, United States, arrived at the port of Napoli by ship. Uncle Peppino with his children went to Napoli to welcome his brother Silvestro and afterward brought him to Casteltermini. At Silvestro's arrival in town, all the relatives went to uncle Peppino's place to meet him. Uncle Silvestro had never seen me before, including in photos, but he recognized me immediately. In fact, he said to me, "Tu sei la figlia di Giuseppina! (You are Giuseppina's daughter)." He brought a lot of gifts for everybody and stayed at Uncle Peppino's home for three months. While he was in town, there were banquets and parties for all the Fantauzzos. Once, he took the youngest nephews and nieces to see the movie *Gone with the Wind*. We were many, and we all had a fantastic time. He was a real nice and affectionate uncle, and he was also the uncle who had sent me many packages when I got out of the orphanage.

MY FIRST VACATION

One summer, I decided to take a break from my hard-working life. I thought that a short escape would be beneficial and also felt the necessity to go away for a while from my hometown. I had never had a vacation in my life, and this would be my first one. I wrote a letter to Agata, my friend from the orphanage years earlier, asking her if it was okay for me to go to visit her, and she gladly answered me yes and wanted to know when I was going. I had never traveled alone. It was really exciting to undertake a trip by myself, and the feeling of doing something that I wanted was wonderful.

As soon as I got the information needed on how to get to Valguarnera, my friend's hometown, I notified my uncle Peppino and some of the relatives of my forthcoming trip. By bus and train, I went to Valguarnera and arrived at the town's railroad station. I found Agata waiting for me. It was great to see each other again, and this was also the first time that we met since Agata had resigned from the orphanage several years ago. From the station, my friend took me to her place where we had a lot to catch up on, but most of all, she was interested to know what had happened to my cousin Giovanni Fantauzzo, whom she still seemed to be in love with.

In Valguarnera, my friend introduced me to her parents who were busy with their business. They had a restaurant, and during my stay, Agata's family wanted both of us to eat at their eatery, which we did with pleasure. After spending five nice days in town, Agata and I went by train to Catania to see one of her friends, Concettina, whom I also knew. While there, we visited a few interesting places, and we all had a pleasant time. After spending a wonderful week with my friends, I headed back to Casteltermini. Regarding my cousin Giovanni, many years later, when his wife died, he wrote me a moving letter. He wanted to know if my friend Agata was still available and where she was living as he was hoping to touch base with her. But unfortunately, she had already died of heart complications.

Back home from my vacation, I learned that my relatives didn't like that I left the town by myself. For the townspeople, it was a big scandal when a girl departed the city alone so that, for a while, there was gossiping. As usual, I didn't care about the chitchats. I was doing my best to live my life in the way I thought it was right for me and for me alone.

AUNT VINCENZINA FANTAUZZO

I was still spending my nights at Aunt Vincenzina's home, as arranged, when I left the orphanage, and I detested the situation from day one. Aunt Vincenzina never gave me the key of her apartment, and many evenings, when I was tired and wanted to go to sleep, I had to wait at my uncle Peppino's place until she got home, which was around 10 or 11 p.m. My god, how nervous, upset, and humiliated I felt. It was an undeniable sad condition.

Before I started my embroidery business, Aunt Vincenzina had changed her mind; she wanted me to live with her during the day too. It seemed that she had some concern in my regards, and she wanted to help me by settling down in a marriage. She tried to do the matchmaking with one of her friends' son who was a tailor working in Milan. One day, she introduced me to the man's parents who became interested in me. I knew the tailor by appearance only because he came to Casteltermini for his summer vacations and walked on the main street. I liked his parents, but I didn't care about him. I was also not ready for any commitment, and my aunt was very disappointed.

Aunt Vincenzina was an old-fashioned lady accustomed to leave the house always with a companion. Now seeing me going out alone was not to her liking at all, and she also didn't approve of some of my friends. For her, I was too free, and for that, we argued a lot. When I went to Valguarnera by myself, she became furious, and that was when I stopped going to sleep at her place. My small apartment, which up to now was used for the embroidery business only, was big enough, so I put a couch in it and felt good about that.

AN IMPETUOUS STUDYING DECISION

On one of the trips with my friend Ninetta Cuffaro, we were coming back from Agrigento to Casteltermini, and in the seat behind me, there were two gentlemen talking about education. One of them was a railroad station master who was worried about losing his job because of the new government's regulations. With the new rules, the gentleman's job required at least the middle school diploma, which he didn't have, so he was considering going to school to get the diploma. I immediately started to think, *If this man who is much older than me is considering going back to school, maybe I could do the same to improve my situation.* The contemplation was short because I suddenly made my mind up. I was also going to get my diploma, and while I was still on the bus, I gave Ninetta some indication of my decision.

As soon as I got off the bus, I went straight to see a lady professor by the name Rafaela Cordaro, whom I knew for quite some time, and I also knew that she was an excellent high school teacher and very well known in Casteltermini. When I met the professor, I told her that I wanted to get the middle school diploma and would like to have her as my private tutor. I also told her that I would like to condense the three-year studies in one year. I knew that what I desired to do was too much for her and especially for me. She looked at me and said, "I am glad to see you." Then she stated that it would be very difficult to condense three years in one, especially at my age for I was almost twenty-five. Also, too many years had passed from my elementary school, and my memory, for sure, has become rusty. However, seeing my enthusiasm, after a while, she said, "Okay, we will try. I will give you all the subjects necessary to obtain the diploma, and for the mathematics, you would need another professor." She gave me the cost of the course and the schedules, and I agreed with everything.

I left the professor's place and went to see Uncle Peppino to tell him of my sudden decision and the expenses that I would incur for the private lessons. His answer was, "If this is your wish, it is okay with me. I will start giving you your money back, and whatever you need, I will always be there for you." He was the only one who always understood me thoroughly and who also had a lot of confidence and trust in me. When the relatives heard of the news, they didn't like it, and the gossiping began. Some of them were concerned that I would lose whatever little money I had because they were sure that I would not succeed. Anyway, I said to those who didn't have any confidence in me that if I don't try now, how will I know later if my decision was right or wrong? I was ready and very determined to take the risk of losing whatever I owned, which was what my uncle Salvatore Butticé had left me.

With my latest decision, I would not have any more time for any embroidery, so I contacted some of the clients to give back their materials for the jobs that I hadn't started yet. I kept the work that was in progress with the intention of completing it slowly. I also told my friend Ninetta Cuffaro that her children could not come to my place to learn the embroidery anymore. Ninetta was very pleased with my decision and spontaneously offered me her son's books, which I gladly accepted. For me, it was great to get some of the used high school books for free. In this way, I had fewer books to buy.

In January 1957, I began to study for the middle school diploma. Professor Rafaela was teaching at the town high school in the morning, so I went to her place in the afternoon five days a week.

It was a tremendous effort for me, and at the beginning, it was really hard to keep my concentration. In fact, while reading, I was falling asleep. In memorizing something, I had headaches, and many times, I could not focus on anything. I soon realized that I was doing too much altogether and I needed to slow down and take short breaks. I started to go to my Butticé aunts to find my cousins Memma and Lina, and then with them, I would take some long walks or go to the movie. After a while, studying became easier, and I was able to focus and spend more hours on my studies. I sacrificed everything. My main purpose was studying, and nothing else mattered. To stay awake more hours a day, I went to Piazza Duomo to get a strong espresso coffee at the bar there. After a few months, Rafaela told me that I was doing just fine. Hearing that from her was a big relief for me.

The math professor named Gugliotta, and whom I knew by appearance only, lived across the street from my apartment, so it was very convenient to go to him. Every time I went for the lessons in the morning, the professor let me wait in his study for more than an hour, making me very uneasy, and after a while, I reached the point that I would not tolerate his behavior any longer. The private lessons were very expensive, and for me, time was like gold, so I got very disgusted and stopped going to the professor. One day, Professor Gugliotta had a talk with a cousin of mine, and he told him that I had made a big mistake in quitting his lessons and was sure that I would fail.

I needed to get a new math professor, but I was so disappointed that I didn't have either the patience or the will to start with a new one. Luckily, I always liked the mathematic subjects; they were my favorite ones, so I decided to study on my own. The mathematic books I had were good, but the study was harder than I thought. Anyway, I put extra effort to it. I remember staying wide awake many nights until the math problems were resolved, and it was in this way that I was able to learn by myself. This period of my life seems incredible, but I am telling the truth.

The undertaking was not an easy one. As a matter of fact, until now, I cannot believe how I succeeded.

In the middle of August 1957, professor Rafaela sent the application form to one of the public schools in Agrigento for my examinations to be taken in the month of September. For the Department of Education, September is known as the recuperation month for the failed subjects. But for me, it was different. My examinations were crucial; no room to fail—succeed or flop. To avoid the daily traveling, I rented a furnished room in Agrigento for a week. On my first day, when I went to the public school for the exams, I felt like a fish out of water because all the students were in their teens, and I was over twenty-five. Anyway, everything seemed fine, and so I spent an interesting but tense examination week in Agrigento. A few days after the exams, I left Casteltermini, and I returned to Agrigento to see the results.

On September 20, 1957, I received my middle school diploma. I cannot describe how thrilled I felt when looking at the public school board and saw the results, which indicated that I had passed all the subjects with mediocre marks. What a big satisfaction! I had successfully completed middle school! I sent a telegram to my relatives in Casteltermini, and they couldn't believe that I had made it, but they were happy for me. In those days, for a girl to travel alone was shocking news for the town, but for me, nothing mattered.

After my success with middle school, I decided to continue studying to get the bookkeeper diploma and wanted to complete two years in one. Of course, this time it would be harder and heavier than before, but I wanted to try anyway. For the private lessons, I went back to Professor Rafaela, and for the mathematic subjects, I went to Professor Schifanella.

In January 1958, I began studying as hard as I could and neglected everything along the way. Then in June, I rented a furnished room in Agrigento and stayed there for the duration of the examinations. Going to school for the test, again, it seemed like I was a fish out of water, but this time, it didn't bother me as before.

A few days after the exams, I returned to Agrigento to see the results on the school board. With disappointment, I saw that I had failed and there was no hope of recuperating any subjects in September. While in Agrigento, I went to see some of the school officials for information on my status, and they told me that I only needed to repeat the second bookkeeper year, so it was not a complete loss. However, instead of paying the two professors for the private lessons, I could have saved money if I had attended the first year at the free commercial public school. But who knew for sure; I was in hurry to get my diploma.

It was summer time, and in a certain way, I was glad that I could relax for a while. I really needed a good break from my demanding schoolwork. Nevertheless, because I still had some embroidery to be completed, I took advantage of the pause to finish and return all the projects to the clients, and that was what I did. I spent my summer months completing the embroidery work and at the same time earning some money, which was very helpful.

My second bookkeeper year started in the month of November 1958. The actual school year began at the end of September, but in order to finish the remaining of my embroidery responsibilities, with a few excuses, I started later. From the Cuffaro's bus services, I obtained the seasonal bus ticket to travel to and from Agrigento six days a week. The commercial public school was in a beautiful and peaceful location, close to the bus stop, the railroad station, and the Valley of the Temples.

This school year was special because it was a repetition. The homework was easy, so for me, it was like a carefree year. Going to school in the morning, on the way to the bus, I bought a small roll filled with panelle (fried omelet made with chickpea flour) for breakfast, and by 7:30 a.m., I was en route to Agrigento. The duration of the ride was approximately twenty-five minutes. The school hours were from 8:30 a.m. to 3 p.m., and the classroom had about forty students who were in their later teens, except three, including me, who were in the middle twenties. Naturally, it was a little strange to be in the class with so many young people. After a few weeks, I felt more comfortable, maybe because one of the professors was of my age and he was very nice to me. As usual, some of the professors' methods of teaching were excellent due to their good knowledge and their easy way of explaining the subjects, and these teachers made the school hours very interesting. Others were boring to the point that I could not keep my eyes open. During the school year, the entire class went for a day excursion in the vicinities twice. I didn't want to miss any occasions, so wherever the students went, I went too. Teachers and students were nice, and I had a great time and felt young again.

One day, en route to Agrigento, Brigadier Combaretto, a high-ranking member of the police force stationed in Casteltermini, was on the bus. I was surprised to see him there and especially when he sat next to me, which seemed to be on purpose. During the trip, he suggested that I should take a day off from the school because he wanted to have a talk with me, so that day, I skipped class and went with him for a stroll. After his introduction, he started to talk about himself, his family, and his hometown. Then he told me that for quite some time, he had been interested in me. He said, "I have often seen Professor Rafaela to get information in your regards, and I know everything about you." I was not surprised of what he was telling me because many times, I had noticed him following me when I was strolling on the town's main street with my cousin Memma. Knowing that a policeman could not marry a family member of a convict, I told him that my brother had been in prison. His reply was that he knew that and it was not a problem because, with his years of services, he could retire if he wanted.

Mr. Combaretto was very serious. He immediately told me that he wanted to marry me and I didn't have to worry about anything. At that point, I didn't know what to say. He had come to Agrigento just to propose to me, and he now wanted an answer. I felt really embarrassed. He didn't impress me nor did I want to try to know him better, and at this time, marriage was the last thing on my mind. Politely, I thanked him for the honor that he had given me, and then I said that I was sorry but I was not ready to settle down. He looked at me with a great disbelief because he didn't expect a negative answer, especially knowing my circumstances. I had no parents and trying to get ahead in a town where there were no possibilities, and especially for a woman, it was a great struggle. Afterward, there was nothing else to say other than good-bye, and the two of us returned to Casteltermini on different buses. When I told some of my relatives what had happened in Agrigento, nobody seemed surprised because they already knew something about Combaretto's feelings in my regards, and they would have liked him to become a member of the family. They all thought that Mr. Combaretto was a very good opportunity for me to settle down. Nobody knew what was going on in mind. In marrying somebody, I would lose any opportunity of going to America.

On June 15, 1959, I received my bookkeeper diploma with good scores. I will always remember this pleasant year, which was the best school year ever in my life. I enjoyed very much going to school and being among the carefree young people. To celebrate the happy occasion, I invited my cousins Memma and Lina to come with me to the Valley of Temples in Agrigento. They gladly accepted my invitation, and the three of us went there and spent a wonderful day.

LOOKING FOR EMPLOYMENT IN TOWN

A friend of mine had told me that there were two openings at city hall, so I applied for a job there. As expected, I didn't get the position because no women had ever worked there. In Sicily, the preference had always been men against women, so the chance to find work in Casteltermini was zero.

Professor Rafaela tried to help me through the political party affiliation that she had. She made an appointment for me, and she also gave me a letter of recommendation to present to one of the honorable members of the Sicilian region at the headquarter in Palermo. I went to Palermo to see the honorable. He was very courteous in receiving me, then he read the letter from Rafaela and, after a short pause, he told me to come to see him again in two weeks. In the way he spoke and looked at me, it seemed that he really wanted to help me get the position. On my second visit, the gentleman was as nice as before and said that he hadn't forgotten me. He gave me more hope. I just needed to have a little patience, and I had to return to see him once again in two weeks. On my third visit, I found the gentleman too enthusiastic. In fact, he made me a proposition. He told me to get an apartment and he would pay the rent. Then he locked his office door and tried to kiss me. At that point, I understood very well his wicked intentions. Infuriated, I told him to unlock the door, and I left his office very disgusted. I returned to Casteltermini with empty hands.

LEAVING MY HOMETOWN FOR GOOD

Several months had passed since I had received my bookkeeping diploma, and up to now, I had no hope in sight of getting a job. One day, my aunt Angelina, Peppino's wife, unexpectedly asked me if I wanted to go to Palermo and temporarily help out her daughter Rosetta who was going to have her third child. It didn't take long for me to give a reply. As a matter of fact, I immediately and happily said yes. This was a great opportunity for me. Once in Palermo, I had a better chance to find a job. In no time, I sold the few pieces of furniture that I owned, prepared two suitcases, gave up the apartment, and left Casteltermini for Palermo.

My mother – Giuseppina Fantauzzo

My Father – Gaetano Butticé

My dear uncle Peppino Fantauzzo

Me, out of the orphanage

Me, teaching embrodery in Casteltermini.
The girls I remember most are:
Palmina Diliberto, and Crocetta and Maria Cuffaro

Casteltermini 1955 - Uncle Silvestro from
America with the Fantauzzo's families.

Outing at the Diliberto' countryhome near Casteltermini
I am on the right next to Carmelina, my
cousin Giovanni Fantauzzo's fiancee

With cousins Lina Fantauzzo and Rosetta Renna
on the balcony of uncle Peppino's home

On a beautiful excursion day in the countryside near Casteltermini.
Top with glasses is cousin Rosetta Fantauzzo.
Then from left are: aunt Peppina Butticé, Concettina,
a friend, cousin Memma and me.

FOUR YEARS IN PALERMO

My goal in going to Palermo was to find employment as a book-keeper. It was March of 1960 when I went to live with my cousins Rosetta and Agostino Giudice. Their place was not strange to me for I had been there a few times before and I also knew their two children, Franca and Giovanni. I liked being there, and I felt wanted, and the warm atmosphere made me feel at home. Agostino was very busy with his executive responsibility at the Agronomic Department in Palermo, and Rosetta, with two small children and one on the way, had her hands full. She really needed some help with the housework.

Rosetta gave birth to Giuseppe on May 16, 1960, and on the same day, I went to the hospital to visit her and see her baby boy who was a bundle of joy! I had never seen newborns, and what a fantastic feeling I experienced! After three days, my cousin came home and, naturally, I was busier than before, but I didn't mind; I was glad to be there, and the days now went faster than usual. After a few months at my cousins' place, I found time to take some courses of study available in the city to improve my job résumé.

Moving from a small town to a big metropolitan city was really a change of life for me, and I liked that. At the beginning, I was timid and found things a little strange. Here, people were enjoying more freedom than those living in small towns and the daily way of life was completely different. But in a short time, I too got accustomed to the city's life, and it was great. I began visiting some of the elegant boutiques and shopping at the big department stores and small shops. In Sicily, it is very important to learn how to bargain with the seller because the asking price for the merchandise, in many places, is often highly exaggerated. I too acquired the knowledge of how to deal with the vendors.

I started visiting some of the beautiful and historic places, and I found one more interesting than the next. Palermo is rich in history, culture, architecture, and gourmet cuisine. The winter weather is mild. As a matter of fact, it was the first winter in my life that I didn't suffer with the frostbite on my fingers and toes, and that was a pleasant surprise for me.

My cousins knew that my stay at their place was temporary. I helped them with the household chores for a while and then began to seek employment in the city. Several months after my arrival, I told Rosetta and Agostino that on my free time, I was going to look for a job. They were not surprised, and concurred with me. They also invited me to stay at their home as long as I needed. I was really lucky because, with no money, I could not have found a place better than theirs.

THE STRUGGLE TO FIND EMPLOYMENT

In Sicily, jobs were scarce, and when you got one, it was like a lifetime opportunity. In my spare time, I was practicing stenography, which I had learned in school, although I knew that I was wasting my time because I was terrible at it and unable to translate what I had written. In those days, excellent stenographers were in great demand because there were no recording machines. As a matter of fact, there were plenty of job opportunities for people with academic degrees, experienced stenographers, or bilinguals. For the rest, the chances of obtaining employment, by way of winning the open competitions, were nearly zero due to the great number of applicants. Because of the high unemployment, many individuals with high education were unable to win competitions and were compelled and happy to accept any jobs available, such as typists and clerks. There were always exceptions to the rules. In fact, if a person was lucky to have some connections, then it was easier to find a suitable position. The connections with high-ranking citizens were very effective in order to obtain recommendations for employment.

My first job in Palermo was an evening part-time position as a statistical typist in a private office. But two weeks later, I quit because I was not paid. My second job was at a doll factory. I didn't like the type of work that was assigned to me, and it was not worth staying, so I quit. Then I found a job at a bookbinding factory in the center of the city. It seemed like a job that would last, so I informed my cousins of the new job, left their place, and moved to a rented furnished room on Via Maqueda. The location was excellent and also a short walking distance to the workplace. It was manual labor, which consisted of putting pages together. Although it was not what I wanted, I thought that for the moment it was acceptable because I started earning some money and was able to support myself. Unfortunately, three months later, I lost this job too.

Without work, I could not get by with the expenses, and I didn't know where to go to, so I found myself in a very peculiar situation. My Giudice cousins had moved to a smaller apartment and far from the city center. The new location was temporary until their new condominium was ready for them to move in.

Subsequently, when other cousins of mine, Franco and Adalgisa Martorana, came to know of my circumstances, they invited me to live with them; they were also residing in Palermo, and I do not remember how they found out about my situation. Anyway, God was good to me, and their offer was very beneficial, and in no time, I moved with them. Franco was always on the go, occupied with his job as an official at the Sicilian Aqueduct and with his involvement in an archaeological project. Adalgisa was taking care of the household chores and their only son, Fernando, who was about three years old. While at the Martorana, I started looking for work again with no luck. My cousins didn't need any help from me; they were doing fine. They were just good and sensitive in my regards and wanted to help me the best they could. I was very grateful for their kindness and generosity, which I didn't expect.

Finally, my Giudice cousins moved to their new condominium in Via Lombardia, and they asked me to go back to live with them. Though my Martorana cousins had been very nice to me, I didn't waste any time to return to the Giudices' home where I continued giving them some help and at the same time, looking for employment again.

At one time, two college students hired me to type their thesis. I did the best I could, but it took too long to finish the job because I was slow and also made too many mistakes. With the old typewriters, the corrections were tedious to fix. Then later, I got another job at INA (Institute Nationale d'Assicurazione) to sell insurance. The location was in Piazzale Ungheria in the center of Palermo, but first, I had to attend a two-week seminar to learn how to sell insurances. The seminar period coincided with an anniversary of the company. It was celebrated at one of the best hotels in Palermo with a big banquet and many speeches. I was also invited to attend the celebration, and I remember how impressive and elegant everything was. At the end of the seminar, I started to work on my assignment, but the hardest part of the job was convincing people to buy the insurance for their children. In good and bad weather, on foot, I went from house to house, up and down the stairs, meeting polite and rude people. I tried my best to sell, but with all my efforts, I was unable to convince anybody, and frankly, I could not be convinced myself that this insurance was a good idea to buy. In three weeks, I only sold one thanks to a colleague of mine. This colleague knew my brother, and in their youth, they were at the Don Bosco in Palermo. We became casual friends and often went for a walk, and our conversation was always about daily happenings and about how hard it was to find a job, which was a big problem for many people, young and old. Anyway, with no sales, there was no gain, so this was the end of my job as a saleswoman at the insurance company.

Many times, I really felt miserable but never to the point of giving up. Well, I also couldn't afford that leisure, so I tried and tried again in the hope of finding some occupation. How much I dreamed of the day of reaching my economic independence goal! Thank God that during these difficult times, I had my Giudice cousins who were unbelievable human beings, who always gave me a lot of encouragement.

One day, Agostino asked his uncle, Dr. Alessio Butticé, to help me find work. Dr. Butticé was married to Agostino's aunt and held the highest position in the National Health Care of Sicily. I had met this gentleman through my cousins who had taken me along each time they had been invited for lunch at the Butticé's country home. A few days later, after Agostino had talked to his uncle in my behalf, I went to see Dr. Butticé at his office in Palermo with great hope. He was very courteous in showing me the chair to sit down, but at the same time, I also noticed his coldness. He knew the reason why I was there. I needed a recommendation and a letter from him, which would have helped me enormously. In fact, I felt with certainty I could have found a good position as a bookkeeper. However, after our brief conversation, he said to me, "Cara Lina, I am really sorry that I cannot do anything for you. I am against nepotism." I couldn't believe how indifferent he was! By chance, my last name was also Butticé, and he already knew that, so he could have saved me the trip and the disappointment too. Anyway, when I returned home, Agostino also was very surprised that his uncle would excuse himself in that way. There was a lot of favoritism going on in Palermo, and my case would not have been unique.

RAYTHEON-ELSI

By a twist of fate, an uncle of mine, Enzo Ricotta, who was married to my father's youngest sister, Marietta, had returned from Casale Monferrato, Italy, to Sicily for good. Because of his brother who lived in Rome, he had gotten employment at the Raytheon-ELSI (Elettronica Sicula S.p.A) in Palermo and was already working there for almost one year. Knowing that I was in search of work, Enzo tried to help me in the best way he could. He started to investigate if there were any openings available at his working place. As soon as he found out that the company was looking for a temporary statistical typist, he informed me of the opportunity. Fortunately, one of the courses that I had taken in Palermo was for a statistical typist, so I immediately applied for the job, and I got it with no problem.

The Raytheon-ELSI was an Italian company established in Palermo but wholly owned by an American corporation. It produced electronic components for defense and commercial use. My temporary job here started in the spring of 1961, precisely one year after I left Casteltermini for Palermo. Although it was a provisional job, I was very happy to get inside this big company. I thought that once in, I had a better chance of getting a permanent employment. It was really a great place to work. The pay was good; the benefits were excellent, but not for me at this time. The meals at the cafeteria subsidized by the company were inexpensive and good too. In addition, the employees had Saturdays off. At that time in Italy, the normal working days were from Monday to Saturday, and at Raytheon-ELSI, in order to have Saturday free, there were more working hours per day, from 8 a.m. to 6 p.m. with three daily breaks. The company was located far away from where I was living, but there was public transportation. So going to work, I took a bus that crossed one of the long stretches of the city—from Viale Liberta to Via Oreto—and then I changed buses to get to Via Villagrazia where the company was located.

From the bus, I could see many interesting and beautiful places, making the trip very enjoyable.

After a few months at Raytheon-ELSI, I applied for a permanent job as bookkeeper and waited for quite some time. As a matter of fact, weeks, months, then years went by without receiving any answer. Throughout my temporary employment, I worked continuously in the accounting department as statistical typist and was occasionally transferred to the engineering department to type some letters and reports. The only difference between the permanent employees and me was that I did not receive the company's benefits nor did I get paid for the vacation time.

With the passing of time, I came to the realization that many people were being hired, and I was still waiting for the permanent job. I began to be very disappointed, and I thought that it was unfair, but I didn't have any other choice other than waiting. Meanwhile, my income for the regular hours and overtime was really great. Of course, the new hired employees had some connections with politicians or Mafiosi through whom they were getting the proper recommendations for the employment. I had no connections, so my expertise and all the time spent at the company didn't count at all.

At the Raytheon-ELSI, the end of the year was the busiest period for the accounting department due to the preparation of the annual reports to be sent to the Raytheon Company in the USA. The chief of the accounting department was Accountant Corradi, who luckily happened to be my direct boss. Not only was he a good gentleman, he also appreciated my work. In one of the long working nights for the preparation of the reports, my boss asked Engineer Profumo, the head of the Raytheon-ELSI in Palermo, who happened to be there that night, to sign an employment application form in my behalf in order to be hired permanently. Mr. Profumo was taken by surprise when he learnt that I was a temporary employee because he had seen me there for quite some time.

Anyway, that same night, Mr. Profumo signed the form for my steady employment.

Therefore, it was at the end of December 1962 when my job as a statistical typist at the Raytheon-ELSI became permanent. It happened so suddenly that I could not believe that I was now a regular employee. It was my lucky day! After so many difficult years, I had finally reached my goal of financial freedom. To celebrate the happy occasion, I invited my cousins with their children for lunch at the best fish restaurant in Palermo. The restaurant located at Foro Italico had a vast variety of local fish, and one of our favorites was the fish egg omelet, a very tasty Sicilian specialty. The year of 1963 started very well. No more looking for employment, and no more worries. I was still living with my cousins without paying a penny, and for quite some time, I wanted to contribute something to cover the expenses, but I could not convince them. Instead, both husband and wife suggested that I open a savings account. What unbelievable relatives they were!

By chance, I found out that a lady engineer at Raytheon-ELSI was getting married and looking for somebody to rent her furnished room apartment because her lease had not expired yet. I told her that I was interested and went to take a look at the place. I instantly liked it, and because I didn't want to miss this good opportunity, I paid the rent right away. It was in an excellent residential area in Via Lombardia. Many buildings in this neighborhood had big apartments, as well as small ones for the domestic help. Some people leased these small apartments when they were available. Subsequently, I told my cousins that the time had arrived for me to live on my own and I was going to leave their place at the beginning of the coming month. They didn't know what to say but were happy for me and also expressed pleasure at the idea that I was going to live nearby.

* * *

I began to love my cousins' children—Franca, Giovanni, and Giuseppe—as though they were my own children. They grew up to be gorgeous and wonderful and never gave me any problems. In fact, even now, I have warm feelings and love for them all. There were times when my cousins went out and left me in charge of babysitting, and each time it happened, I enjoyed cooking the meals for them. They ate whatever I gave them with a hearty appetite because the food had been prepared by Aunt Lina. Occasionally, I took Giovanni and Franca with me to one of the parks in the city, a pizza restaurant, or an ice cream parlor, and once to the UPIM. The latter was a big department store in Via Maqueda where Giovanni saw a keyboard and immediately started to play. I suddenly noticed many folks around us looking at Giovanni with interest, applauding and asking me if I was the boy's mother. I was so proud of him, but I was just his aunt.

There are some of the episodes of Giuseppe's childhood that, after so many years, are still vivid in my mind. He was over two years, and though very smart for his age, he was not talking yet; but I remember when, for the first time, he said, "Lina." Often, my cousins left the boy alone with me to watch over him. A few times while hiding, I tried to let him speak by telling him to say "Lina." One day, as he was looking all over the apartment for me, he called my name. I cannot describe my immense joy and couldn't believe it. As soon as his parents returned home, I happily conveyed to them what had happened. Of course, for them, it was almost normal, but for me, it was an extraordinary event. Another time, my cousin Lina from Casteltermini came to Palermo with her baby boy Vincenzo. He was Giuseppe's first cousin. At the sight of me taking Vincenzo in my arms, Giuseppe became very jealous and started crying uncontrollably. He was not giving up while holding on to my dress. Very irritated, he was telling his little cousin to go home because Zia Lina is his. Giuseppe was about three years old, and his mother always kept the entrance door locked to make sure her son would not go out alone, but more than once, my cousin accidentally left the key in the door so that Giuseppe took the key, locked the entrance door from the outside, and went to the street. One day, it happened that I was at the window and heard Giuseppe's voice from the street. He was telling me, "Zia Lina, tell mamma not to worry because I have the key." I could not believe what a naughty boy he was, but then again, to me, he was always special. It seemed that he had some intuition because when I used to come home from work, it was his habit to stand on the chair, looking out the window, waiting for my arrival while his mother worried about his dangerous position. Then from far away, I could hear his loud voice, saying, "Zia Lina is coming. Zia Lina is coming!" And he would run toward the door. I remember a particular day; I arrived there wearing a new, beautiful, elegant yellow dress, which I had just bought. Giuseppe came running toward me and embraced me with his dirty chocolate hands. Imagine the conditions of my dress, but I didn't care. His warm welcome was more important to me than anything else. He was making me very happy, and at the same time, he was making his mother upset. On several occasions, I took him to the store or to my apartment. At my place, he knew where I was keeping his sweets so that when he went in, he always went straight to the drawer. Anyway, whatever Giuseppe was doing or saying, he gave me a great joy that I cannot forget. I have been talking about Giuseppe because it was the occasion of his birth that brought me to Palermo, and afterward, my life started to change for the better. I became very attached to him. I had never been with little children so close before, and this was the first and last most beautiful experience in my life.

* * *

Going to live on my own and at the same time be close to my cousins and their children was really fantastic. My new residence in Via Lombardia was at number 3, and my cousins were at number 12. Except for the night, nothing had changed in my daily routine. In fact, every day after work, instead of going to my new place, I continued going to my Giudice cousins' home where I was always warmly welcomed. During summer time, wherever my cousins went with their children, they always took me along

For the Christmas holidays, a few times, I went to Casteltermini with Rosetta and her family, where we all stayed at Uncle Peppino Fantauzzo's home. All of Peppino's children were married and out the house, but the place was not big enough to accommodate the six of us—Rosetta, Agostino, their three children, and me. For sleeping, I could have gone to my Butticé aunts but Uncle Peppino insisted that I remained at his place, so every evening, during my stay there, he set up a bed in the living room for me. What an incredible man he was!

THE NATIONAL HEALTH INSURANCE

I had an episode that I think is worth mentioning. One time, I started to have some health problems. I had low fever that would not go away, strong heart palpitations, and a rough voice. I had all three things at the same time. After several days at home from work, my cousins suggested that I go to see a cardiologist for the palpitations. Thus, I made an appointment. The doctor who belonged to the National Health Care examined me briefly, and with no other evaluations, he concluded that I had a serious heart problem and told me that I had about six months to live. Then before leaving his office, he prescribed some medications to alleviate my trouble. I cannot describe the big shock I experienced. I could not believe that what the doctor said was true. To make a long story short, I was very demoralized and went straight to my cousins' home. I was about thirty-one years of age and convinced that I didn't have long to live so that I started to feel sicker than before seeing the cardiologist. I was taking all the prescribed medications with no results, and I also started being depressed. After a while, my cousins recommended that I go see

Dr. Cannella, a friend of theirs. They made the appointment for me, and when I went to see the doctor for my low fever and rough voice, he discovered that my tonsils were severely infected. He was surprised at what he saw and said to me that I needed to have surgery immediately, so he prepared the proper papers for my hospitalization. The hospitals didn't have any beds available, and in addition, there were many sick people ahead of me, waiting for their chance to be admitted, so I didn't know how long I had to wait for my turn to be admitted. My cousin Agostino telephoned his uncle Dr. Alessio Butticé, telling him of my health condition and the hospitalization difficulty. As I mentioned before, he was a very important person in the National Health Care; in fact, as soon as his secretary made a call for him in my regards, I was immediately admitted to one of the best hospitals in Palermo, and I also got a private room with two beds. Subsequently, my aunt Marietta accompanied me there and stayed with me until I was discharged. It was incredible how well I was treated during my hospitalization due to my last name because they were convinced that I was related to Dr. Butticé. After the tonsillectomy, I remained in the hospital for three days until my temperature was normal, and then I was released.

For two weeks, I couldn't eat or talk and my cousin Rosetta encouraged me to stay at her place during my convalescence. When I went back to work, I started my daily job with no concentration. I was constantly thinking that I didn't have long to live! Those were the words of the cardiologist. Not long after my tonsillectomy, I went to Dr. Cannella for a routine visit. He found me much better than before the surgery. As a matter of fact, he said to me, "I don't find anything wrong with you." But I was convinced that I had a cardiac problem. Before leaving his office, Dr. Cannella told me that his father was seeing a private heart specialist who was considered one of the best in Palermo. He was very expensive and didn't belong to the National Health Care. I told him that I wanted to see this well-known doctor and the money was not a problem for I could afford to pay the high fee. Dr. Cannella himself made a call to the specialist, and I went to see him on the same day. The moment the new doctor saw me, he asked where the sick person was, and I answered, "Doctor, it is me." After his examination, he told me that I was in good health. The only thing he found was a light murmur, which, according to him, was not a real problem, and subsequently, he got rid of all the medications that I had brought with me. What a huge relief! I left the cardiologist's office like a new person, and from that day on, I felt great again.

* * *

During the summer, I often visited my aunt Marietta and uncle Enzo Ricotta, and sometimes, I stayed at their house for the weekend. They had two teenage sons, Elio and Gino, whose favorite pastime was going fishing. On the outskirts of Palermo, there were many good and peaceful places for that sport, so on Saturdays or Sundays, weather permitting, the three of us joined the boys in some rocky and remote location. There, we all had a picnic with good food that Marietta had already prepared at home. I spent a few enjoyable weekends in this way. One time, I invited Aunt Marietta to go to the movie with me, and this time, I insisted that I would buy the tickets. Going in, there was no problem, but when we left the movie house, I noticed that some-body had stolen the wallet from my pocketbook. At Raytheon-ELSI, the office employees were paid monthly, and my wallet contained the entire month's salary. I was very mad, but there was nothing I could do. It was gone, and I had no way of tracing it. In the old days in Sicily, some men had very disgusting and vulgar behavior and took advantage when they were in crowded public places where the women couldn't move at all. These guys were pinching, touching, or stroking the women, and when the ladies turned around to face them, they pretended to be innocent, making the women ill at ease. This is probably how my wallet disappeared.

On the job, I met an accountant who started to have some special feelings for me, and in order to have the chance of knowing each other better, we started going out together. He took me to nice restaurants, café shops, movies, and so forth. During our long walks, he did most of the talking, and when he became self-confident, he started to tell me about his personal life and his intentions in my regards. He seemed to be a fervent socialist and was three years younger than me. I liked him as a friend, and that was all. I also thought that he was too young for me. I told my cousins about this young man, and they advised me not to make any hasty decision, and the age difference should not be a problem. He was a nice, serious man and also had a good job, so I wanted to give him a chance. So we continued going out together with the intention that maybe I would fall in love. I tried, but after a while, I was convinced that we were not made for each other. There was no chemistry between us, and we were two different individuals with nothing in common. Anyway, at the end, I let him know my final decision, and with no hard feelings, we remained friends.

* * *

I remember that November day in 1963 when President Kennedy was assassinated. Elvira Scaffidi, a colleague of mine at Raytheon-ELSI, knocked at my door to tell me about the assassination of the American president. I didn't know that Elvira was also living in the same building where I was, and she had the same apartment arrangement as mine. During our conversation, she told me that soon she was going to live in New York where her entire family had already moved. She also told me that she was engaged to Enzo Sollima, a designer in the engineering department. I knew him because he was also working at Raytheon-ELSI, and at one time, he was interested in me and I was not, but I didn't tell Elvira anything. I just kept listening to what she had to say, and thereafter, for a short time, we became friends until she left for the USA.

For the 1963 New Year's Eve, two colleagues of mine convinced me to join them to celebrate the special event at a nightclub in Palermo. Elegantly dressed, I went with the group to the nightclub where we stayed from 11 p.m. to 5 a.m. The festivities were exuberant; the meals were good, and there was dancing, drinking, and lot of commotion that went on all night long. It was really something to remember. Strangely and without knowing, this New Year's Eve celebration was my first and last one spent at a nightclub in Palermo.

*   *   *

During 1964, my brother Vincenzo returned to Casteltermini for good. Some years back, he had come to town where Uncle Peppino had offered him work at his factory. He stayed for one or two weeks and then disappeared, and nobody knew where he went. Through a friend of his, Vincenzo met Maria from Reggio Calabria, he fell in love, and without any consideration, he hastened to marry her. Vincenzo and Maria got married in the early summer of 1964. The wedding took place in Condofuri Marina, her hometown, and the ceremony was held in a very old and characteristic town tradition. I didn't attend the event because Uncle Peppino didn't want me to go for the reason that the place was a little peculiar. But three of our cousins went to the ceremony— Gino Fantauzzo, Enzo Martorana, and Silvestro Fantauzzo.

I met the bride for the first time at our cousins Rosetta and Agostino's place, where the honeymooners had been invited for lunch. Then after a short honeymoon in Palermo, my brother brought his bride to Casteltermini without any thought. While Vincenzo was away from Casteltermini and happily busy with the marriage and the honeymoon, the family was very concerned about an odd situation. My brother was bringing his wife to an empty apartment in Casteltermini where he also had no job. Anyway, before the honeymooners arrived in town, Uncle Peppino, Butticé aunts, and I took care of furnishing the place. The bride's dowry had already arrived, and the apartment was ready for them. In addition, through a recommendation, my brother also found employment at the Montecatini. How lucky Vincenzo was! He had gotten everything for free, but most of all, he was fortunate for having found a strong and wise wife who was going to put him on the right path. I am sure that our parents were watching on him! Thank God for the lucky ending!

MY TUMULTUOUS MONTHS IN PALERMO

It all started during the month of June 1964. At Raytheon-ELSI, I was transferred from the accounting department to the electronic engineering division to type reports and whatever was needed. Typing was not my favorite task because dealing with the carbon paper inserted between the pages to produce extra copies made it difficult to fix the typed mistakes. Luckily, in this division, I found some nice people who had patience and good manners too. They helped me overcome the discomfort that I felt at the beginning of my transfer. Here, I met a very attractive engineer. I will call him Federico since I don't want to disclose his real name. We casually looked at each other, and something just clicked. I had never felt that way before in my life. Straightaway, I remembered the nuns in the orphanage who often advised us not to look at the men in the eyes when going out for some occasion, making us believe it was dangerous. I tried to avoid Federico's glance because the feelings I felt for him were frightening, but the strong attraction was mutual. In fact, shortly thereafter, we both fell in love and started to meet each other secretly.

After a while, Federico told me that he was married and had two children. Momentarily, I didn't have any reaction whatsoever for my love for him was blind. Soon, the knowledge of his marital status started to make me feel miserable, and consequently, the secret meetings troubled me even more, and finally, the realization began to sink in. I had no future with him. At the beginning of our relationship, I didn't ask him if he was married or not. The attraction was so strong that I was unable to think clearly so that in part, it was my fault. I should have been more careful and smarter, but I was not. All my life, I had been waiting for something so magical like this—falling in love, having my own man and my own family. That was my biggest dream, and now that it happened, the person was not free. I had met the wrong man! I loved him very much, but I had to get out of this complicated situation. I tried to stop seeing him several times with no success. Working in the same department, naturally the situation started to be difficult, especially when he was giving me some of his work to type. We tried to avoid any kind of conversation, except when it was related to the job. Quitting my job was not possible because there were no other jobs available. I remembered the time when I was looking for employment and how difficult it was. Anyway, for the time being, the only thing I could do was to ask for a transfer to another department, then think how to stop seeing him, which, for me, was a must. At this particular time, there were two employees who were having an open love affair. He was an accountant and was also married with children, and she was the secretary of one of the department managers. His wife often came to the Raytheon-ELSI, complaining about her husband's affair and wanted to get his salary. It was an odd and shameful situation, and everybody was gossiping about the matter.

I met Rosetta Ciaramitaro, an accountant in the payroll department, through my uncle Enzo Ricotta. We started to have lunch together and soon became friends. She talked about the daily occurrences at Raytheon-ELSI and about her family. I spoke very little about myself, but one day, I asked her if there were any openings in the payroll department, and she said yes, just one for a bookkeeper. The next day, I went to see the head of the personnel and asked him if I could get the position available in the payroll department, and I also showed him my bookkeeping diploma. He didn't care about my paper; instead, he told me that there were others ahead of me for that position. Of course, the others were men, and in Sicily, the preference was always for the males.

I had to find a department manager who was willing to ask for my transfer. Luckily, I had met Accountant Ragusa when I worked in the accounting department. He was the manager of the purchasing department, so I went to him to see if he could request my transfer to his department, and so he did. This department, located on the main floor, had a lot of commercial correspondence in French, English, and Italian, and here, the typists were all women. I was assigned to type one of the men's French and Italian correspondences. I had studied some French in school, and now, it was like practicing the French language. At the beginning of September 1964, the work load was extremely light, and the days at the office were boring and seemed like an eternity, so I decided to go to Mr. Di Gesú, an engineer whom I had met in the engineering division. Without thinking, I asked him if he had any work for me. Mr. Di Gesú's position was higher than Mr. Ragusa's. Consequently, when Mr. Ragusa came to know that I had gone to his boss to ask for work, he was very disappointed and, from that day on, became incredibly unpleasant and rude to me. I suddenly found myself in an awful situation; nonetheless, I tried not to pay much attention. Maybe Mr. Ragusa was right, but there was no activity for anybody in the department, and I was getting bored and sleepy by doing nothing.

On the same purchasing department floor, there was also a small computer division. It only consisted of a computer programmer who had just arrived from Northern Italy, a keypunch operator, and two machines—one for punching and the other for verifying the cards. The verified cards were then sent to the IBM Computer Center in Palermo, which was unique at that time.

I became friendly with the keypunch operator by the name of Angela Richichi who had just broken ties with her fiancé and was living with her widowed father. She had neither sisters nor brothers, and she really needed somebody to talk to, so I became her confidante. Angela invited me to go to Mondello Beach with her a few times, and whenever I accepted, she came to pick me up at my apartment, and we went to the beach together. I liked her for she was a very sweet, nice girl, but I never shared my confidences with her. Concerning the keypunch machine, it was a novelty for me. At a certain point, I was taken by curiosity and wanted to know how the piece of equipment operated. On my breaks, I started going to Angela's workplace, and one time, I asked her to show me how to punch the cards, and so she did. Once I learned how to operate the machine, I regularly went there and practiced out of curiosity.

THE OPPORTUNITY TO GO TO AMERICA

About the middle of September 1964, I got a call from my aunt Marietta Ricotta. She was inviting me to her apartment for dinner. At her place, I found two of her distant relatives from America, whom she was eager to have me meet. They were the Pomponios. The mother was Maria, and the son was Vincent. Maria spoke a little of the Sicilian dialect, and Vincent spoke English only. Marietta's intention for the invitation was very clear. Some time ago, I had expressed to her my desire of going to America. She didn't know anything about my current secret life. Anyway, after the introduction, Maria and Vincent seemed to be interested in me, and during their stay in Palermo, he took me around the city by bus. It felt strange going out with him because he was extremely shy and childlike, and besides, we could not communicate with each other due to the language barrier. I didn't like him at all. Furthermore, there was no comparison whatsoever between Vincent and Federico. Anyway, my behavior toward the

American man was very courteous. During this time, I was doing a lot of thinking, and while my mind and heart were in turmoil, I was convincing myself that the only way to forget the man who was in my heart was to go to America. Shortly after meeting Vincent, I told Federico that I had fallen in love with another man and told him my determination to go to the USA. At first, he didn't think that I was telling him the truth; then when he saw me with Vincent, he started to convince himself, and little by little, we distanced ourselves. Of course, it was not so easy for me to pretend, especially since we were working in the same company where there was no escape from meeting each other.

The Pomponios returned to the USA after their Sicilian vacation. Vincent started sending me affectionate letters written in Italian, and I presumed that it was his mother who wrote the correspondence for him since he didn't know Italian. Anyway, I politely answered all of his letters and certainly not in the same amorous way. In no time, Vincent sent me a proposal of marriage, which I accepted with one condition; the wedding had to take place in America. I immediately received a happy response from mother and son for my request was also their desire. I didn't know anything about Vincent or what kind of man he was, but I imagined that he was not an interesting person. Nevertheless, I had the nerve to give him a chance to know him better, with the hope that maybe in time, I would become fond of him and forget Federico.

Soon after the agreement with the Pomponios, I started to be fully engaged with the preparation for my trip to America, where I only could go as a tourist. It was already the end of October 1964, so I started planning to be there by Christmas. For the trip, I needed the following documents, which took almost two months to obtain:

1. An Italian passport, which was my first one
2. A letter of guarantee from the Raytheon-ELSI Company for the American Consulate stating that I would have my job back on my return to Sicily

3. A certificate from the Health Department—this was a must document to give assurance that I didn't carry any contagious diseases.
4. A certificate of vaccination
5. A letter of sponsorship from the Pomponios—without this, I could not have gone to the USA. When I received the letter, the family also wanted to send the money for the trip, and since I could afford it, I didn't allow them to pay.
6. A tourist visa from the American consulate in Palermo—I ran into some difficulty, but at the end, I obtained a visa for six months.
7. A around trip airline ticket

When I went to the American Consulate Office for the visa, I found lots of people waiting in line for the interview. When turn came, during the cross examination, the general consul asked me why I wanted to visit the USA. I answered him that I had a big desire to see the "New York World's Fair." It was just during that time of the fair, which ran for two six-month seasons in 1964 and 1965. I noticed that he was not convinced by my answer. Anyway, he said to me that he had to think it over and told me to return in two weeks. When I went back two weeks later, he was not there. In the office was his substitute, the vice consul, who asked me a few questions because the general consul had put a question mark on my application. Suddenly, the vice consul said, "Have I seen you before?" Then he asked me, "Do you live on Via Lombardia?" My answer was yes. We just lived across the street. At this point, there were no more questions, and I got the visa to travel to America.

I knew that Adele Carriglio, who was also working at Raytheon-ELSI, had lived and worked in America several years back and obviously spoke the English language well. I asked her if she would give me a few English lessons in order to get some knowledge of the language. She said yes, and I went to her house twice a week for four weeks. The time was too short, and I learned nothing. At my departure for the USA, she gave me a gift plus her friend's telephone number to call when I was in New York.

Before my departure, I sent a trunk full with my dowry to the Pomponio's address in New York City. Then I gave up the apartment, and I went to stay with my Giudice cousins for the remaining days. From my behavior, my cousins were convinced that I didn't have any feelings for Vincent Pomponio. In fact, every time his name was mentioned, I always tried to avoid any conversation because I didn't know what to say about the man. I remember when they were telling me, "Lina, are you sure that you want to go through with your huge decision? You have time to change your mind. At least here, you have a good job, which you tried very hard to get, and you also have all of us who care about you." My mind was set to go, and I never told them about the wrong man I had fallen in love with. I was bringing my secret to America.

I went to Casteltermini to say good-bye to my relatives and friends. Everybody wanted to know something about Vincent, but I didn't have much to say about him. I visited my cousin Giovanni, whose wife, Carmelina, was recuperating from breast cancer, but that was the last time I saw her. While in Casteltermini, with the occasion of my departure, I asked Butticé aunts if they could give me the money of my father's legal part of the house. There was no problem. They gave me whatever they thought was the value. Going away to an unknown world, I was sure that it was a good idea to have as much money as possible.

On my last day at Raytheon-ELSI, I visited all the departments where I had worked, including the engineering department where I also said good-bye to Federico, the man who was in my heart. For my departure, the colleagues gave me a farewell party and many gifts and cards, and at the end, I left with great sadness. By the way, because of the market difficulties and the lack of business, Raytheon-ELSI closed in 1968, just four years after I had left Palermo.

90

The last get together with my father's family was a few days before leaving for the USA. The occasion was the christening of Maria Gabriella, which took place in Palermo. Maria Gabriella was my cousins Franco and Adalgisa Martorana's first girl. At the celebration, besides the beautiful baby girl, I was also the center of attention. I was asked a lot of questions concerning my going to America, and noticing my coldness, everybody was convinced that I was not going to marry Vincent. I told them all not to worry about me for everything would be just fine.

* * *

On December 22, 1964, I left Sicily for the United States of America. That morning, Uncle Peppino Fantauzzo, my brother and his wife, and other relatives from Casteltermini came to Palermo to the Giudices' house, bringing more gifts, which were small in size but great in value. Then when the time arrived for my departure, four cars full of relatives accompanied me to Punta Raisi, the airport of Palermo. That day, little Giuseppe's behavior was incredible. At home, he followed me everywhere I went, then on the way to the airport, he sat on my lap all the time, and when the time came to say good-bye, he didn't want to let me go. Giuseppe embraced me with all his strength and began to cry because he wanted me to take him with me for I had promised him so. I was very much touched! At the airport, the farewell was very emotional for everybody, and for me, it became more painful when, from afar, I saw Federico who had also come to the airport to waive good-bye. I boarded the Alitalia flight without looking back. I couldn't turn my head because it was too much for me to bear. Then from the window, I could see everybody waiting for the plane to take off.

What a gloomy day it had been, and it was not over yet since the worst part of the day was waiting for me. Anyway, I was going to an unknown world with the determination to begin my life all over again.

Palermo 1960 - My cousins Rosetta and Agostino Giudice

1961 – On an excursion with my cousins Giudice and friends.

1964 – Franca Giudice's birthday
Next to Franca in the center is her brother
Giovanni and behind him it is me.

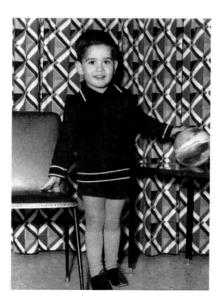

1964 – Giuseppe Giudice

Me, at thirty years

December 1964 – The Baptism of Maria Gabriella Martorana
This was my last reunion with the Butticé
and Martorana' families in Palermo

THE FIRST YEARS IN AMERICA

I arrived at the New World on December 22, 1964. Although it had always been my dream to come to America, without knowing why, now that it materialized, I felt miserable instead of being happy because the reason for my coming was an unpleasant one.

The direct flight from Palermo to New York City was lonely and long, and this was also my first time on an airplane. My seat was next to the window. The plane was not crowded, and nobody was sitting beside me. During the long and exhausting flight, my mind was bursting with countless recollections, and the melancholy that overpowered me was unimaginable. I cried a lot, and to keep my composure, I pretended to read the magazines found in the front seat. At that time, the atmosphere and service on the airplane were excellent. Meals and drinks were first class, and besides blankets and pillows, they were giving slippers to the passengers to wear during the flight, but I was so distraught that I didn't care about anything. When the plane was approaching Manhattan, it was already dark, and from the window, I could see the vast illumination all over the town. In better circumstances, the view of the skyscrapers and other buildings illuminated for the Christmas holidays would have looked fabulous, but for me, it was too depressing. In fact, I was hit by a deep melancholy from which I tried to recoup before the landing.

I arrived at the airport and went through immigration, and with strong heartbeats, I met the Pomponios. To my surprise, I only saw Vincent's parents who welcomed me warmly, but he was not there. I asked the family why Vincent had not come with them to the airport, and their answer was that he was busy at work due to the Christmas Holidays. In my opinion, this should have been a special day for him especially that I was coming from far away. For sure, this was not a good sign; although, I was glad that he was not there.

Coming out of the airport, the weather was depressing. That morning, I had left the beautiful and mild weather in Palermo, and here, I found plenty of snow, ice, and a very cold temperature. At Kennedy Airport, we took the bus to the city and then a taxi to the family's apartment located on Second Avenue and Third Street in Manhattan.

* * *

The welcome at the Pomponios' home was the most rude and unpleasant I had ever experienced in my life. As soon as I entered the apartment, Rosa, the Pomponios' daughter, took her coat and left in a fury, screaming and slamming the door. I didn't understand what she was saying and why she behaved in that terrible way toward me. The parents were very embarrassed of her action, but at the moment, they didn't say a word. Next, Mary, Vincent's mother, showed me my bedroom, which was nice and simply furnished. Afterward, we sat down in the living room for a while.

Vincent came home around 9 p.m., and when he met me, it was like he was seeing an old friend. Frankly speaking, I was glad of his behavior toward me, but I questioned myself, am I going to settle down with this man? The answer was "no way!" Anyway, we had supper during which there was little conversation. Except a few words that Mary exchanged with me and her husband, the atmosphere at the dinner table was depressing. Vincent practically didn't say a word. His father who seemed to be a kind person spoke very little, and his sister Rosa had gone out soon after my arrival. After supper, everybody went to the living room to watch television. I excused myself by saying that I was tired, said good night, and retired to my room. What a melancholic day it had been for me!

My first night in America was like a nightmare. I didn't sleep at all and could not stop crying. My tears poured from my eyes and ran down my face like running faucets. I was immersed in my thoughts, on how miserable I was feeling, thinking what I had left back home, what I found here, and what was waiting for me thereafter. The following day after breakfast, Mary showed me the apartment, which consisted of three bedrooms, two baths, a living room, and a large kitchen with a big terrace. It was a comfortable place on the sixth floor of a condominium building. Mary also explained to me what was going on in the family. First of all, the apartment belonged to Vincent, and currently, his parents and his sister with her fatherless child were living there. Moreover, Vincent was working for the US Post Office, and was supporting his sister Rosa with her child. The bedroom that they gave me before my arrival was Rosa and her child's bedroom. Now they had to use the living room for sleeping. It was very clear why Rosa had behaved in that awful way. My arrival was of great inconvenience and was troublesome for her, and also, her future was undetermined.

For Christmas Eve, the entire Pomponio family was invited to one of Vincent's brothers living in Manhattan. There I was introduced to everybody and got a warm welcome. That evening, they served plenty of food and drinks, and they also exchanged presents. I also received some gifts from Vincent and his parents. In Palermo, a friend of mine had told me of the Christmas traditions in America so that, because my coming to the USA coincided precisely during these holidays, before my departure, I bought some expensive gifts for Vincent and his parents. That evening, I distributed whatever I had brought, except I kept the gold Swiss watch that I had bought for Vincent. It was a long and boring evening for me, and there were loud laughs and talking, and I didn't understand a word. Anyway, I tried to do my best to be pleasant with the company. Then for Christmas Day, the entire family was invited to another of Vincent's brothers living on Long Island. We all went there by train, and then somebody came to the railroad station to pick us up. There were, again, more introductions, more food, and more talking. It was another long and tiresome day. For New Year's Day, all the close relatives came to the Pomponios' place in Manhattan for dinner.

The apartment was terribly hot. To be able to sleep, I had to keep the window ajar, but the cold that was entering from the little opening was too much. I was not accustomed to the very hot inside and terrible cold outside, so I caught a cold that lasted until the summer. I was glad when the evenings came because I would go to my room and be by myself. After spending many restless nights, little by little, I became exhausted and was able to fall asleep. Being more relaxed, I started to be realistic of my situation in America. I had come here with the determination to forget the past, and at this point in time, I had no actual plan to put forward, but with certainty, I knew that I needed to have a lot of patience and be stronger than ever in order to face whatever difficulties were yet to come for me in the future.

At home, there was not much to do other than watching television, which for me was very boring because I didn't understand anything. Sometimes, I tried to help Rosa with the house chores, but that made her extremely angry. Numerous times, if I was watching television, Rosa changed whatever channel was on, and when she was washing the floor, she constantly cleaned under my feet. Whatever she was doing, she certainly did her best to annoy me. I often went out to get away from her, though I didn't know where to go. I had no friends to talk to, so I just walked and thought. I didn't tell Mary about her daughter's behavior toward me because, knowing that she had several health problems, that would have aggravated her condition even more. Living with the

Pomponios would have been much better if it had not been for Rosa who was an intolerable person. Vincent's parents were good and honest people and were wonderful to me—Mary in particular. Rosa resented her parents and her brother's kindness toward me terribly.

Mary sincerely did her best to make me feel at home. She took me out whenever weather permitted, asked me what I wanted to do or what I needed, or prepared my favorite food. One day, I told Mary that I wanted to buy the map of New York City and an Italian/English dictionary. She told her son, so Vincent bought me the map and the dictionary. After the Christmas holidays, I asked Mary if there were schools in the vicinity that I could attend and learn English. It was essential for me to have a break, so going to school for the English language and, at the same time, getting out the house brought a great relief to my daily life. The only free public schools were in the evening and not far from where I was living, so the first day, I went there with Vincent's mother, and subsequently, I went by myself. At school, I didn't understand anything, and most of the students were speaking Spanish. Although I realized very quickly that the school was not for me; nevertheless, I continued going in order to be away from home.

In Palermo, Adele Carriglio had given me a telephone number of one of her friends living in Manhattan, so after a few weeks in America, I made the phone call. I don't remember the gentleman's name anymore, but anyway, he asked me if I were available for dinner the coming Saturday, and I agreed. I was free. Soon after, I told Vincent's mother that I was going out with a friend, and she said okay. It seemed that she didn't mind. The following Saturday evening, the gentleman came to pick me up, and together, we went to a nice restaurant in New York City. I remember how cold that evening was and also how much ice was on the streets! During dinner, most of his talk was about Adele. He wanted to know a lot about her, but I didn't have so much to say because I didn't know anything about her private life. He casually asked me what I was doing in America. I didn't have much to say because, for me, he was a stranger. Adele and this gentleman knew each other very well, and they had been close friends when she was living in the USA. In my opinion, he was in love with her. The evening went smooth, and I spent a pleasant time in the company of a person with whom I was able to have a normal conversation in Italian. After dinner, he took me home by taxi, said good-bye, and I never saw him again.

Every day, Vincent used to buy the *New York Times*, so to occupy my mind, I scanned it and often tried to understand something with the help of the Italian/English dictionary. The lack of knowledge of the English language was terrible. At this time, people that I met were only speaking in English, and sometimes, to please me, they were trying to speak in Sicilian dialect. Because of the various foreign controls, there are several dialects spoken in Sicily; consequently, there were times when I could not understand some of the dialects either.

VINCENT POMPONIO

The man I was supposed to marry in America seemed to be somewhat introverted. At my arrival, whether it was lack of self-confidence or the language barrier between us, his welcome was definitely out of the ordinary. Anyhow, once the Christmas season was over, he started taking me out on his days off from work. Together, we visited several places in Manhattan. Once, he took me to see a show at Radio City. Another time, he brought me to the Hayden Planetarium near Central Park. I remember the Planetarium in particular because I enjoyed looking at the spectacular celestial mysteries of the stars without understanding a word of the related narration, and I was sure that this was Vincent's favorite place. I tried to communicate with him through gestures and expressions to make him realize that I didn't understand what he was talking about, but he kept talking in English. It seemed that he was not making any effort to understand what I was telling him. Maybe he was not smart enough. At home, in the evening, Vincent's hobby was looking at the stars through his telescope on the terrace. With a lot of enthusiasm, he was often calling me to join him on the balcony to watch the stars in the sky, and to make him happy, I always joined him.

Every time Mary saw her son and me together, I noticed how delighted she was. Her big desire was to settle her son down as soon as possible. Vincent was a good man but extremely timid, and in my opinion, he had never been alone with a woman. He was older than me, but his behavior was not of a mature person. As a matter of fact, it was his mother who was telling him to kiss me. I remember how repulsed I felt when he tried to kiss me, and at the same time, I was sorry for him because he was a nice fellow!

Rosa knew some Sicilian dialect, but when it was really necessary, she always spoke to me in English. She was a mean person! Anyway, she did the best she could do to keep any warm feelings from starting between her brother and me. She knew precisely what she wanted—me out the way and her brother to continue taking care of her and her child. During my stay there, I thanked God that Rosa went out to play cards at some of her friends' home or went, who knows where, and returned home after midnight. For the time being, the circumstances were complicated, and there was no choice for me other than to stay there, be thankful, and ignore Rosa.

*   *   *

Three months had passed since my arrival in America, and I knew, more than ever, that Vincent was not the man I wanted to spend my life with. I also knew that I could not live at the Pomponios' place for long. I had to make a decision and soon. However, being alone in an unknown land was not an easy situation. I needed a little time to come up with some strategy, and the first step I took was to get familiar with the city of Manhattan. I studied the map of NYC, the routes of the buses and subways, and started going to the city center by myself, taking along the map and the Italian/English dictionary.

It was already the spring of 1965. The weather was much better now, and it began to warm up. That brought a huge lift to my life. Just when I was thinking of how to get out of my current situation, Vincent's mother started to talk about the wedding of her son and me. It was very awkward for me to tell her that I didn't have any feelings for her son. From my behavior, she already had some intuition that nothing was going on between her son and me. I told Mary that I was deeply sorry, but Vincent deserved somebody better than me. In addition, I told her that as soon as possible, I would leave their apartment. God bless Mary because her answer was that it means it was not God's will, and then she said to me, "Do not rush to move out of my place. You can stay as long as you need."

Mary was a special lady and was also fond of me. In fact, on more than one occasion, she told me that she would have loved to have had a daughter like me. How happy she would have been if the wedding had taken place, but she also knew that her son was not behaving like a grown-up, maybe due to his timidity or who knows. The entire family had been incredibly good to me except Rosa.

Regarding the marriage, my uncle Peppino Fantauzzo was supposed to come to New York on my wedding day to bring me to the altar. Instead, I wrote him a letter to let him know that no ceremony was going to take place. In receiving my news, Peppino started to worry and wanted me to go back to Sicily, but that was out of question for I had made up my mind to remain in the USA. Other Italian relatives were not surprised of my decision because in advance, they had already imagined that I wouldn't marry Vincent and once in America, I would make an attempt to stay.

When a few of Mary Pomponio's Italian-American friends, to whom I had already been introduced, found out that I was not going to marry Vincent, they wanted to play the matchmaker with some of their relatives. But respectfully and with a smile, I declined their proposition. They were good and simple people who wanted to help me by settling me down with a greengrocer, a shopkeeper, or others to remain in the USA. They meant well. It was never my intention of getting married just to stay here and divorce later. In fact, if the case was that, I could have done so by marrying Vincent who was not a stranger to me. I was not the kind of person to take advantage of anybody because it would have been a very dishonest action on my part.

1965 – CHANGED USA VISA FROM TOURIST TO STUDENT

My tourist visa had two more months to go, and after that, I had to return to Italy. To extend my stay in the USA, at least temporarily, I needed to have the visa changed from tourist to student, and to do that, I didn't want to wait until my current visa expired. I spoke to Vincent's mother about my intention, and she contacted a friend of hers who knew an immigration lawyer by the name of Cusumano. I went with Mary's friend to the lawyer's office in downtown Manhattan. After I spoke to him about my USA status change, he told me that the student visa application would only be valid for one year stay, and to obtain that, I needed a sponsor who would take full financial responsibly during my stay in America. The Pomponio family willingly provided the letter of sponsorship for the immigration, which in my case the paper was just a formality because I fortunately had the means to support myself, at least for the time being. The savings that I had in Italy was now very useful. The lawyer also recommended that I attend the Spanish American Institute, which was an inexpensive school.

While waiting for my student visa, I started looking for a furnished room in the *New York Times*. I got one on West End Avenue near Eighty-fourth street. I wrote down my questions translated in English, and then I made the phone call to find out if the room was still available and what the price was. The landlord answered that the room was vacant, and the weekly rent was thirteen dollars. By myself, I took a bus on Second Avenue to Forty-second Street. There, I changed buses to go to Broadway and Eighty-sixth Street, and afterward, I walked to the building on West End Avenue. I went to see the landlord who showed me a large room with a big window and modest furniture. The place had some inconveniences. For instance, the bathroom in the corridor and the refrigerator in the kitchen both had to be shared with the other tenants, and there was no cooking in the facility. However, it had some positive factors, such as the excellent location, the nearby public transportations, and the reasonable weekly rent. After a short consideration, I concluded that the place was fine for me, so I paid for the room and left. Back at the Pomponios' home, I told Vincent's mother that I had already found a place and that I temporarily needed to leave the trunk that I had brought from Palermo at their place. She said that was okay with her. Subsequently, I prepared my suitcases, thanked everybody, and left the Pomponios' place. Mary, who was related to one of my relatives in Sicily, felt like it was her responsibility to see that I was doing fine. She told me to let her know whatever I needed and also invited me to go to her place for lunch every Sunday. Mary didn't have to behave in that way toward me, but she did because by nature, she was a remarkable person.

When I moved to my new place, simultaneously, I received my student visa from the immigration. This was great news because I had left the Pomponios' home before receiving my status change in the USA. Subsequently, I enrolled at the Spanish-America Institute located in Uptown Manhattan. The school hours were in the evening, and the fee was ten dollars a week, so far, not too bad. The students were of all ages; they all spoke Spanish and were attending the class just to stay in America with the student visa. Some of the students had been in this country for more than five years, and they still could not speak English. In my opinion, this school was a joke, and the pupils were not interested in learning. But whether I liked it or not, with the student visa, I had to go to school. Then for my furnished room, I just bought a radio, a few pans and plates, and an electric burner for cooking in my room, and because of the limited facilities, I started buying what was easy for me to cook at the supermarket. Anyway, I did my best to eat at home and save some money. Sometimes, I went to eat at some cafeterias in mid-Manhattan, and once a week, I started going to Tad's Steakhouse in Times Square where the steak, potato, garlic bread, and salad were very tasty.

Every Sunday, I went to the Pomponios' home for lunch. Everybody was glad to see me, including Rosa. Since I had left their place, Rosa's behavior toward me had changed. Now she didn't have to worry about her brother supporting her and her child anymore. I was out of the picture, so everything returned as it was before my arrival in the USA. After a few Sundays, I stopped going to the Pomponios' because, from Vincent's behavior, I noticed that he still had a little hope. In fact, once, he went to some Caribbean islands for a vacation and was sending me cards one after the other, inviting me to join him there. I felt really uncomfortable, so I decided not to go to their place anymore.

LIVING ON MY OWN IN MANHATTAN

It was a great challenge living in a big city like Manhattan. Taking the bus was fine, but traveling by subway was another thing. At the beginning, I was missing many of the subway exits, or I was taking the wrong train and consequently was ending up in strange places. Every day, I tried to go out to keep my sanity, but being alone, it was very difficult. I remember when I was strolling on some of the city avenues, looking at the countless unfamiliar blank faces while listening to the whispering of the many spoken languages and observing the big crowds going in all directions. It really seemed like I was on another planet, and the loneliness around me was unbearable. From the world I left behind, a lot of memories were invading my mind like uproars. The city atmosphere was depressing. I felt empty, indifferent, and cold to everything. But with the passing of time, things started changing, and as a result, my reasoning improved too. Little by little, I started going window shopping.

The language was my biggest obstacle. With the help of the dictionary, I tried writing down a few simple questions before asking for directions or something else, and afterward, nobody understood me because my English written questions were constructed terribly. However, I was often lucky to meet kind folks who stopped and made an effort to help me. Other times, it was real unpleasant to see people looking at me and then disregarding me and going on their way. Hard as it was, I managed going on in this way, and my willpower to succeed was always stronger than ever. Since I was not working and with the evening school only, I had plenty of free time on my hands, so I often bought the *New York Times* to keep me a little busy. I liked to look through its pages and then tried to get some understanding.

I do not remember how Elvira Scafidi, a friend of mine from the Raytheon-ELSI of Palermo, got in touch with me. Anyway, she invited me to her wedding, and I gladly accepted the invitation. When the day arrived, I happy went to the ceremony, which took place in the Bronx, New York. There, I met Elvira and the rest of her large family. Elvira's relatives were incessantly talking to me in the Sicilian dialect. They had a lot to tell about their family members living in the old country, their jobs and their workplaces in New York City, and so on.

Enzo Sollima, now Elvira's soon-to-be husband, had been transferred from the Raytheon-ELSI in Palermo to the Raytheon

Company in Boston. For the wedding, Enzo invited a few people from his workplace, and at the wedding banquet, my seat was at the table reserved for the Raytheon's personnel. One of the gentlemen sitting at the table remembered to have seen me years back at Raytheon-ELSI in Palermo, and in Italian, he asked me what I was doing in New York, and I answered him that I was studying English and also looking for a job. Then before leaving the place, he gave me a telephone number of an Italian company to call. With the knowledge of the Italian language, he thought that they could employ me. The following Monday, I called the number that I had just gotten. The company was in Downtown Manhattan, and somebody from the company gave me an appointment and also instructed me on how to get there. The office building was in the Wall Street area. I arrived there and was interviewed by an Italian gentleman, and from the questions, I immediately knew that I was not the right person for they needed a stenographer who spoke English and Italian perfectly. Anyhow, they told me to contact them as soon as my English had improved. After the interview, one of the employees invited me to have lunch with him, and because I didn't have anything to lose, I accepted the invitation. I didn't know why I was treated so cordially, but maybe it was due to my acquaintance with the man from Raytheon!

* * *

For one reason or another, I often went to see my immigration lawyer, and one time, he introduced me to one of his Italian clients who, soon after, invited me out the following Sunday. I don't remember the client's name, but anyway, on that Sunday morning, the man came to my place, and we went to the Bronx Zoo where I had never seen so many animal species. The visit to the big zoo was very interesting, and I really enjoyed looking around the place and also having the opportunity to speak in Italian. After a while, the man started to talk about some activities that didn't make any sense and what he would have liked to do in the future to make money. I was listening carefully without saying a word and understood very well what his ideas were and what kind of man he was. His intentions were criminal activities to make money, and I felt ashamed to have met a person with such a dangerous mind. I was really surprised that the lawyer had introduced me to this individual. On the other hand, I was sure that he didn't know anything about the Italian guy. Anyway, I didn't want to spoil the day. In the afternoon, the man took me to a very nice restaurant in Brooklyn where he ordered lobster, among other things, for both of us. I remember this occasion because it was the first time I ate lobster, and I liked it. Toward the evening, when he took me back home, he told me that he wanted to see me again. I answered him that I was too busy with other engagements, which were just excuses. Then I thanked him for the lovely day and said good-bye. He understood that I was not the person that he was looking for.

My money from Italy was dwindling. I had to pay for everything, room, school, food, transportation, and more. Though the food was inexpensive in comparison with that in Italy, it was costly for me, and being on my own, I had to ration everything. Many times, I walked instead of taking the public transportation to save a few cents. I went to the Alitalia Airline to get the reimbursement of the half around trip ticket that I had purchased when I came to the USA. I also wrote to my Giudice cousins in Palermo to withdraw and send me some of the money that I had in my saving account.

WORK PERMIT DENIED

Being in the USA with the student visa, I needed a permit from the immigration office in order to get job. When I realized that my money reserve started shrinking, I went to my lawyer to apply for a part-time job authorization. He did, but the request to get my work permit was denied. As a foreign student, I was not allowed to work in America. In many circumstances, the immigration office gave work permits, but my case was different for I had been sponsored by the Pomponio family who were completely responsible for my stay here. At the wedding of Elvira and Enzo, I had learned that Elvira's sisters were working in a garment factory on Thirty-fourth Street in Manhattan as pieceworkers. In the middle of June 1965, I called the sisters and asked them if they could get a job for me at the factory. They replied that they would talk to their boss for me. They did, and their boss told them that it was okay for me to go there, and the only thing that I had to bring was my social security card, which I didn't possess.

THE SOCIAL SECURITY CARD

The way I got the card was never my desire, but I had to. With no work permit and no social security card, it was impossible to find any job, which I needed badly. After some thought, I decided to try the next step. I found out where the Social Security Office was located and went there with my dictionary. Of course, after waiting in line for some time, it was my turn, and the social security employee wanted to see my Green Card, which I didn't have. Anyhow, I didn't tell him that I was a foreign student; I just said that I had left my Green Card at home. Fortunately, he believed me and gave me the forms to fill out. Until now, I cannot forget this particular episode since it was my life's biggest lie. I didn't have any other choice. I needed a job in order to survive in America. Thank God, two weeks later, I received my social security card in the mail.

MY FIRST JOB AT A GARMENT FACTORY

Toward the end of June 1965, I went to the factory, applied, and got the job. With a pay of forty-five dollars a week, I was so glad that I would now make some money! The factory's manager who spoke to me in Italian seemed to be a nice gentleman, but the factory was a very hot place, and for me, the conditions were even worse because all day long, my work assignment was turning woolen sleeves of men's suits. Besides the tailors and dressmakers, many of the employees were pieceworkers whose job, in my opinion, was a piece of cake. Simply put, the faster they went on the sewing machines, the more money they were earning. At the factory, I met a nice lady by the name Carmela who became my friend. Subsequently, she invited me to her daughter's wedding and more than once to her house in Brooklyn. She was a warm and kind person and was also a big moral support at this workplace where I met some very unfriendly people who made me feel uncomfortable. During the summer, working at the factory was too much. I was losing weight due to the unbearable summer heat and also from the hot steam emitted by the pressing machines used for the ironing. I was observing other workers, and it seemed like that work condition was normal for them, and I could not understand it! However, there was also another problem with me. I was going to work wearing dressy clothes, like going to a nice air-conditioned office, and this made my situation worse. At this time, I didn't have any casual clothing, so wherever I went, I was always dressed up with the clothes that I had brought from Italy, and many times, I really felt awkward going to certain places. Because my future was unknown, I didn't want to spend any money to buy some comfortable dresses. I was indeed saving every penny. After a short time at the factory, I went to my immigration lawyer and asked him if he could find a job for me. I didn't tell him anything about my social security card or about my work at the garment factory. A few days later, the lawyer called and informed me that there was a young couple with a child in Queens, New York, looking for a babysitter. I told him that I would try that position. Not knowing if I would like my new job or not, I kept my furnished room, and at the factory, I told my boss that for personal reasons, I needed two weeks off from work. The boss consented, and I got the time requested without pay.

THE BABYSITTER

It was sometime in 1965 when I tried this new job. The child's parents were full-time working people, and they certainly needed a person who would do a lot for them. Anyway, during the day, I started to be occupied with whatever they wanted me to do, and in the evening, I went to school in Manhattan. I soon realized what this couple expected from me was more than just babysitting; they also wanted me to do the house chores. This kind of arrangement was not for me, so before the two weeks were over, I told the folks that I was quitting, so they paid me for two weeks, and I left.

I returned to the garment factory where I continued doing the same silly work, turning sleeves, but at least here, I knew how many hours a day I was supposed to work, and then I was free for the evening school and more. About a month later, I had a talk with the manager. I asked him if he would give me a piecework job, and he said that he would think about it. A few days later, my boss called me in his office and asked me if I was available that weekend as he wanted to take me to his country home. I couldn't believe what he had just asked me. I was so surprised! He was in his fifties, and I had already met his wife and niece who were working at this same factory. As matter of fact, his niece had invited me to her apartment in Brooklyn for dinner. Anyway, my answer was that I had other engagements, and the conclusion of this episode was that instead of getting the piecework job, my boss's behavior toward me changed drastically. He was no more courteous and kind toward me as before, and my situation there started to be very unpleasant. I was sure that sooner or later, he would find some excuse to fire me.

MET AN OLD ACQUAINTANCE BY CHANCE

It was during the month of September 1965 when one day I went to a pizzeria to have something to eat, and there, I heard one of the employees speaking in Sicilian dialect. Being in a foreign country and hearing people speaking your language, you suddenly feel nostalgic. I approached that employee and started to talk to him in Italian. We were from different towns, but both belonged to the same province of Agrigento. He told me that his girlfriend came from Palermo, but she was not Sicilian. I asked him if by any chance her name is Frances Diamond. "Yes," he said, and then he added, "How do you know her?" Just to make it short, I asked him for her telephone number, which he didn't want to give me because he wanted to ask her first if she wanted to contact me or not. However, I gave him my name and telephone number. The following day, Frances called me, and I cannot describe how happy I was that she had remembered me. Since we were both busy during the week, we agreed to get together on the coming Sunday. On Sunday, I met Frances in person at the YWCA where she was residing, and from there, we went together to a cafeteria in mid-Manhattan. We spent a few wonderful hours in animated conversation, with a great nostalgia. We talked a lot about life in Palermo and people that we both knew there. At a certain point, she asked me what I was doing in New York City, and I answered her that for the moment, I didn't feel like talking about myself. Then she started telling me her personal life and about her boyfriend and her job. She was working as a secretary for an American shipping company in Downtown Manhattan. The time we spent together at the cafeteria was very pleasant and went quickly. In fact, Frances realized that it was already past the YWCA curfew time. We left the place, took the buses, and each of us went our separate ways.

Frances was born in England. At the age of seventeen, she left her country and moved to Italy to study art. Painting was her passion. After spending many years in Northern Italy, she moved to Sicily where she stayed for a few years before going to the USA. While in Sicily, with her good knowledge of the English language, she got a job at the Raytheon-ELSI in Palermo as the secretary of Mr. Kaminsky, an American engineer. Though we both worked for the same company and on the same floor, we were just acquaintances. We saw each other almost every day, and we casually said hello. Then I didn't see her anymore because she had gone to America.

I was overjoyed to have found Frances. To meet a familiar person from the old country in a foreign land is really fantastic, and we soon became friends. We met each other whenever possible. We were both busy—Frances with her job and boyfriend and me with work and school—but we often spoke on the telephone, and that was great for me. At least I had somebody to talk to. Our conversations were always in Italian, and that was good for her because she liked to speak in Italian, while for me, it would have been more important to speak in English. Frances was a sincere and warm person, and I liked her friendship. She had several friends, and most of them were Americans with good jobs and boyfriends. I was her only Italian friend, and she liked that very much because she was fond of the Italian people in general. She would often talk about the happy years she spent in Italy and all her Italian romantic stories.

More than once, Frances asked me why it was taking so long for me to learn English. In a certain way, she was right. Frankly speaking, I was trying hard to learn English, but I didn't have much talent for the language. In addition, I hadn't had a good opportunity to really practice it. For example, when I lived with the Pomponios, they were only speaking to me in Sicilian dialect. At the garment factory, people spoke in Sicilian dialect, in Italian, or in Spanish. At the Spanish-American Institute, the students were speaking in Spanish or in Portuguese. At the current workplace, my job didn't require much speaking. At home, I always kept the radio on, which was hard to understand. For me, it seemed that they were talking too fast. Anyway, until now, I had managed the situation reasonably and was continuing to do the best I could to improve my English.

After a month from our first meeting at the YWCA, Frances moved to a residential hotel in the Upper West Side, at Seventieth Street and Broadway. The new location was better for both of us because we were now living closer to one another. When she was available on Saturday, I went to her hotel, and there, we decided what to do for that evening. More than once, we went to the night club called CORSO on the East Side. Frances was good with meeting people, and by nature, she was a very friendly person. I was the opposite of her, very reserved, and my English was of no help either. Most of the time, I just went to please Frances; otherwise, she would not have gone to any place without company. Once, a Greek man invited me to dance at the CORSO Night Club. He thought that I was from Greece, and I was not surprised at that because other people that I had met in New York City, so far, had also thought that I came from Greece. In their opinion, my face had Greek features. Though I was neither a dancer nor a talker, I danced with the man who, before leaving the club, asked for my telephone number. A few days later, he called and invited me out the next Saturday. When he came, he took me to a Greek restaurant and afterward brought me back home. My first impression of him was positive. He seemed to be a nice and pleasant person to be with. I remember when, at the garment factory, I told my friend Carmela about this man, and she told me to be watchful because he could be one of those men looking for fun only. Again, the Greek man invited me out for the following Saturday, and I accepted. He took me to a restaurant and then to the movie; afterward, he wanted to take me to his apartment. From his behavior, I understood clearly what his intentions were, so I wanted to take a taxi to get home, but with insistence, he accompanied me to my place. I never heard from him again, and that was the end. From that day on, I found it humiliating and degrading to go to any night club, and Carmela was right. Most men think that women go there looking for men to have fun and not to meet real, decent people.

MY FIRST GOOD JOB OPPORTUNITY FOUND THROUGH THE NEW YORK TIMES

I came to know this newspaper when I was living with the Pomponio family, and since then, although I didn't understand much, I became convinced that it was a good paper where one could find any kind of information. I bought the *New York Times* from time to time, and lately, I bought it almost every Sunday. With the help of the Italian/English dictionary, I soon began to understand the contents of some of its sections. It was in the middle of October of 1965 when my eyes caught the job classifications section. It was full of advertisements and plenty of companies looking for experienced keypunch operators. At Raytheon-ELSI in Palermo, I had learned how to punch the cards with the IBM machine.

Anyway, I could not believe that there were so many jobs available for specialized people like keypunch operators! I started to think; *perhaps I could get a job as keypunch operator.* I got the telephone number of the E. H. Hutton Brokerage House from the *New York Times.* Then I wrote down what to say on the phone in English. The following day, I made the call to the keypunch department and asked if somebody spoke Italian there. The answer was yes, and as a matter of fact, they gave me the department supervisor who was from Napoli, Italy. We spoke in Italian, and I told him that I knew how to punch cards, but I didn't have any experience. I also told him that my English was not good. In short, he told me to go there for a test and instructed me how to get to their place. Subsequently, when I went to the E. H. Hutton Brokerage House in Downtown Manhattan for the test, I was a little nervous and not so sure that I would get the job. The friendly supervisor introduced himself and, after a brief inter-view, gave me a test containing numbers and a little of English to punch on cards. It was really an easy test. The interview and test went fine, so the supervisor told me that my starting pay would be at eighty-five dollars a week and the working hours would be in the afternoon from 4 p.m. to 12 p.m. Afterward, he wanted to know when I was able to start working there, and my answer was, "Is next Monday okay?" It was reasonable. On the same day I got the new job, I changed my current Spanish/English school for another one located in midtown Manhattan. The new school was a little more expensive and was not better than the first, but it had classes in the morning, and my new job was in the after-noon. I could not enroll to a good English school yet because it was too expensive for me, and as long as I had the student visa, I was compelled to go to school. I went to the factory and hap-pily quit my job. Knowing that my English was bad, the man-ager and everybody was surprised that I had found a much better employment. Subsequently, I walked from the factory to Macy's Department Store, where I bought some casual clothes. I finally could afford to spend some money on myself. I had felt so tired and ridiculous for going around all dressed up. Then I went to the Tad's Steakhouse to have a good meal, and afterward, I took a walk on Forty-second Street in a very good mood. I could not believe what had happened. For me, it was something unrealistic, being in a city as big as New York, and I had found a job with no recommendations whatsoever, just through the *New York Times*!

At the end of October 1965, I started working at E. H. Hutton Brokerage. The environment was nice and comfortable. What a huge difference in the atmosphere and work conditions in com-parison to the garment factory! In addition, my supervisor was a very nice person. I didn't have any problems with my keypunch job as it was easy and I did my best, although in the beginning, I was really slow. My weekly pay increased from forty-five to eighty-five dollars. Considering that I had learned keypunching from just being inquisitive, I felt very fortunate that my salary was almost doubled. Who knew what a great improvement this would have on my life!

After a while at E. H. Hutton, the supervisor introduced me to an employee who was of Italian origin and spoke some Italian, and we started dating. On Saturdays, and sometimes on Sundays, he took me to the movies, to restaurants, and to the beach in Coney Island and in Staten Island. One day, he took me to a party at one of his friends' house in Brooklyn for a celebration, which I don't remember the occasion. There among the friends were also some of his relatives to whom I was introduced. There was a swimming pool and some of the guests enjoyed jumping into the water. I had told my friend that I didn't know how to swim. However, later, he stupidly pushed me into the pool where, if I had not been rescued, I would have drowned. Coming out the water, I was really enraged but was also able to control myself because I didn't want to spoil the festivity. I remained there until the end of the party without saying a word. There was something disgusting about this friend. His finger nails were always soiled, making me nauseated when looking at his hands. I also didn't like his manners, and the pool occurrence was the conclusion. From that day on, I didn't want to see him again.

* * *

I remember the evening of the Northeast blackout, which occurred after the rush hour in the month of November 1965. I was on Broadway, walking toward home and had ten more blocks to go when life in the city suddenly stopped. All became black. Everything fell into chaos, and the crowd rushing home or going to other places was much disoriented. Fortunately, there was a bright full moon over the city, providing some aid to the millions who were plunged into the darkness. The buses were running, but the subways had stopped. The television and the radio stations in the New York metro area went dead too. I walked home, and when I got to the dark building, it was hard to find my way in.

Fortunately, people were helping each other. I don't recall how long the blackout lasted because once in bed, I fell asleep.

A few days before Christmas, Vincent's mother called and invited me to her home for a holiday dinner. Instead of spending the day alone at home or going to eat outside by myself, I accepted the invitation. There, I got an unexpected warm welcome and also found Rosa completely changed for the best. Then everybody wanted to know how I was doing and what was new in my life. I was glad that I went to the Pomponios' home where I spent a nice day in a friendly atmosphere.

The year of 1965, which was my first and most difficult in America, ended reasonably well and also gave me hope for the future.

For the arrival of the year 1966, Frances and I decided to celebrate the first day of the New Year at a luxurious place where we could enjoy some extravagance. A few weeks earlier, Frances took care of the reservations at the Plaza Hotel Restaurant in Central Park South and Fifth Avenue. All dressed up, we went to the restaurant for lunch. We remained a little surprised because the place was almost empty. Probably the customers were tired from the celebration the night before. We started with champagne, and then we ordered the best of everything. The ambiance was great. The food and service were excellent, and the place was very expensive too, but for that day, we didn't care. It was later in the afternoon when, satisfied and a little tipsy, we left the restaurant and went home by taxi.

At the beginning of each January, all non-USA residents were compelled to register so that 1966 was my first year to register with the Immigration and Naturalization Office as an alien.

THE 1966 NEW YORK CITY TRANSPORTATION STRIKE

It was called by the union workers at their contract expiration date, which began on New Year's Day, and lasted for twelve days. It happened at the beginning of Mayor John V. Lindsay's Administration. Millions of commuters were affected by the strike, and since there were neither subways nor bus services, the City of New York was completely paralyzed. To go to work was a big problem because of the difficulty to get any ride. All the cabs were full because they were taking as many passengers as they could for each trip. Between taxis and many private cars going in all directions, the traffic was so congested that nothing was moving smoothly. It was really a crazy time. At this precise time, most people were helping each other. As a matter of fact, it was normal for people with private cars to stop and help anyone who needed a ride to get to work, if the passengers were going in the same direction. I was living on West End Avenue, and to take a taxi to go to work, I walked from my building down one block to the corner of Eighty-fourth Street. There I tried to get a taxi and then another, but it was useless. They were all either full or going in different directions.

While I was waiting for the chance to get transportation, behind the taxi that I had just stopped was a red car that had also stopped at the corner of Eighty-fourth Street. Inside the red car were two gentlemen. The one sitting on the passenger seat inquired where I wanted to go, and I told him, "Wall Street."

"So do I," he replied. Then with a beautiful smile, the man said to me, "Can we give you a lift?"

"Yes," I answered. Subsequently, after I got inside the car, the man who had spoken to me introduced himself. His name was Andrew Janovitz. I instantly liked him very much. This was an extraordinary event that I will remember for the rest of my life. On this day, I got a lift and also met the man who would become my husband. On the way to Wall Street, Andrew did most of the talking. He asked me a few questions, which were difficult for me to understand. Anyway, I tried to answer him, and who knows what I was saying. Then he asked me if I knew the French language, and I answered, "Very little." I liked that he knew French, and to continue the conversation, I asked him, "Do you French?" instead of saying, "Do you speak French?" Andrew and the driver burst into laughter. I looked at them questioningly, not sure what was so funny. They laughed even more. Much later, I learned the meaning of my silly question, and Andrew never forgot it. While in the car, Andrew asked for my telephone number, which I gladly gave to him. They took me to the entrance of the E. H. Hutton Brokerage House building where we said good-bye, and afterward, they continued for Bankers Trust on Wall Street. Andrew and I were living on the same block, just two doors apart, but we had never met each other before.

Two weeks later, I got a call from Andrew, asking me if I were available on the coming Sunday to go to the movies, and without any hesitation, I answered, "Yes, I am free." I was so happy that he had remembered me! We met outside my building and walked toward Broadway and then to the movie. He asked me if it was better for me to communicate with him in French, and I said yes. I thought that in French, it would have been much easier for me to understand him than in English. He slowly started to speak in French, adding a few words in Italian and some in English. For the time being, this was the only way I could communicate with him. It was really awful, but he didn't seem to mind. After the movies, he took me to the entrance of my building where I thanked him for the invitation and said good-bye. He didn't say anything about meeting each other again. I thought that maybe he was disappointed with my poor language skills. It was very hard to express myself, but I could not help it! Then two months later, I got another call from Andrew. He again asked me if I were free on the coming Sunday to go out with him, and again my answer was yes. Subsequently, we met outside my building, walked toward Broadway, and then he took me by taxi to a French restaurant on Seventy-second Street and Broadway. At the restaurant, he asked me what I wanted to order, but I didn't know anything about the French cuisine, so he ordered for me too.

It looked like we liked each other, and again, it was terrible for me not be able to have a normal conversation. I was talking like a little child. Nevertheless, I understood when he told me that he was not married, was born in Czechoslovakia, and was Jewish. After enjoying his company and dinner at the restaurant, he took me to my building door where we said good-bye and nothing else. That evening, the word *Jewish* began to resonate in my mind. I started to remember the Good Friday in my hometown when, from the church pulpit, the priest was preaching about the life of Jesus, his death in the hands of Pontius Pilate, and the Hebrews who put Christ on the cross. In my childhood, I came to believe that the Jews were wicked people because at that time, the church was unreasonable toward them. I never thought that one day I would meet a nice Jewish man and subsequently would have very deep feelings for him. How strange it was now! Andrew was the first American man whom I came to be fond of. He had good manners, a beautiful smile, and was attractive too, and since I met him, I began to feel happy and also felt like I were a different person, but really, I didn't know anything about him. Andrew continued to invite me out, and it was always on Sundays. Naturally, it didn't take long for me to imagine that he was involved with someone else, but I accepted his invitations anyway.

SHARING APARTMENT IN NEW YORK CITY

For the Memorial Day weekend, I had hoped to spend some time with Andrew, but it didn't happen because he already had other plans. In fact, through a mutual friend, I found out that he went away with his girlfriend to a resort in Upstate New York.

LINA BUTTICE-JANOVITZ

Although he had never told me that he had some feelings for me nor did he know of my feelings for him, I became very disillusioned. As a result, I decided to change my residence to be away from him as we were living too close to each other.

It was through the *New York Times* that I found an apartment to share at 900 West 104th street, between West End Avenue and Broadway, and without delay, I went there to look at the place. The apartment was in an elegant upscale building with a doorman, and my first impression was that it was fantastic. I arrived there and the doorman called the person who had put the advertisement in the paper. Then I went to the fourth floor where the apartment was located, and there I met Jean. To help with the expenses, Jean was sharing the place with two other girls. One of them had already left, and she needed a replacement. The beautifully furnished apartment contained three large bedrooms, two baths, a living room, and a big kitchen. The largest bedroom with a full bath was occupied by Jean, and that made sense because she had the lease and the responsibility of the place. Then Jean showed me the available room and the second bath with a shower to be shared with Betty, the other girl. I liked the size of my room, which was nicely setup. It had a big window looking out onto the street. For Jean, I was all right. My part of the rent would be eighty-five dollars a month, which included the expenses for the cleaning woman once a week. Because I was enthusiastic about the place, I immediately paid the monthly rent and left. On that same day, I called one of Andrew's friends, George Koskoris, who came with his car and helped me move to my new place. In the evening, I met Betty, the other roommate, and she seemed to be a nice lady. At the new place, I felt really comfortable. There was nothing to compare with the previous old furnished room. What a big difference between the two, plus the security of the building was good, and the subway station was nearby.

As soon as I felt settled in the new apartment, I telephoned Mary, Vincent Pomponio's mother, telling her that I had moved to a new place, which had room for the trunk that I had left at their home. With her usual kindness, Mary told me not to worry because she would take care of everything. On the following weekend, Vincent and his father brought the trunk to my place in a minivan. I didn't know how to thank them for being so kind to me and also for paying to transport the trunk. As I described before, the Pomponios were very good people, and now Vincent was also pleased to see me. Not long after my trunk arrived, my roommate Jean didn't like to see it in my room, and she started to complain that my room looked too busy and I should bring the trunk down to the basement. I ignored her completely because the trunk was new and I had covered it like a piece of furniture. In addition, it was in my room. When the old trunk from Italy arrived in the USA, it was in such a bad shape that I had to buy a new one.

*   *   *

One evening, on my way home from work, while I was on the subway platform in the Wall Street area waiting for the train, I met Andrew who was also on his way home. He came near me and politely asked me how I was doing; I answered "fine." He was already well informed of my new place because his friend George had told him when I left the old furnished room. After a simple conversation, he asked for my new phone number, and I, once again, gave it to him with no hesitation. I was happy to see him, and for months, he had constantly been on my mind. We both took the same train home, and his subway stop was earlier than mine. Before leaving the train, he asked me if I would like to join him for a drink, and I said yes; so instead of continuing the trip home, I got out of the train, and we went together to his apartment. That evening, due to my poor English, our basic conversation went on for quite some time until it was too late for me to go home, so I remained there for the night. The next morning, I went to school from there, and Andrew went to work. A few days later, he called me just to say hello.

For Christmas's Eve 1966, Maria Majoros invited Andrew and me to dinner at her place on Seventy-sixth Street in Manhattan. I didn't know Maria; Andrew had asked her to invite me, and I gladly accepted it. Andrew and Maria knew each other for many years. They both spoke Hungarian, and I assumed that she was his confidant. For the three of us, Maria prepared a real Hungarian dinner, which, in my opinion, was first-rate. After eating, with a great surprise, I got a sewing machine from Andrew as a birthday/Christmas present. This was the first gift I had ever received for my birthday, December 25, and to this day, I still have the machine as a memento. Before the holidays, Andrew had asked Maria what I would most appreciate as a gift, and she had suggested a sewing machine. I don't know why she had that idea, and I wondered what he had thought about the machine, which was an expensive present to give to a friend. Anyway, for the occasion, I had also brought gifts for them, but they were nothing special. I spent a lovely Christmas Eve, and with Andrew at my side, I felt very content. After midnight, Andrew took me and the sewing machine to my place by taxi, then we said good-bye, and he left. The following day, he called to wish me a Happy New Year.

*   *   *

The meetings with my friend Frances Diamond had become distant due to my busy schedule. She believed that I was doing too much and had no enjoyment, and she suggested that I take it easy. To add some pleasure to my life and to try meeting more people, her advice was reasonable. However, Frances didn't understand my current situation for she was an American citizen and I was not. With the student visa, my status here was on a temporary stay so that I had an uncertain future. I didn't want to miss any opportunity to earn as much money as possible and save for a rainy day. Frances was working for the Commercial Costa ship line, an Italian company in New York City.

One day, one of the captains of the Costa line invited Frances to have lunch on the boat, and she could bring a friend. She chose me to take along. The following Sunday, Frances and I went to lower Manhattan and got aboard the ship where the captain and another officer were waiting for us. After Frances introduced me to the captain and the officer, we all started to converse in Italian. It was wonderful to hear people speaking the same language. The captain gave us the tour of the ship, which I found very exciting. For me, it was the first time I was on a boat. Then lunch was served at 1 o'clock precisely. I don't remember what we ate, but for sure, the food was delicious, and the company was pleasant too. During lunch, I noticed certain sadness in the captain's expression, and later, I learned that he had recently lost his wife in an automobile accident in Rome. Anyway, after eating, the atmosphere on the ship became cheerful. It looked like the officers wanted to have some fun. Obviously, we paid no attention, but at this point, we weren't interested in staying aboard any longer, so we decided to go ashore. The captain insisted on taking us home, but we begged to be excused, then we thanked him for the lovely lunch and pleasant time spent on the ship and left the place by taxi.

During summertime on Saturdays, Frances and I often went to Central Park West, which was just a short distance from her residential hotel. Once there, we joined the crowd like the rest of the people, sat on the grass, and enjoyed the free public entertainment. It was very pleasant and relaxing, but we left before the end of the show because it was too long and tiring for Frances. Throughout the summer, Central Park hosted many musical events, and there was something for everyone to enjoy among the extensive concert lineups.

I remember the day when I introduced my friend Andrew to Frances. She already knew something because I had told her whatever I knew of him and about my feelings for him as she had become my confidante. A few days after the introduction, Frances called and told me that she didn't like Andrew and advised me to forget him. Strangely, he disliked her too. Whether my meetings with Andrew were often or seldom, Frances thought that, while I was seeing him, I would not be interested in meeting anybody else, and on that, she was right.

One Saturday, Frances convinced me to go with her to the Corso Night Club. It happened on this evening that she met Haim Glasner. He was born in Israel but for several years lived in America. After a while at the club, the two left together, and I took a taxi home alone. From that day on, Frances and Haim started dating, and shortly after their brief relationship, they decided to get married. Frances asked me to be her witness at the civil marriage, and I agreed. For me, that was great honor. The ceremony took place at City Hall in New York City. Haim's witness was his brother Jack, and I was the witness for my friend, then after the formal procedure was over, we all went to a restaurant for refreshments. For the Jewish ceremony, I was not invited. Only a few close family members were in attendance.

Frances and Haim settled in a nice apartment in Washington Heights, Upper Manhattan, and after a while, she invited me to her new place for supper. The day of my visit, Frances appeared to be happy. She was standing next to her husband who gave the impression of being a good, loving man. It was a big adjustment for her; she was not free. The absolute freedom that she had enjoyed all her life, starting at the age of seventeen, moving from country to country, was now suddenly gone. After the wedding, Frances and I saw each other much less than before but kept in touch by telephone. In 1967, Frances telephoned me to announce the birth of her baby girl. A few days later, when I went to visit her, I saw a radiant expression on Frances's face that I had never seen before. She was really a happy and proud mother. The special gift that I had brought for her little Ruti was just perfect. I felt very glad and wished Frances many more happy occasions.

*   *   *

Since I was doing pretty well economically, I decided to go to a better school. In January 1967, I enrolled at the New York University for the intensive pre-university course in American English intermediate level. The course was a three hundred-hour program, six hours a day in the morning, five days a week. It was a very expensive course, but I was glad that I finally could learn the language properly.

To frequent this school, I needed to have more free time available for the study. Nobody knew that I was in the USA with the student visa, but everybody knew that I wanted to learn English. At E. H. Hutton Brokerage House, I went to my supervisor and asked him to let me work there part time for the duration of my English course. He approved my request with no problem. Subsequently, I went to school in the morning, and in the afternoon, I went to work for six hours, then at home, I did my homework until late in the evening and went to bed for just a few hours' sleep. On the weekends, I tried to catch up with my study; although my daily schedule kept me extremely busy, I was very satisfied with my life.

The school was really great. I was attending classes with eagerness. The hours spent there flew by very quickly, and the daily homework was heavy and interesting too. We had three professors: one for English grammar, one for pronunciation, and one for the elements of the American history. The grammar professor was a pleasant lady and also an excellent teacher. For the pronunciation, besides a professor, we had a recording machine to listen to. There were several small cubicles furnished with special machines containing recorded English lessons that we had to listen to, and afterward, we had to repeat the English sentences. The students of all ages were mostly Europeans, and every one of us was enthusiastic to learn English as fast as possible. Every day after school, I took a stroll in Washington Square Park to stretch my legs and pleasantly look around the area. Among the monuments there, I saw, with surprise, one Giuseppe Garibaldi. I wondered why this military and political Italian hero was here! To this day, I don't know the reason that monument was there. At the park, I also sat on a bench to eat my lunch and then studied until it was time for me to take the subway to go to work. I completed the course in the spring of 1967 with a B grade. The grammar professor suggested that I should continue with the study. I would have liked to do that, but it was not possible. Between school, work, and my uncertain status with the immigration, it was too much for me to deal with. Anyway, my English improved enormously, except for the pronunciation. As a matter of fact, people still had difficulty understanding me and vice versa. They were talking too fast and didn't have the patience to pay any attention to what I was saying.

* * *

After the NYU class ended, I called Maria Majoros to find out something about our mutual friend Andrew. She told me that for quite some time, Andrew had a girlfriend from South America, and her family, who had recently immigrated to the USA, was treating him like a prince. They had become fond of him and wanted him to become part of their family. Besides being kind, Andrew was also a generous man and was happy when he could help others. Such was the case with him and the girl's family.

Andrew's calls continued to come. They were just short conversations or invitations to go to the movies, to dinner, or for a walk together. We enjoyed each other's company, and between us, in my opinion, there was something more profound than just friendship. I didn't tell him that I had spoken to his friend Maria, and I now knew about his Spanish girlfriend. I had already decided to consider Andrew my friend and continue seeing him as such, but going on with my life was not going to be so easy. I couldn't ignore my feelings for I had fallen in love with him! Anyway, at that time, there were things in my life that I wanted to resolve by myself, and also, I didn't want to interfere with Andrew's private life.

AUTOMATIC DATA PROCESSING (ADP) AND THE IMMIGRATION AND NATURALIZATION

One Sunday, while going through the job classifications section of the *New York Times*, I saw that ADP was looking for experienced keypunch operators, with a starting pay of 105 dollars per week. The following day, I called ADP to inquire about their job openings. They told me to come for an interview. The place was just located across E. H. Hutton, the company where I was then working. I went for the interview during my lunch hour; after which, I got the job as keypunch operator. I gave E.H. Hutton two weeks' notice and also told them the motive for me leaving the place. Besides payrolls, ADP was also a brokerage service. It was processing the daily volume of transactions of the major stock brokerage houses in the Wall Street area. At that time, many companies didn't have their own computer centers, so they were sending their transactions to ADP for processing.

It was in the summer of 1967 when I began working at ADP. The hours for the keypunch operators were from 12 noon to 8 p.m., and as benefits, all the employees received a few of the company's stocks on an annual basis. The work load was very heavy and so was the overtime for the keypunch operators so that when it was late at night, the company paid and sent us home by taxi. As supervisors, I had wonderful people who were very nice to work with, but I cannot say the same for the head of the keypunch department. He was a very unpleasant man. Because in this period I was not going to school, I had plenty of time on hand, and the opportunity to make extra money was really great for me. To influence the keypunch operators to work harder than usual, the department established rewards; they began to weigh the deck of cards that each one of us punched, and based on the weight, we started receiving nice bonuses, which were added to our paycheck. I always got the reward. At this time also, if a keypunch operator worked the entire year without missing a day, except for vacations, that person got another bonus. The only time I tried, two days before the end of the year, I got terribly sick with the flu and missed the bonus. Among the keypunch operators, I became friendly with only one girl from South America by the name Maria Diaz. She was a pleasant person and never worked any extra time. She did just the hours required to keep her job. One day, Maria met an Italian man, and after a brief courtship, she got married and moved to Vienna, Virginia. We kept in touch with each other by mail.

While punching the transaction information from the brokerage house on cards, I started noticing that certain stocks were doing extremely well. One day, I called my friend Andrew for some advice related to stocks. His workplace was nearby, so we met and afterward decided to go to a brokerage agent where I bought a few of the Occidental Petroleum stocks, and a few months later, also bought some of the IBM stocks at a very high price. Unfortunately, I was not lucky with my first investments; in 1969, the Oxy Petroleum stocks started to plunge due to the coup d'état and afterward the creation of the socialist government in Libya, and many years later, I sold the Oxy stocks for pennies. Regarding IBM, in 1969 the US government launched an antitrust suit against the company, and the IBM stocks also started to plunge. For many, many years, I saw my stocks loosing value until I sold them with losses.

For years I had been asking myself, what are the possibilities to have my status changed to permanent resident in the USA? I was sure that something existed and I was not aware of it. I needed to find out, but how? The *New York Times* was my answer. Going through the paper and looking at the job classifications section, my attention was always on the keypunch operators, which were in great demand. I started to think that perhaps the knowledge of the keypunch operator work was the opportunity that I was looking for. In the past, when I went to see my lawyer, I often asked him what the possibilities were to submit an application to the immigration for my US status to be changed. His answer was, "There are no chances for you in America. Your only solution is through marriage." After I got my first job as a keypunch operator at E. H. Hutton, I mentioned to the lawyer again and again what my work was like, but his answer was always the same: "There are no chances for you other than getting married." This time, when I went to his office, I insisted to let me see the list of the job qualifications for foreigners in demand in the USA. Though he didn't like my resolve, he reluctantly showed me the paper, and to my surprise, I saw the keypunch operators on the list. When I pointed out to him what I had just seen on the list, he wanted to know where I had learned that specialization. From the first time I went to this lawyer, we spoke in Italian, and that was good for me because at the beginning, I didn't speak any English. Coming from Sicily, he imagined that I was behind the times and unaware of the fast development in the electronic field. Perhaps he thought that the progress was only in America. In a few words, he demonstrated that he had never paid any attention when I was asking him or telling him something. I was taking into account that he was expensive and I paid every time I went to see him. As disappointed as I was with the lawyer for having ignored me all this time, nevertheless, I now couldn't say anything because I needed his help. I asked him what kind of papers I had to provide for the immigration, and he told me I had to submit a letter from the company where I was currently working.

It was toward the end of 1967, and ADP was the only company that could help me by providing me with a letter for the immigration. But I had a big problem that I first had to resolve with the company. Up to now, wherever I went and was hired for a job, I showed my social security card to the new employer. I let them to believe that I was working in this country within the law. In reality, I was working illegally because the immigration had refused to give me a part-time work permit, and subsequently, I had gotten my social security card by lying to the Social Security Administration Naturally, during all this time, I had paid taxes in full like any other USA resident. The time to tell the truth had arrived. Very embarrassed, I went to see one of the big bosses at ADP. I don't remember if he was the owner or the founder of the company. I explained to him my situation in the USA in detail, and at the end, I told him that I needed his help. Thank God he remained calm and politely asked me, "What can I do for you?" I answered, "A letter for the immigration office stating that ADP needed me as a keypunch operator." I had seen him many times before because the computer main frame and the keypunch department were located on the same floor. I am sure he remembered my face too. He was a real gentleman. He didn't show any disappointment. Maybe he noticed how uncomfortable I was. Anyway, he told me, "You will have my letter by tomorrow." The next day at work, the boss secretary gave me the letter, and on that same day, I brought it to my lawyer who, afterward, took care of the rest.

A few weeks later, I received a notification from the lawyer, informing me that the immigration had approved the request from ADP. That meant that I was on the immigration professional quotas and had to wait until my turn arrived to be called for the USA normalization procedures. The whole process could take years because it all depended on the type of immigrant categories and the country of birth. Anyway, for the time being, I had the hope of being legalized, and that was a huge moral relief for me. But even though I was already living in America, I now needed a temporary permit to remain here while my immigration case was pending. Subsequently, I went to Congressman William F. Ryan's office in Upper Manhattan, and there I met Mr. Ryan. After a brief conversation, I told him that I needed his help to obtain a temporary stay permit. He was a nice gentleman who understood the situation and took my case. About a month later, I got the provisional stay permit through the congressman.

I could not believe that I had fewer worries with immigration, and I was not compelled to go to school anymore. What big improvement! From now on, I had just my job to think about, and so I continued working and earning as much money as possible. At ADP, my working hours were from 12 noon on so that in the morning, I had plenty of free time to do whatever I liked. Twice, I took the subway from home to Battery Park, and there, I took the ferry to the Statue of Liberty. On the island, I followed the crowd or walked around by myself and enjoyed the view of the majestic and impressive skyscrapers of Manhattan. By 12 noon, I was at ADP and ready to start my daily job.

Working in the same Wall Street area, Andrew and I often met on the subway platform in the evening, waiting for the same train home. Now that I didn't have any more problems with my English, it was much easy to communicate. I kept Andrew informed of my happenings, including the involvement of the ADP with the immigration on my behalf.

*   *   *

At this time I just had a job, which was too easy and monotonous, and that started to make me restless. I felt the need of doing something more stimulating to engage my mind. I thought to try getting a job as a statistical typist, which, in reality, was not better than my current work. It was only a change. I told Andrew that I was considering finding a job as a statistical typist even though I knew it was the wrong idea for the fact that I could not quit my job at ADP while my US Immigration status was pending. Andrew didn't like my stupid idea at all because he already knew me for some time and thought that I could do much better than statistical typist work. He told me that at Bankers Trust, one of his colleagues was studying to be a computer programmer, and he would try to get some information from him for me. In addition, he told me that something in the computer field would be just right for me.

A few days later, Andrew came to my apartment bringing with him some booklets containing computer programming information from La Salle University correspondence courses. At that time, I didn't have any idea what computer programming meant. We talked for a while, and then he left, leaving the booklets with me. In no time, I started to read the booklets, and the more I read, the more I wanted to know. The assembly language, the bits and bytes, words, codes, and so forth got my attention, and I found the information very interesting and out of the ordinary. As soon as I finished reading, I decided that I wanted to become a computer programmer. The following morning, I went to New York University to inquire if they had courses for computer programming. Yes, they had, but at this particular time, the courses were twice a week and for two to four years. For me, it was too much time. I wanted to complete the course as fast as possible because of my unsettled situation in the USA.

Through the *New York Times*, I found a school for computer programmers. I don't remember its name anymore. Anyway, it was on the first floor of the Empire State Building at Thirty-forth Street, and I went there to find out more. The school had intensive courses for four to six months, which was precisely what I was looking for. It was equipped with several desks, a few key-punch machines, and a small IBM System/360 computer center. Once there, I enrolled, bought the books for the course, and paid the full tuition. Here, the classes were in the morning from 9 a.m.

to 12 p.m., five days a week, and for me, it was fine because ADP agreed to let me start work at 1 p.m.

In January, 1968, I started attending the computer programming course with a lot of enthusiasm and the expectation that this school was as good as the NYU, where I had had an excellent experience. But I soon realized that it was not the case. All the students were men and most were veterans of the Vietnam War. I was the only woman. We had a teacher who seemed to have no experience in the computer field; as a matter of fact, without the textbooks in front of him to read, he was lost. I remember when the students were asking the teacher to give some examples on the chalkboard; he did his best by writing down the precise information from the textbooks. It was really ridiculous for there was nothing new to see. It was an unfortunate situation because, at this particular time, the only school I was able to find was this one. Luckily, the textbooks were excellent, and the positive thing about this place was that we had the facilities to test our programs as many times as necessary. Therefore, I did my best to get whatever was possible from this course, and I studied harder in the evening at home.

I learned the assembly language, wrote test programs on special coding sheets, punched the information on cards, prepared the DOS/JCL (Disk Operating Systems/Job Control Language) cards, and lastly executed the assembly test program. At the beginning, all my programs never ended properly; instead, they went into a loop, which meant in order to bring the loop to an end, the computer operator had to stop the execution. Afterward, I found out what was wrong, made the fixes, and repeated the test. The end result on the printed reports was really exciting. After four months of school, the exam of the assembly language was done with the quiz. It was the first time in my life that I dealt with quizzes, and I didn't like that because I found it hard to understand the questions. Anyway, I passed the exam with mediocre results. Although I had already paid the full tuition for the entire course, after the assembly language exam, I decided to quit school. I bypassed the COBOL language because, in my opinion, it was useless to continue attending class and have the same teacher.

I now had to find a job as computer programmer trainee, but no firms were looking for trainees. All the companies in New York City were in search of programmers with at least one year of experience, and I didn't have any.

At ADP, I went to talk to the big boss. He was the same gentleman who had given me the letter for the immigration. I told him that I had just finished a computer programming course, and then I asked him if I had to go outside the company to look for the new job. He said that he had to talk to the manager of the systems division, and he would give me the answer soon. One week later, in the keypunch department, somebody from the systems division approached me and said to follow him. Then in his office, he interviewed me briefly. The meeting went okay. The system division accepted me, but because I didn't have any experience, if I wanted the job, I had to start with a salary of 100 dollars a week. It was an enormous cut from my keypunch operator job where I was making 145 dollars a week plus overtime. At the same time, this was a big opportunity for me to become a computer programmer, and I didn't want to miss it, so with a great enthusiasm, I said, "Yes, it is fine with me." I knew how difficult it would have been to find a trainee job, and I also knew how well the programmers with some experience were paid.

* * *

I started my new job as a computer programmer trainee in the summer of 1968. The working hours were from 9 a.m. to 5 p.m. The systems division was located on the second floor, and the division was comprised of twelve people: systems analysts, programmers, and the division manager. Everyone had their own office, except I had to share the room with a young man by the name Emmanuel. The systems division was a very busy place and was also the right place to get good experience. I was assigned to Terry Peterson who was the analyst in charge of the computer systems maintenance and was also the troubleshooter. Here, most of the computer programs were written in assembly language, which was the only one I had studied. Since my first day, I didn't like Terry. She was an arrogant and disrespectful young woman, but for now, I had to swallow my pride and consider myself fortunate to have gotten the trainee job.

I had the entire evening free and was not accustomed any longer to have lazy evenings. I had to do something to keep myself busy, and I also wanted to make up for the pay cut at my new trainee job. Through the *New York Times*, I got keypunch operator work from 6 p.m. to midnight on Forty-second Street so that the two pays together equaled my previous earnings.

A few months later, I got lucky in the systems division. I now had a new boss by the name Bernie Kaplan. He was a senior systems analyst in charge of developing new computer systems. How glad I was for not having to deal with Terry Peterson any longer! Working with Bernie was a pleasure. He was a kind person, and his knowledge in the computer field was quite extensive. Through Bernie, I absorbed a lot. I also had the opportunity to learn and write programs in COBOL, and it didn't take long for me to become a computer programmer. The systems division was incredibly busy, and so was I. In fact, I was working long hours every day and often taking work home. Thanks to Bernie, I got two pay increases in less than a year, and although I was not getting a good salary yet, I had to quit my evening job because I didn't have any more free time.

For Thanksgiving, all the employees at ADP got a turkey, and Emmanuel gave me his because his family could not eat that type of meat. Emmanuel was the computer programmer with whom I was sharing the office. He was an Orthodox Jew with a nice personality, and we got along very well. I now had two turkeys and no idea what to do with them, and I also had nobody to give them to. I decided to give one to Andrew who would give it whomever he wanted to (in my mind, it was his Spanish friend's family) and to keep the second one in the freezer at Andrew's apartment. Therefore, the turkey matter was resolved. Then one Sunday, I went to Andrew's place to cook the turkey, but I didn't know how. Anyway, I tried my best. I baked it, and the outcome was impossible to eat. In conclusion, I threw the dry and burned bird out, and we went to eat at a restaurant. That was the first and last time I tried to cook a turkey.

* * *

In September 1968, Andrew was going on vacation to France. On his departure day, I accompanied him to Kennedy Airport, and there, we found a lady waiting for him. I immediately understood who she was, and Andrew, who didn't know that I was aware of his girlfriend, looked embarrassed, but he didn't have any other choice other than to introduce Julia to me and vice versa. I just smiled at her. She seemed to be shy, very nervous, and was trembling too. Anyway, he finally departed, and I said goodbye to Julia and left. Andrew sent me many beautiful cards from Paris, but with regards only. I felt bad meeting Julia at the airport, and on my way home, I thought of going away.

I decided to take a week's vacation from ADP to travel to Vienna, Virginia, where my friend Maria Diaz Lucas resided. In the past, Maria had invited me many times to visit her and meet her Italian husband and their two children. I went by Amtrak from Manhattan to Washington DC. At the railroad station, I found my friend waiting to take me to her home. The couple's house was big and located in a nice residential area.

At home, I met Louis, who was Maria's husband, and their children—a boy and a girl. They all were very pleasant. During my stay at their place, Louis was busy at his government job, and

Maria, who was bringing along her children, was taking me to Washington DC by car. Together, we went to the Arlington

National Cemetery where we visited the John F. Kennedy Eternal Flame, and after that, we went to see some other places.

I soon realized that it was too much for Maria to take me out, so I decided to go to Washington DC by myself. I used the city map that Louis had given to me. One day, in DC, I joined a group of tourists and went to the White House. It was interesting to see the place in person rather than in photos or on television. When the tour was over, I decided to walk in the vicinity of the White House. It happened that I was going southeast, and after a while, I didn't know where I was anymore. I felt lost. All people living there were black people. They were looking at me strangely, and I didn't see any white people around. I finally took a taxi, and the black driver asked me what I was doing there. He saw that I was disoriented. He then asked me which country I came from, and I told him that I was from Italy. At this point, the driver started to recall his military time when he was stationed in Italy, and with a lot of enthusiasm, he began to talk about Italy, the Italians, the food, and so on. It was very pleasant to listen to him, and I felt safe. Then the taxi driver made sure that I would not get lost again. He took me precisely to the bus stop en route to Vienna. He was a real gentleman. After spending an interesting week with Maria, Louis, and the children, I returned to New York City by Amtrak.

* * *

During the month of September 1969, I found a note in my room one day while returning home from work. It had been left under the door of the apartment, and Jean, my roommate, had put it in my room. The note was from the Amorellis, an Italian couple who was at the end of their honeymoon in America and wanted to surprise me by coming to my place unexpectedly. The note said that they wanted to see me before going back to Sicily. They also wrote down the name of the cruise ship and the time of sailing, which was the next day at 5 p.m. The following day, I went to the cruise ship to meet them. The ship's terminal, located on the Hudson River in New York's Upper West Side, was not far from my apartment so that, in no time, I arrived there where I found the couple waiting for me. The meeting was very emotional; I knew her but not her husband. Nena, a close friend of mine from my hometown, introduced me to her husband, Frank Amorelli. Though I had never met him, it was like he knew me for a long time. Frank was a pharmacist, and he had spent many years in the USA, but he had to return to Sicily because his parents needed him back home to take over the family business. The couple took me aboard the ship where we had lunch together. Afterward, we spent the rest of the time on the deck, taking photos and talking intensely. They wanted to know everything about me and my future plans. I told them that for the time being, I was doing fine; regarding my future, I, myself, didn't know what to say because I was waiting to hear from the immigration and naturalization. When the departure time came, we said good-bye with tears, and then I disembarked the ship and waited at the port until the vessel left for Italy. The time spent with my friends was wonderful, especially because they were the first folks from my hometown I saw in New York City after almost five years.

* * *

Last time I saw Mary, Vincent Pomponio's mother, was for Christmas day in 1968, then I noticed that her health condition was poor, but as always, she welcomed me with open arms. Later in 1969, I got a telephone call from Vincent who, with emotion, told me that his mother had passed away. I went to Mary's funeral, and afterward, I followed the Pomponio's family and went to the place where they were holding the mourning. Here, all those who knew me wanted to know how I was doing, and they were surprised in the way I was answering them in English. Anyway, I remained there for a while and then said good-bye to everybody and left. This was the last time I saw Vincent.

* * *

In the early part of 1970, my friend Frances was thrilled when she called to tell me that she was moving to Israel for good. After five years in the USA, Haim, Frances's husband, decided to go back to Israel and temporarily leaving his family behind to follow him a few months later. Haim had spent his youth in Israel, and his parents were still living there also. When Frances left for Israel, it was a big loss and sad day for me. Besides being my best friend and confidante, she was also the only close friend I had in America.

UNEXPECTED EVENTS

ANDREW JANOVITZ

Andrew was the man I met during the 1966 New York City transportation strike. Though Andrew and I had often seen each other as friends, it was more than three years after our first meeting that our relationship became more frequent and interesting too. As a matter of fact, every time his friends invited him to parties, weddings, dinners, and so forth, he proudly took me along with him. One Sunday, he brought me to Queens to meet his aunt Margaret who, after our introduction, looked at me from top to bottom and only gave me a pleasant smile when her nephew told her that I was Italian.

I had never told Andrew that I loved him nor did he, but his behavior was more than words. Everything seemed to be going wonderfully. I enjoyed his company enormously, and whether he was still seeing his girlfriend or not, I didn't care. I had reached the point that nothing bothered me anymore. On many occasions when I was talking about my pending situation with the immigration, I noticed that Andrew always tried to avoid the subject. It looked like something was troubling him, but he never said anything to me except when I was expressing concern about my uncertainty in the USA. He was telling me not to worry about it and that everything will be fine.

PROBLEM WITH THE IMMIGRATION

The problem arose suddenly at the beginning of August 1970, when I got a surprise letter from the immigration department stating that I had to leave the United States within thirty days; otherwise, I would be deported to Italy. Being on the immigration foreigner professional quota since the end of 1967, I never anticipated receiving this shocking news. It was really dreadful for me. The setback with the immigration was due to the bad economic situation in the USA, which caused the quotas for immigrants to be closed or frozen. That happened during the administration of President Nixon. Consequently, I had only thirty days to remain in America, not much time left to think of anything. Anyhow, I soon reached the conclusion that there were two options. Option 1 was to return to Italy. I thought that with the knowledge of the English language and the experience of more than two years as a computer programmer, it would be easier for me to find a good job in Northern Italy. Option 2 was to have a talk with Andrew. This was not as easy as it seemed, and that gave me a lot of concern. Even though in the last few months we had been more than just friends, yet it seemed that he didn't realize that I was in love with him, or maybe he pretended not to know. Up till now, I had been proud of myself and wanted to have my status with the immigration settled before initiating any serious conversations with Andrew.

I decided to try option 2. I telephoned Andrew and told him that I needed to talk to him as soon as possible. When we met at his apartment and I showed him the letter from the immigration, his expression changed. He looked profoundly disturbed, very nervous, and didn't say a word. He knew that the only solution for me to remain here was to marry an American citizen. At his apartment, there was also his friend, George, who precisely knew how his friend felt with my immigration situation. Later on, I learned that my case was almost identical to the circumstance that led Andrew to his first marriage. After a while, George told

Andrew, "If Lina wants me, I will marry her." The room fell into a complete silence. Then after regaining his composure, Andrew coldly said to me, "All right, we will get married." At first, I didn't know what to say. I tried to control myself by remaining as calm as possible, and then I told him not to worry because if he wanted to divorce me later, it would be fine with me. Imagine how difficult his decision was and also how big my disappointment was! Without wasting any time, we had the blood test, applied for the marriage license at City Hall, and then I went to Forty-seventh Street to buy the rings.

CIVIL MARRIAGE, SEPTEMBER 22, 1970

That morning, Andrew Janovitz and I met at City Hall in New York City where we were married with two strangers for witnesses. We were very nervous, didn't look at each other at all, said what there was to be said, and exchanged the rings in a dark and depressing room. This is what I now remember of that day. Then after leaving City Hall, each of us took a different direction. He went to work, and I despondently went home.

On my way home, I felt awful and started to recall some of the events in my life from childhood to that day. For many folks, the happy occasions were always celebrated with a lot of cheerfulness, but I could not say the same for myself. For example, in the occasion of my first Holy Communion and later my confirmation, I was the only one in the orphanage who had no family members present. How could I forget that! Not to mention the preparations for the wedding. Although the civil ceremony is not the same as the religious marriage, for me, this civil ceremony should have been a happy event. Instead, it was very sad and gloomy. I would have never imagined that Andrew's reaction would have been so strong! He just could not overcome his bad experience of the past, and now everything happened so fast that he didn't have much time to digest his decision. I should have been grateful to him for his effort in trying to help me resolve the problem with the immigration, but I could not help myself in the way I felt toward him. Maybe because it was never my intention of marrying him, just to settle my status in the USA, I could have married someone else beforehand. I had loved Andrew from the first day we met, and since then, he had always been on my mind. Although in my entire life I had always struggled for everything, after a while, I started to reflect on my real situation, and for an unexplained reason, I was sure that in time, things would change for the better.

Anyway, to some extent, both of our lives had been incredibly challenging, and now the event of that September day will never be forgotten. Strangely, until my husband's death almost forty years later, I never remembered that peculiar anniversary day. It was Andrew who remembered it, but of course, he didn't like when I recalled the bad experience of that day. Several times, he told me that he didn't want to lose me. It was just that he hated the circumstances so much.

A few months later, when I got the marriage certificate, instead of going to my lawyer, I went directly to the immigration office. Fortunately, my case was assigned to Mr. Ruggiero, a very kind gentleman. I presented him the letter that I had received from the immigration and my marriage certificate. He helped me fill out the forms, and afterward, he told me that the normal procedure is that I should wait outside the USA until my papers are finalized by Immigration and Naturalization. Then he added, "Because you have been in the country for some time and currently you are fully employed, you would get a temporary permit to stay until the final approval by the immigration is reached." He also told me to come to see him in case I needed further information. I found it easier and cheaper to go directly to the immigration office rather than to go to my lawyer. Thank God! It seemed that everything was going to be all right, and moreover, during this unsettling time with no friends anywhere, it was my job that kept me mentally and physically occupied.

At the beginning of December 1970, Andrew called to tell me that he was going to Santo Domingo for the Christmas holidays. I hadn't seen him nor heard from him for over three months, so I wondered why he was telling me that he was going away. I was really surprised that he just telephoned to let me know that he would be away for the holidays. I didn't know what to say other than, "Have a nice vacation." He had been invited by an old friend of his who left New York and had moved to Santo Domingo.

* * *

In the meantime, sharing the apartment with two women was not an ideal situation. Betty was okay. I didn't have any complains with her. She minded her own business, and we got along very well. Jean, who had the contract on the apartment, was something else. She was not an easy person to get along with because she always found something to complain about. For example, I seldom cooked at home, but when I did, I always invited Jean to join me, and all the time, she accepted the invitation. She enjoyed my cooking and always complimented me. Then a little later, she complained on the cooking smell in the house. Most of the time, she was unemployed, and when she worked, she did it only for a few months so she could get unemployment checks again.

Jean was a good-looking blonde, spoke fine English, and was also an American citizen, so it was up to her to have and keep a good job. She had all the opportunities at her disposal. There were times when, coming home from work, I found the desk drawer in my room all messed up. I noticed that because I always place things in a way to have easy access at any time. Among the items in the drawer was my savings bank book, and for sure, Jean had seen it. She resented me, and more than once, she said to me, "You foreigners have good jobs and make more money than we

Americans." She had chosen an easy and lazy life when, instead, I was very busy with study, work, and no pleasure.

At the end of December 1970, I moved to Bretton Hall Hotel. After Andrew left for Santo Domingo, I decided to change my residence. More than four years had already passed, and I had become tired of sharing my apartment. There was no reason for me to stay there any longer. I started to look for a new place at an affordable price and where there was little work for me to do. I went to see several places in New York City, and the one that I liked most was the Bretton Hall Hotel, which was between Eighty-sixth Street and Broadway in Manhattan, so I decided to take a room there. Back at the apartment, I told Jean that I was leaving her place at the end of the month. Betty had already left, and Jean now needed two roommates to replace us.

My hotel room was nicely furnished. It had a walking closet, and a kitchenette. The monthly rent was reasonable. The location was excellent. Outside the building were the subway stations, the bus stops, a big supermarket, and stores. The daily hotel service was fine too. Altogether, it was a comfortable place, and I just needed to buy a television and a few other small items.

Knowing that I was going to spend Christmas Eve alone, Maria Majoros invited me for dinner at her place. There, I found another guest, an English gentleman who was friendly, cheerful, and pleasant to talk to. He had also brought three small Christmas fruitcake boxes, one for each of us. The entire evening, Andrew's name was not mentioned, and I believe that was done on purpose. Anyway, I was glad that I went because I spent an enjoyable evening with good company.

JANUARY 1971–THE TURNING POINT OF MY LIFE

At the beginning of January, Andrew, back from his vacation, called my old telephone number, and my former roommate told him that I had moved to Bretton Hall Hotel. He then called the hotel and asked for my room number, and when I answered the phone, he told me that he wanted to talk to me in person. I told him, "By all means, come to the hotel."

Almost four months had passed since our civil ceremony at the city hall, and this was the first time we saw each other. I immediately noticed a huge transformation in him. He had come back from his trip a different person. Who knows what kind of reflecting he had done during that time. He was now very pleasant, relaxed, and easy to talk to. For sure the vacation had been beneficial to his heart and mind. Looking at Andrew, my bitterness started to dissipate. He was very warm and full of enthusiasm so that little by little, our conversation became interesting and intense too. To make the story short, we concluded our reunion with a wonderful and happy decision. We would live together as husband and wife as soon as possible. For the time being, we would see each other on a daily basis until further decisions were made.

*   *   *

It didn't take long before my relationship with Andrew, now my husband for real, started to become stronger. His apartment was a small place, and besides that, I didn't like to move there because it was in a town house not well kept, and the entire building was also infested with roaches. In New York City, the problem with the roaches is well known and especially with old buildings. I told Andrew that, for now, if he liked, he could move with me at the hotel where the room was big enough to accommodate the two of us. He liked my idea. Therefore, instead of renewing his lease, he gave up his apartment, put his furniture in a warehouse, and moved in with me at the hotel. For the moment, the arrangement seemed fine. We lived together, went to work together, and whatever we did together were great.

One day, upon entering my hotel room, I noticed that the lock of my trunk was broken, and when I opened it, I saw that nothing had been touched, except the contents of the jewelry box were gone. The jewels, all in 18-karat gold, were gifts that I had received from my relatives and friends when I left Italy. I was very upset, and Andrew, who happened to be there, called the police immediately. When the police came, they asked me what was missing. In conclusion, I never recuperated any of my jewelry.

Some months later, Andrew and I began looking for an apartment on the Eastside. Through the *New York Times*, we found several places to look at, so on the weekends, we went to see a few apartments and soon realized that the places were much too expensive. We started to ask ourselves why we had to waste so much money for a small and high-priced apartment when we can have our own home!

In the meantime, I gradually began to know my husband much better. Once he became more receptive of me, he started to talk about his family and his past.

* * *

Andrew was born in Kosice, Czechoslovakia, and was the only child of Arthur and Maria Janovitz. He had a happy childhood until his parents divorced. After that, he spent most of the time with his father in Kosice and some time with his mother in Budapest. He studied and graduated in Czechoslovakia and spoke Czechoslovakian, Hungarian, French, English, and German fluently. In addition, he understood some Russian, Polish, Italian, and Spanish. During World War II, when the horrendous atrocities and persecution of the Jewish people was in full scale, Andrew's father was arrested and sent to one of the concentration camps where he was later gassed. In Budapest, some local people, who were spies, reported his mother to the Gestapo who shot her on the spot while she tried her unsuccessful escape. Andrew, who was living in Budapest at that time, was soon alerted of the tragic death of his mother and of the Gestapo who were all over the city. An uncle, his mother's brother, helped Andrew by finding him a hiding place with a Catholic priest's family. Unfortunately, this uncle didn't succeed in helping his own family and himself. Andrew remained in hiding until the end of the German occupation.

Most of Andrew's relatives perished in the concentration camps. Just a few survived, including the uncle who helped Andrew find a hiding place and a cousin, Lila, who still lives in Prague. At the end of the war, precisely when Eastern Europe became part of the Union Soviet Socialist Republic, Andrew escaped from Czechoslovakia and went to Austria. Because of his knowledge of several languages, he found work as a translator in Salzburg at the American intelligence office and remained there for two years.

After World War II, the only family members Andrew had left were those living in America—his paternal grandmother and two married aunts. He contacted them, and they started to communicate with each other. Near the end of December 1957, Andrew travelled to the USA as a refugee and temporarily went to live with his Aunt Margaret in Queens, NYC, where he was received with indifference. His grandmother who was living there was mentally ill, and his aunt and uncle were cold toward him even though they didn't have any children and Andrew was their only surviving relative. The uncaring behavior of this family toward Andrew made me think of the affection of Uncle Peppino Fantauzzo toward me. What a huge difference between Andrew's relatives and my uncle!

About five years later, in New York City Andrew married Magda, who was in America with a tourist visa. Andrew had met Magda in Budapest, Hungary, long before coming to the USA. At the beginning all seemed fine, but the reality was that she just married him to stay in America.

The many unpleasant circumstances had a profound effect on Andrew's life that, unfortunately, would not be easily erased from his mind. For Andrew, it was very difficult to trust people. He had become a skeptical human being, and, in my opinion, he was right to feel the way he did. I loved my husband profoundly. He was a loving, good, kind, and generous person, and what he needed was trust, understanding, and love, which was what I also needed.

Even though we were exactly right for each other, there were some difficulties to overcome first. We were already two mature people who, for a long time, had lived an independent life and had enjoyed freedom, and now everything began to change. At the beginning, living together was not so easy. For a while, we had plenty of disagreements. By nature, I am a very strong-willed person, and generally speaking, in order to get along with people, I have to put a certain effort to come to the realization that we each have our own individuality. Thank God, my husband was softer than me, and that made our personal adjustment period easy to deal with. Therefore, slowly and with mutual respect and understanding, we became accustomed to each other wonderfully. I had finally reached what I had wanted most in all my life, being economically independent first and then settling down with a loving, caring, and good-mannered man. I was so proud of him.

* * *

The ADP Company had been very good to me, and I was grateful to the owner who had helped me more than once, starting with the immigration request and then for giving me the opportunity to get the experience in computer programming. I had been in the systems division for over three years and had already become a good programmer, but I was underpaid. Due to the high inflation in 1970, the congress passed the Economic Stabilization Act, which gave President Nixon the power to impose wage and price freeze, and this control lasted for a while.

At this point, I had no hope of getting any salary increases, and in addition, I was not getting any overtime pay either because of my job classification. Luckily, I had a wonderful boss, Bernie Kaplan. He had asked the ADP's management for my pay increase several times, and because he didn't succeed due to the Economic Stabilization Act, he advised me to look for a job outside the company where the starting programmer's salaries were based on experience. Thanks to Bernie, I had acquired very good experience, had written programs in assembly and COBOL languages, and done some systems maintenance too.

In the systems division, one programmer had to stay for the nightly computer processing on a weekly rotation basis. The programmer's duty was to assist the computer operator by temporarily resolving problems in case of need—in other words, be there as a troubleshooter. The actual problems were fixed the following day by the systems division personnel. One day, during my lunch hour, I went to an employment agency, looking for a job as a computer programmer, and after I filled out the application, the agent told me that I would hear from them, but I never did.

MY FIRST RÉSUMÉ FOR COMPUTER PROGRAMMER

I prepared the resume the best I could since it was the first one I had ever written. It was simple; I just put down my experience as a computer programmer and the company where I was working. (ADP was an excellent reference place. There you had to be good and dynamic or you couldn't last on the job for long). At the bottom, I put a note, saying, "Although my English is not perfect, it wouldn't interfere with my work performance."

Then, as in the past, by way of the job classification section in the Sunday issue of the *New York Times*, I found two companies whose locations were convenient for me and decided to send my resume directly to them. One went to the INMONT, which was headquartered in mid-Manhattan, and the other went to the American Express headquarters in Downtown Manhattan. To my surprise, I could not believe that both companies answered me with telegrams. I was astonished that they equally replied in that way. Was it real? I started to remember the old times in Italy when I was looking for work and how hard it was to find one. How lucky I was now to be in America! Then I happily showed the telegrams to my husband who could not believe it either. Anyhow, I phoned the INMONT Company first because it was closer to my residence, and somebody from the systems division gave me an appointment for an interview. It was just the right time because the meeting coincided precisely during the week of my nightly shift at ADP.

At INMONT, I was interviewed by two senior systems analysts and someone from the personnel division. Afterward, one of the analysts asked me how much I wanted for the position. I was amazed that he had asked me how much I wanted and that was incredible for me! I also didn't have any idea what the salaries were for computer programmers. Anyway, the analyst understood that I was a little puzzled and gave me an offer, which was more than double of my current pay. The offer was very appealing, and I accepted it readily. At the end, the interviewer asked me when I could begin to work there, and I answered in two weeks. On that same day, when I went to work, I gave my resignation. I felt bad leaving ADP, but I didn't have any other choice. I didn't know how long the wage and price control would last, and fortunately, I had now found a better-paying position. Then I called American Express to thank them for their answer and told them that I had already accepted another job offer.

In the middle of 1971, I began working at INMONT as a computer programmer. INMONT was a chemical company with its headquarters in New York on Sixth Avenue and Forty-third Street, and the manufacturing center was located in New Jersey.

During the interviews, someone mentioned that the company was going to convert their systems from the IBM to the Burroughs computer system, and at that time, because I was offered a high-salary job, I didn't pay too much attention to it. Before being hired, I first had to pass a complete physical examination for which the company sent me to some place for the tests.

The systems division was small. People were kind, and the work load was lighter than at ADP. Altogether, it was a nice and pleasant environment. Most of the programs were written in COBOL and RPG languages, and here, I learned the RPG. Then the company decided to move its headquarter from Manhattan to New Jersey where its industry was located, and to attract its employees to move with them, they offered to pay the expenses for the move. It was pleasant to work at INMONT, and I told my husband that I wanted to remain with the company, so we both decided to look for a house in New Jersey.

Living in New York City, we didn't need any car. We were using the public transportation, which was fine for us. Now it became necessary to have our own transportation in New Jersey, so we bought our first car, a Chrysler Plymouth. On weekends, my husband and I went to New Jersey to look at the available homes, and after several trips there, in the hope of finding something reasonable that we both liked, we concluded that New Jersey was not the right place for us. All the houses that the real estate agents showed us, taking into consideration the locations and the type of constructions, were really overpriced. Furthermore, the real estate taxes were extremely high. In addition, there was another important factor to consider. The company was going to convert their computer mainframe from IBM to Burroughs, and that was something I wasn't interested in.

A colleague of mine, by the name of Bob Feldes, told me that he could show me a few houses in Hollis Hills where he resided, which was a section of Queens, New York. He was a computer programmer at INMONT and had a part-time job at a real estate agency in Queens. The following three weekends, my husband and I went to Queens where Bob showed us several houses and where we finally found the one that we both thought was right for us.

It was an attractive large Cape Cod house, and comparing its construction, location, and taxes to those seen in New Jersey, this was paradise. This house was in a beautiful well-kept residential area. The price was reasonable, and the real estate taxes were low because the property was within the limits of New York City. Although on a two-fare zone, the house was on a one block street, and at the end of the street was a Union Turnpike bus stop. The only bad part was that the house required a lot of work. It had been on the market for over a year, and it had been neglected for quite some time. Nevertheless, because the house had the second floor nicely finished, my husband and I thought that it had some good possibilities, so we decided to buy it on the spot. However, for some unforeseen difficulties, it took several weeks to get the mortgage from Bankers Trust. After my husband applied for the mortgage at Bankers Trust, where he was currently employed, the bank left him waiting for weeks with no explanation for the delay. Subsequently, we realized that we could lose the house if we waited any longer, so I decided to put my name on the mortgage application, and almost immediately, we got the loan. I found it a little strange, and was asking myself why the bank didn't give Andrew any answer regarding the loan. Two years later, I got the answer. Anyway, our wish was to put a 50 percent down payment, so I sold my ADP stocks to come up with the required amount.

OUR FIRST HOME IN QUEENS

It was in the middle of November 1971 when we finally closed the contract. Soon after receiving the key, we went straight to our new place. What great satisfaction and a wonderful feeling we both experienced in unlocking the door and entering our own home! We stayed for a while and looked at the place inside and outside, and we were so enthusiastic that we didn't see anything wrong. Then we happily left our home and returned a few days later to move in.

To begin with, in our new home, my husband brought his furniture and paintings from the warehouse, and I brought whatever I had from my hotel room. Then we bought some essential things just to get by. Although the house was almost empty and in bad condition, that didn't bother us. We felt very happy, and together, we were starting a new life with a bright future ahead. On Saturday, following our move to Queens, we went to visit my husband's aunt Margaret. Afterward, with a big surprise, Margaret learned that we had gotten married and had also bought a house not far from her house. Anyway, the way she behaved made my husband believe that she liked me. As a wedding gift, she gave us money to buy a complete set of dinnerware. Furthermore, she was so eager to introduce me to her Italian friends that without wasting any time, she invited us to come the next Saturday. As scheduled, we met her friends that day at her home. They were interesting people, and to please me, some of them started to speak in Italian. Then cheerful Aunt Margaret served coffee, cakes, and drinks to the guests sitting at a nice decorated table. Altogether, it was a very pleasant evening.

When my husband and I lived and worked in Manhattan, the traveling to our working place was a short distance, but now that changed. Besides the two-fares zone, the trip was really long. The duration of a one-way trip for me was one hour, and for my husband it was almost two hours. In the evening, by the time we were getting home from work, especially during wintertime, it was too late to do anything other than have supper, watch a little television, and go to bed.

Because this was our first house, we didn't have any idea of the problems that we would encounter after moving in. We had no house-buying experience; therefore, we did not have the house inspected before the purchase. Though we knew that the house required a lot of work, we didn't expect to have serious troubles from day one. We were already in the month of December, so we took care of the most crucial things to get by. We got some contractors to fix the leaking roof, the broken window panes, and the leak in the basement, and also replace all the valves on the radiators. Then the heating system stopped working too, and the house got ice cold. To replace it would have cost us a lot of money, so the contractor made a temporary repair to the unit. The cost of the repairs and replacements was more than we had ever imagined.

Our first Christmas holiday as husband and wife and also in our new home in Queens was fantastic. Even though we were alone, it didn't make any difference because to have each other was like a wonderful dream comes true, and for me, it was hard to believe. What a year 1971 was! I can only say that it was the happiest year of my life.

After we got settled in Queens, I decided to notify my Italian relatives that I had gotten married. I briefly wrote them of my new status and sent them my new address. Up to now, nobody actually knew of the many ups and downs that I had endured in America. They assumed that everything was going smoothly. In receiving my sudden good news, they were very surprised and happy for me at the same time. Even though it was an unusual situation, I was glad that nobody asked me for any particulars.

* * *

At the beginning of January 1972, I got a telephone call from an employment agency. This was the same agency I had contacted a year earlier to get a computer programmer's job, but I never heard from them. At that time, in all probability, they ignored my application because of my heavy Italian accent. Surely, they thought that it would have been impossible for me to get a job. The person who called me was the same agent I had met the previous year, and he was now well informed of what was going on at INMONT. I asked the agent how he found out where I was working. Instead of giving me an answer, he asked me how I had gotten the job at INMONT. I told him I found an AD in the *New York Times*. Then he said that INMONT was planning to move to New Jersey and if I didn't want to go there, sooner or later, I would be looking for a job again. At INMONT, the environment was good; the location in midtown Manhattan was excellent, and my job was interesting too. However, I also knew that there were changes on the way, such as the conversion from the IBM to the Burroughs computer mainframe. In addition, it would be stressful traveling from my home in Queens to INMONT in New Jersey. To make it short, the agent insisted and convinced me that I had nothing to lose if I went for an interview at the company that was searching for good computer programmers. I agreed, and a few hours later, the agent called to let me know that he had already made an appointment for my interview.

The company was TIAA-CREF (Teacher Insurance and Annuities Association–College Retirement Equities Fund) located at 730 Third Ave in New York City. The following day, I went to TIAA-CREF for the interview during my lunch hour.

It was just a short walk from where I was working. There I was interviewed by the personnel agent and by two senior systems analysts—Richard Wagner and Diana Axelrod. All the questions were technically related to computer programming and were very easy to answer. During the meeting, I said to one of the interviewers that I would prefer to work with men rather than with women. I had no idea how Terry Peterson just came to my mind, but I remembered the bad experience I had with her at ADP. I later found out that my work preference request was kept in my personal file. That same afternoon, the agent called me to tell me that I was offered the job and wanted to know when it was a good time for me to start working at the new place. The benefits and my new salary at TIAA-CREF were very attractive, so I accepted the job. Back at INMONT, I told the systems manager that I was leaving the company, and I gave him my six weeks' notice. Because we were in the middle of implementing a computer system, I wanted to finish what had been assigned to me.

TIAA-CREF

What attracted me most to this place, in addition to the big salary increase, was the four-day weeks during the summer months—Monday through Thursday with extra working hours each day. Here, also, the benefits were excellent, and the employee cafeteria was good and very inexpensive because it was subsidized by the company. Anyhow, I thought this was a dream place at which to work. On my first day, I was assigned to a systems analyst who gave me something to read and then some specifications to write programs in COBOL. In no time, I started to be very busy. In the systems division, there were plenty of projects going on, and everybody was extremely busy. As matter of fact, after a few weeks on the job, a person from the systems division asked me if I could bring other programmers to the company, and as a reward, I would receive a bonus for each person I brought in. However, at that time, I didn't know any programmer looking for work.

In those days, the job of a computer programmer was not as easy as it is today. In addition to writing programs on special coding sheets, the programmer was also responsible for the preparation and the execution of the job stream. Bear in mind that we were dealing with cards, magnetic tapes, and disks. The most unpleasant task for any computer programmer was the handling of the job stream cards kept in boxes. The systems division personnel had a special pass to enter the computer room because there were times when we, especially programmers, had to run the job stream personally or assist the computer operator during the processing.

What a big relief the computer terminals brought to the computer personnel, especially to the programmers! The terminals, which were introduced in the early 1970s, made the punched cards obsolete little by little.

*   *   *

In the early spring of 1972, my husband and I began the maintenance work on our house. With our full-time jobs, most of the work was done on weekends, holidays, and vacation days, and when the days were long, we worked late into the evening. To save some money, we decided to do the inside work by ourselves. My husband did all the tedious repairs. For him, everything had to be done with perfection. We argued a lot because I wanted to finish as quickly as possible. I would say, "Before starting the job, I wanted to see the end of it." I didn't have any patience with that kind of work, and I hated it. It was too much for me and for my husband too. I had also started on my new job at TIAA-CREF so that I had other more important things on my mind than that tedious work. Andrew and I had thought that the inside work would have been done in two to three months. Instead, it took more than a year of hard work to finish it. Anyway, hard as it was, we did our best. We accomplished a lot, and at the end, we said *never* again would we do such unpleasant work.

Even though the work on our house was hard, my first year at TIAA-CREF was fantastic. The three-day weekend during the summer months seemed like having a short vacation every week. Therefore, with the week off that I got from work, my husband and I decided to go to Grossinger, a Resort in the Catskill Mountains. This was our first vacation together, and I cannot describe what a wonderful time we had there. For me, it was like a dream. Soon, it was already the end of 1972, so for Christmas, we invited Aunt Margaret to our house for dinner, and in turn, she invited us to her house for the New Year celebration.

In the spring of 1973, we were still busy with our home. We replaced the carpet in all of the rooms, bought new furniture, and started with the outside maintenance work, which took some time for the contractors to finish. On my free time, I made the curtains for all the windows. The sewing machine that I received as present from Andrew on Christmas 1966 was now very handy.

Next, my husband started to have troubles with Bankers Trust. For quite some time, he was telling me how he felt about the management and the atmosphere of anti-Semitism at the bank. He was of the opinion that he was being discriminated again.

Eventually the ordeal with the bank started to take its toll. Andrew began to have sleepless nights, started to smoke a lot, and became very tense. Other health problems emerged too. I felt terrible to see my husband in that condition, and I tried to convince him to quit and look for another job, but I didn't succeed. He had spent many years at Banker Trust, and he was over forty-nine years of age, so he didn't feel like starting to look for jobs again. I was sure that my husband's troubled situation could not last for long and sooner or later something was going to happen. As a matter of fact, for some time, something was gradually taking place. I now remembered the 1971 episode when Andrew applied for the mortgage for the house and the bank left him in waiting with no answer at all.

One day during the summer of 1973, I got a call from a TIAA-CREF security employee, telling me that my husband was in the lobby waiting for me. When I met him, I noticed from his expression that something bad happened to him. Then with stress in his voice, he said to me, "I was fired." In that instant, I didn't know what to say. Next, I told him that I was glad that his troubles were over and kissed him. On one hand, I felt very bad because I imagined how shocking it was for him to suddenly be fired and then having to give me the unpleasant news. On the other hand, I felt relieved for I knew very well what he was going through, especially lately. It was not worth continuing on in that way.

That day, I left the office early, and we went home together. Along the way, we talked, and I tried to encourage him by letting him know that it was not the end of the world. I had a very good job, and economically, there were no worries for both of us. I reminded him that my position at TIAA-CREF was in part due to his credit. He was the one who had given me the idea to become a computer programmer. After many years of service, Bankers Trust gave my husband only one year of severance pay and a miserable pension in later years. Anyway, for the time being, the most important thing for him was to recuperate mentally and to digest the bad feeling of being fired. Subsequently, he gradually started to relax and began doing what he liked to do most. Andrew often came to see me at TIAA-CREF, bringing croissants and coffee. Once he was in Manhattan, we had lunch together, and afterward, he went to see a movie or just took a walk in the city. Around 5 p.m., he would come back to my workplace, and we would go home together.

FALL OF 1974 – OUR FIRST EUROPEAN TRIP

With a full-time job, I didn't have much time available during the week so that the weekends were always welcome. To be at home with my husband and doing whatever pleased both of us was really great. At the beginning of 1974, my husband and I started considering, and soon after, we decided to take a trip to Europe, which would be beneficial for my husband and fantastic for me. Going back to Italy for the first time in almost ten years was really a brilliant idea. The countries that we liked to visit were Italy, Hungary, and Czechoslovakia. Not being accustomed to travel, the planning for the trip, which was for one month, seemed a little complicated as there were many things to take care of.

At TIAA-CREF, I was getting two weeks' vacation, which was not enough for the trip. Therefore, I asked my manager if I could get some extra time off. I got two more weeks with full pay because he knew that I had worked a lot of unpaid overtime. Next, besides notifying our families of our upcoming visit, we had to prepare our wardrobes, purchase gifts for everybody, and we had also to obtain several legal documents:

1. The Passports: Andrew's American passport was up-to-date, but mine had to be renewed, and for that, I went to the Italian consulate office in Manhattan where they had me pay ten years of back fees.
2. The Czech visa: We both applied for it, and subsequently, I got the visa with no problems. However, my husband's request was rejected because he was still considered a fugitive. In the '50s he broke away from Czechoslovakia after the communist regime took over the country.
3. The Hungarian visa: We both applied for and received the visas without any difficulties.

We flew from New York to Palermo, Sicily, aboard Alitalia Airline. The flight was long but pleasant and comfortable. Just by chance, this was the last Alitalia direct flight from New York to Palermo. Approaching the airport at Palermo, my husband was amazed at the spectacular view of the city with its surrounding mountains and sea. The sunny day made the view more beautiful. The landing was smooth. Then after going through the Italian security, we found many of my relatives waiting for us at the airport.

The welcome we got was incredibly warm. Everybody was very happy to see me after so many years, and they were also enthusiastic to meet my husband for the first time. Among the relatives were my uncle Peppino Fantauzzo, my cousins Rosetta and Agostino, my brother with his wife, my aunt Marietta with her husband, and many others. Rosetta and Agostino took us from the airport to their apartment in Palermo, and the rest of the relatives followed us. At home, I found Giuseppe, my favorite nephew who was four years of age when I left Palermo, and now he was 14. I also found Giovanni and Franca, who had grown beautifully, and for the first time, I met the young Tony who, because of his parents, seemed to already know me. I was very happy that everybody seemed to be impressed with my husband.

Toward evening, with my brother, we left Palermo for Casteltermini. On the way to Casteltermini, at the Acquaviva-Casteltermini railroad station (eight kilometers from the town), with a great surprise, we found many cars full of relatives waiting for our arrival. Everybody got out of their cars to welcome us. Many of them had tears of joy, and some of them, I didn't recognize because in ten years, they had changed a lot. Prior to the trip, when I notified my relatives that I was coming to town with my husband, some of them invited us to stay at their homes because they had bigger and better homes than my brother's apartment. They wanted to make a good impression on my husband, but I said no and thanked them for their kindness. I didn't have to impress my husband with anything. In fact, I had already told him that whether my brother's place was comfortable or not, we would stay at his apartment, and he agreed with me completely. It was out question to go to relatives rather than staying at my brother's place where my sister-in-law was waiting for us enthusiastically. Anyway, after a long and exhausting day, we finally arrived at my brother's place almost twenty-four hours since we left New York.

For fifteen days we stayed with my brother in Casteltermini. What a strange and pleasant situation it was because this was the first time my brother and I were staying under the same roof since the death of our parents. That evening, we met my brother's two children, Giuseppina and Alida, for the first time. Then the hosts gave us their bedroom, and in no time, we went to bed.

Although the apartment was very small and modest, we felt comfortable. The way the guests feel all depends on the hosts. The beauty of a home alone is nothing in comparison to a sincere and warm atmosphere.

The first morning, when we got up and opened the bedroom door, we found my nieces sitting on the floor behind the door, waiting for us quietly. Seeing these beautiful young faces with curly hair and big eyes looking and smiling at us gave us such joy! That same morning, my uncle Peppino came to see us, bringing fresh fruit from his country house. Unfortunately, we were unable to see him because we were still sleeping.

For the first few days, many relatives and friends came to my brother's place to visit us every afternoon. With pride, I introduced my husband to them, and everybody liked him instantly. As it is customary, many of them invited us to their homes for lunch or supper, but we could not accept all the invitations. There were too many, and we had to decline with no offense. Here, everybody considered us as we were on our honeymoon. Prior to anything else, I told everybody to speak in Italian and not in Sicilian dialect. In this way, it was easier for my husband to understand. I was doing a lot of translation and was often getting mixed up with it. I was talking in Italian to my husband and in English to the others. Among the friends who turned up at my brother's place were Frank and Nena Amorelli. This was the couple who came to my apartment in New York City at the end of their honeymoon, and I went to meet them on the ship en route to Italy. They brought us a full tray of cannoli, Sicilian sweets, and after I introduced my husband to them, Frank and Andrew immediately started to talk in English. The opportunity for my husband to speak English made me very happy.

I remember Uncle Peppino's promise when I left Sicily for the USA with the expectation of marrying Vincent Pomponio in 1964. Then he said that he would have come for my wedding to America to take me to the altar. I never told him or anybody else about the strange and painful circumstances that I encountered in the new world. Now Uncle Peppino was the proudest of all. In fact, when he tried to talk to my husband about me, with his typical warm smile, there was so much enthusiasm in his voice and in his eyes. In other words, he was very happy for me, and he also liked my husband a lot. Andrew turned toward me and said, "So this is your uncle Peppino who you loved so much!"

"Yes," I said happily. "Isn't he wonderful?"

In our honor, Uncle Peppino Fantauzzo gave a big party at his country house. There was Aunt Angelina (Peppino's wife), three of their children (Giovanni, Gino, and Lina) with their families, my brother with his family, and many more. My cousin Lina did all the preparations. She was a real good cook, and she enjoyed it when my husband complimented her for everything. What I liked most was the way all the relatives were treating my husband. Everybody liked him enormously, and referring to him, they told me, "Lina, che bell'uomo!" (Lina, what a good-looking man!) Although Andrew didn't speak Italian, he understood that he was the center of attention, and I was sure that he felt good in that warm atmosphere. In fact, he tried to communicate with my family with the best of his ability. We spent an enjoyable evening among pleasant company, warm conversations, tasty food, toasting drinks, cheerfulness, and confusion too. The party lasted until after midnight.

My Butticé aunts also gave another party at their home in our honor. Present were Aunts Tina, Pina, Arcangelina, Rosina, and cousins Memma, Lina, and Enzo. Also present were my brother with his family and some other relatives. There was plenty of food, toasts, talking, and merrymaking. It was really great, and my husband was always the center of attention. Everybody liked him very much, and when he tried to speak to them, they were listening with great interest.

In addition, some of my close Fantauzzo cousins—Giovanni, Gino, Lina, Silvestro, Pino, and Elvira—who were all married and with children, invited us to their homes for lunch or dinner with insistence, and afterward, they gave us nice gifts.

Before leaving Casteltermini, I wanted to show my husband some of Sicily. With my brother and his family, we went to the Valley of the Temples in Agrigento where we visited some of the ancient Greek remains. Then we went to a restaurant where the selection of food was not great. All together, we spent a delightful day in Agrigento. During our stay in town, we didn't have any free time. We were always on the go, and when we took a short walk on the main street, we were continuously stopped. Everybody was glad to see me, meet my husband, and congratulate me. This is what happens in a small town where everybody knows each other. Anyway, I was very pleased. Andrew also saw the way most of my family members were living. They had beautiful homes and had the best of everything. At home, my brother and his wife didn't know what to do first to please us. For them, nothing was enough, but they did a lot for us. Among relatives and friends, we spent a wonderful and memorable time in Casteltermini. What a pity that the days went so quickly! At the end of our stay, my brother drove us to Palermo.

In Palermo for three days we stayed at my aunt Marietta and uncle Enzo Ricotta's big and beautiful apartment in the center of the city. Whatever my aunt did for us, it was from the bottom of her heart and with a lot of exuberance.

Uncle Enzo took us to Mount Pellegrino where the view of Palermo, with its surrounding mountains and sea, is spectacular, and Mount Pellegrino is also described as the most beautiful promontory in the world. Here we reached the Sanctuary of Saint Rosalie, who is the patron saint of Palermo. He also took us to visited the Monreale Cathedral, which is a national monument in Italy and one of the most important attractions of Sicily. The cathedral inside is dark, but when entering the place, you may be enchanted immediately by the darkish golden brightness of the mosaics; a blend of medieval Christian and Muslim architecture. With Marietta and Enzo we had marvelous time in the city.

For me, Palermo is a beautiful city, and I love it, maybe because I liked living there. It is so enchanting and rich in everything. To appreciate the city entirely, you need to visit there at least one month.

While in Palermo, my cousins Rosetta and Agostino, and their son Tony, came to my aunt Marietta to take us to visit the Chinese Palace. This is a historic palace, which was built for a king as a summer residence and is situated in the middle of the large Favorita Park. After the visit, we went to a restaurant for lunch. On the same day, my cousins took us to see the famous fountain in Piazza Pretoria. This is located on Via Maqueda, in the old district of Palermo. The setting of the fountain is fantastic, and it also contains many nude statues. I enjoyed the stop here, but mostly, I liked to look at my husband whose enthusiasm showed on his face. For him, everything was new, and he greatly appreciated it all.

Anyway, our sojourn in Sicily was terrific, and the knowledge of my husband's captivation of everything he saw made me very happy. At the end, we flew from Palermo to Rome.

In Rome, we stayed at a bed and breakfast for two days. With a guided tour, we visited the Basilica of St. Peter, which is too beautiful and complicated to describe; and the Pantheon, which, after almost two thousand years since it was built, its dome is still the world's largest unreinforced concrete structure and has an impressive central opening to the sky. Rome is a magnificent city and the only one of its kind in the world. It requires plenty of time to discover all its enormous richness.

On our second day in the city, we got a nice surprise. Since we didn't have the chance to see each other while we were in Sicily, my cousin Franco Martorana, who had come from Palermo to Rome for business, took the opportunity to come to see me and meet my husband at the bed and breakfast, and that gesture pleased me a lot.

From Rome airport we took the Malev Airline flight for Budapest.

We stayed in Budapest for seven days. Upon our arrival at the airport, we registered with the Hungarian authority. At this time, Hungary was a communist country, so they had to verify our passports and our visas, and then they also wanted to know where we were staying in order to keep track of us. The atmosphere was oppressive; everything looked subdued, and the cold temperature that we also found here made the situation bleaker. However, we were warmly welcomed by my husband's six relatives. The family meeting was emotional because most of his relatives were tragically gone. Andrew introduced me to his Czeck relatives who had come to Budapest just to meet us. They were first cousin Lila and her two children, Joska and Irene. Then he introduced me to his aunt Maria and to her two sons, Laszo and Janos. Maria was the second wife of Andrew's only surviving uncle from the concentration camps and who was now deceased. This uncle was the one who helped Andrew find refuge with a Catholic family, and for that, he remained grateful to his uncle's family for the rest of his life.

From the airport, we all went to Maria's small apartment in Budapest. Maria served lunch, which was a sandwich with the goose liver that she had already prepared in advance. The way the Hungarians prepare the goose liver is really something special, and its fat is tastier than the liver. After eating, the Czech and the Hungarian animated conversations began. Cousin Lila spoke Czech, Hungarian, and a little of English. Her children spoke only Czech, and Maria's family spoke just Hungarian. My husband spoke all the languages, and I just spoke English, besides Italian that no one knew. They had plenty to tell about their families and their current life under the communist regime.

I didn't understand anything, but I knew that now was my turn to be silent and patient because Andrew had done his part with no complaints when we were in Italy with my relatives. Although there was the problem with the language, I felt comfortable with these new relatives. They were pleasant and warm, especially Lila. In the evening, Andrew and I went to a housing area, which was registered with the Hungarian authority. We got a tiny room with no private bathroom. We had to share the only toilet with the other visitors. Lila and her children also went to a different housing area similar to ours.

In Budapest, the grocery stores were just open for a few hours a day until the shelves were empty. People had to go to the store early in the morning and wait in line outside in order to get in at the opening of the stores. The food selection was okay because we noticed that Lila bought things that she could not get in Czechoslovakia. The Americans were not allowed to send dollars directly to the people. Only through a government-approved agency could money be sent, and then the money had to be spent in selected stores. The black market was in great vogue for those people who were getting dollars clandestinely.

Budapest was beautiful as a whole, and the opulence of the past was still evident. It seemed that the city was now neglected because many buildings were damaged from the war, and the holes on the walls from the bullets were still intact. We took the public transportation to go around, which was fine and on time. I like to emphasize that at that time, while all the public transportation in New York City were full of graffiti, the subway stations and trains here were impressively clean. Everywhere we went with the relatives for lunch or dinner, the meals at the restaurants were excellent, but the service was terrible. In all, the time spent in Budapest was nice, and I was glad to have met my husband's small family. We then flew to Vienna.

In Vienna, we stayed at a hotel in the center of the city for two days and decided not to take any tours. Up to now, our trip had been wonderful, except for the little stress that came along the way due to the language barriers. We were finally by ourselves and had two full days to enjoy the magnificent city of Vienna. What a wonderful feeling to do whatever we wished! We took pleasant walks along the boulevards, visited a few beautiful gardens, and went to some Viennese cafés where we savored the famous Austrian sweets, read newspapers, and relaxed at the same time. Then we flew from Vienna to New York.

This 1974 vacation will be remembered as one of the best European trips ever because I returned to Italy for the first time since I came to America, and I introduced my husband to my family, and traveled to Hungary to meet Andrew's relatives.

* * *

As soon as our European trip was over, Andrew started sending resumes to several banks in New York City. Sadly, he was not successful in getting answers. Therefore, at the beginning of January 1975, he went to an employment agency, and soon after, he was sent to several banks. Wherever he went for the interviews, they were telling him that he was overqualified for the position available. The entire year of 1975 went on this way, and the situation seemed hopeless to the point that Andrew became very discouraged. What started to trouble me most was Andrew's health. I tried to keep his optimism alive. I told him not to be apprehensive about the job. If it happened, it was okay, and if didn't, it was also okay since financially, we were in good shape. Nobody could have understood my husband's situation better than me. In fact, until now, year 2012, I often dream of being in search of employment without any success. That situation is still like a nightmare, and when I wake up, I thank God that it was just a dream. I experienced that same situation when I was living in Sicily in the years 1960–1962. I remember going for interviews with a lot of enthusiasm and then little by little starting to hate the process and how depressed I felt! Anyway, on weekends and holidays, to break the gloomy atmosphere at home, we took daily trips. We went to NYC and visited the Metropolitan Museum, which was one of my husband's favorite places, or went elsewhere.

THE 1976 CANADIAN VACATION

One morning, while Andrew was getting up from bed, he couldn't because he felt dizzy and had vision problems. Our doctor lived one block away from us, so I called him and described my husband's symptoms. He came in no time and subsequently diagnosed Andrew's problem. It was vertigo, and he prescribed some drugs. The problem lasted for quite a while so that between the vertigo and the job hunting, there was very little I could do for my husband until I started talking about a trip to Canada, even though I knew that he could not drive the car and I didn't drive. Incredibly, Andrew suddenly started to feel much better and was soon ready to undertake the trip. It was a diversion for both of us despite the fact that I had some hesitation regarding Andrew. We thought traveling on our own would be the easiest and the most enjoyable way of going from place to place. We would then be free to stop wherever we wanted. In the middle of May, we began our trip to Canada.

We stayed at a hotel in Niagara Falls for two days. On the American side, we took the Niagara Falls Maid of the Mist boat ride. Before going on board, all passengers received a garment to wear. The boat started off at the calm part of the fall and then went into dense mist of spray! What a great experience it was! Twice, we had lunch at the Skylon Tower Restaurant where the food was good and the view of the American and Canadian Falls from the revolving dining room was breathtaking.

We spent three days in Toronto. In this large city, we didn't know what to visit first, so we decided to take the guided tours to see more places, and also, it would be less stressful for us. One of the things that impressed me most was the tall glass buildings, which looked like mirrors reflecting the surrounding areas. In one of our strolls in the park of Toronto, Andrew started to have a serious and enthusiastic conversation. He was telling me maybe he should try to go in business for himself instead of continuing to look for work. Then he gave me some of his ideas about how to start it. I was aware that the job hunting had become a nightmare for him, and I also knew of his desire of having his own business for some time, and I hadn't paid any attention. Now it was different because he was trying hard to convince me with his idea. I knew my husband too well, and he was not the person to be in business for himself. I felt bad, but I could not agree with him. Years back, in Austria, he bought real beautiful, unique leather wallets and some elegant European shirts for men. In the hope of doing some future business, he was keeping in touch with those Austrian merchants. He tried to sell the wallets to some elegant stores in Manhattan, and because they were unique, the stores' managers gave him the chance. Many customers liked the wallets displayed in the windows, but they found them to be very expensive, so after a while, the wallets were sold with no gain for my husband. I still have two of those wallets, and every time I see them, I remember my husband's dream and our disagreeable conversation in Toronto.

We stayed in Ottawa for three days. Here we took a sightseeing bus tour of the capital, a scenic river cruise along the Ottawa River, and a guided tour of Parliament Hill, which is the Canadian government complex. Altogether, it was a very interesting city.

The next stop was Montreal, where we spent five days. In the city, my husband had a friend, Henrietta, from the old times when they both lived in Salzburg, Austria, and prior to our trip, Henrietta had invited us to her home for a few days. Our arrival at the end of May happened a few weeks before the start of the 1976 Summer Olympics. Here, we went to see some of the pre-Olympic competitions for swimming, hokey, gymnastic, and others. We went to see some acrobatics performed by the Chinese, and they were unbelievably great, but their music made us fall asleep. At that time, there were no problems with security, so having tickets, we were able to go everywhere in the Olympic grounds. In Montreal, we had a marvelous time. The selection of restaurants was excellent, and most of all, Henrietta had been a wonderful hostess.

Andrew drove all the way to Canada and back to New York. He was a good driver! On the way back home, I was very sleepy. I tried hard to keep my eyes opened but couldn't, and I fell asleep in the car. I felt guilty that my husband was driving, and I was sleeping, but he didn't mind. With that warm smile, he was telling me not to worry about him, that he was doing fine, and it was okay for me to sleep. Then when we got home, we noticed that our lawn was completely yellow, burned! During our absence, there had been no rain, and we had no sprinkler system for watering the lawn automatically so that the hot temperature, which was unusual for that time of the year, destroyed the lawn completely.

* * *

Toward the end of June 1976, on the way to Downtown Manhattan, Andrew met on the train an old colleague from Bankers Trust who was now working for the European American Bank. They started to talk about the past, and among the other things, Andrew told him about the hardship that he was having in finding a job.

Subsequently, through this colleague, he got temporary employment at the European American Bank. It was not what he had hoped to find, but it was better than nothing, and he was glad that he finally had a job. The day he started going to work, I remember how enthusiastic he was and how relieved I felt in seeing him content and relaxed again. On July 3, 1976, I went to the bank where Andrew was now working to look at the parade of the ships in the New York Harbor. First of all, he introduced me to some of his colleagues and then took me to a window to watch what was going on down the Hudson River on East Manhattan. The US Bicentennial Celebration was in full swing; there were ships of all sizes, old and new, beautiful and mediocre, and they all were making their way in the parade. The view from the high window was spectacular.

AUNT MARGARET

After we got married and moved to Queens, Andrew and I went to visit his aunt Margaret every Saturday with the hope that aunt and nephew would start to have a warm relationship, but our efforts were in vain. Starting from the time when Andrew was single, Aunt Margaret never invited him for the Jewish holidays or for any other occasion. The only communication between them was a phone call, which was seldom. Although my husband knew that his aunt was not fond of him, we were going to see her anyway because she was the only relative he had in America. She was his father's sister.

Apparently Aunt Margaret liked me, but I distrusted her because I came to know her better and concluded that she was not sincere; she was a person with two faces.

Nonetheless, we got together for the Jewish holidays at her house, and for the Christians holidays, at our home. Through Aunt Margaret, we met Mr. Sam Kay and his family (Willy and Barbara Kravitz and their children), who were Aunt's best friends. They were all warm and pleasant people, and occasionally, we got together at our home or at theirs.

THE AMAZING TWIST OF MY LIFE

Hard to believe how my life had made such a dramatic turn of 180 degrees! Up until now, I had been so busy that I had little time to reflect on just how far I had come from that orphanage in Sicily. From my perspective, I don't think anyone in my family or the people in my hometown of Castletermini would have imagined that one day, that young unfortunate girl they knew could achieve so much in her life. For now, I had become a woman with an enviable record of accomplishments, working for a major company as a computer systems analyst with demanding assignments, including several programmers reporting to me.

I remember on a visit to Castletermini in 1974, we were at my cousins', Lina and Enzo Arnone's, for dinner. With all the relatives present, Andrew, in broken Italian and with a grin on his face, told them that I was actually doing better than he was back home in America. Given that the men of Sicily were chauvinistic, they were intrigued by the fact that I, a woman, had risen to such an enviable position. This generated many questions about my life since I left Sicily as well as how I met Andrew and what sort of position I had in America. As I was probably the only person in the entire town with knowledge of computers or programming, explaining my job was difficult, and it seemed almost like a foreign language to them. Later, when I asked Andrew why he felt it necessary to say that I was doing better than him, he answered me, "I am very proud of you and want your family to know just how far you've come."

However, the one person, more than all my relatives, who realized just how drastically my life had changed for the better and could really appreciate my good fortune, was uncle Peppino Fantauzzo. So, it was with great regret that I remember that his trip to visit me in America did not materialize because of his poor health. How much I would have enjoyed to have him join me, to show him parts of America and at my home, where he could see for himself the transformation of his dear niece Lina.

The memories of those days brought to mind just how far I had come and achieved. I was now content with my life, had a good husband, a rewarding job, and time to enjoy extended vacations.

THE 1977 TRIP TO ST. LOUIS

The only relatives I had in America were those living in St. Louis, Missouri. They were my two first cousins whom I had never met, Rosa Fantauzzo Pona, and her sister, Lil Fantauzzo Sala. Both were born in Casteltermini, Sicily, and immigrated to the USA with their parents at a very young age. Rosa, now a widow, had three married children—Joan, Marie, and Jim. And Lil, married to Charlie Sala, had no children. Many years had passed since their father, Silvestro Fantauzzo, my mother's brother, had gone to Sicily for a visit while I was still living in Casteltermini. With the nearing of my vacations, I told my husband that I would like to go to St. Louis to get to know my cousins, and he agreed. I wrote a letter to Rosa, explaining who I was—the daughter of her father's sister, Giuseppina—and about my desire to meet all the relatives and to introduce my husband to her and to the rest of the family. In no time, Rosa answered me with a warm invitation to stay at her house. In St. Louis, when we arrived at my cousin's place in the center of the city, I cannot describe the warm welcome we received from Rosa, Lil, and Charlie. It was unbelievable how happy they were to meet us for the first time. Then came the amusing part, my cousins thought that we had come from Italy to the USA for our honeymoon. Knowing nothing about me, they tried to speak in the Sicilian dialect but were surprised when I answered them in English. I had to talk in English because my husband didn't understand the dialect. They liked my husband very much, and they wanted to know everything about both of us. After a while, I told the cousins that I had already been in the USA for over twelve years and explained some of the details of my past ordeals in America. They remained really surprised and disappointed that I hadn't contacted them beforehand. If they had known that I was struggling alone in this country for years, they could have helped me in many ways. But during those hard years, it never occurred to me to contact them because the only American person I knew was Uncle Silvestro, their father, who was already dead. From their father side, I was the first relative that they met in the USA. The rest of the family members were all living in Sicily. Afterward, my cousins showed me many family pictures and wanted to know all about the old Sicilian folks, and, with a lot of nostalgia, expressed their desire to visit their native country. In fact, they wanted us to inform them of our next trip to Italy because they wanted to travel with us.

We stayed at Rosa's home in St. Louis for eight days, and we received the royal treatment. The following Saturday, Rosa's daughter-in-law, Jim's wife, invited us out for a ride. When we came back, we found the house full of relatives who enthusiastically welcomed us. We remained very impressed because we didn't expect to find so much affection in St. Louis. Next, Rosa introduced us to her two daughters—Joanne and Marie—her son Jim and the rest of the big family who had just come to meet us. My cousins had invited all the St. Louis relatives to come to the surprise welcome party As a matter of fact, besides the relatives, we also found a long and beautiful decorated table with plenty of Italian food and drinks. What a successful and unforgettable surprise party it was!

While in the city, with Charlie we visited the Saint Louis Cathedral, which looks like a church in Roma, the St. Louis Union Station, and the Gateway Arch. One day, cousins Charlie and Lil took us to the steamboat on the Mississippi River for lunch. The food was good; the weather was tranquil, and the rest of the day was very pleasant. Another time, the cousins took us at their farmhouse where we spent two wonderful days. The farmhouse, located not far from St. Louis, was on a nice and peaceful piece of land, and there were a few beautiful horses, a brook, and two black dogs. At that time, I didn't know how to drive, so Charlie showed me how to drive around the farm with the cart. I had a ball with the cart.

What a wonderful time we spent in St. Louis! The family's atmosphere was great, and the things that my cousins did for us were the best a person could receive from kind and sincere relatives. Anyway, we left the beautiful city of St. Louis with a fantastic experience and warm feelings.

* * *

Back in New York City, as soon as we arrived in Queens, my first thought was to go down to the basement to check for any water leaks on the floor. During continuous heavy rains, many times, our basement got some water, and up to now, no contractors had been capable of fixing the problem. While going down the stairs leading to the basement, one of my shoes got tangled on a step. I lost control and went to the bottom of the stairs, hitting my head against a rocky wall. For one or two minutes, I had a very strange feeling. It was like a fast bright light going through my brain, and then my vision was blurry. Meantime, my husband was calling and looking for me all over the house, and when he came to the basement, he found me with a bleeding head. Not knowing what had happened, he immediately took me to the Long Island Jewish Medical Center emergency room where I got several stitches and medications. Thank God, it was not serious. The stairway to the basement didn't have any railings, and what I remember was that I didn't have anything to catch and hold on to. After my accident, the first thing we did was to get a contractor to install the railings.

1978 – THE AMORELLIS AT OUR HOME IN NEW YORK CITY

During the month of September, we received a telephone call from our friends Frank and Nena Amorelli and believed that they were calling us from Sicily. Instead, they were in New Jersey and staying at one of their friends' home. I was glad to hear from them, and while we were on the phone, their friends invited us to their home in New Jersey for supper. We didn't know them, but we gladly accepted the invitation. The following day, my husband and I went to New Jersey to meet our friends, and when we arrived there, we received a nice welcome and found ourselves among many Sicilian people. It seemed that everybody knew us. Then the Amorellis introduced their two young children and all the Sicilians present. After a while there, the guests sat at a long dinner table, and soon, a good supper was served. Since everybody was Sicilian, most of them were speaking in the Sicilian dialect, except for a few who, because of my husband, spoke in English. After supper, with enthusiasm, Andrew and I invited Nena and Frank to spend the rest of their vacations at our house in Queens, and they immediately accepted our request with a big yes. Therefore, they packed their suitcases and came with us.

I didn't know why, but upon arrival at our place, the Amorelli were very happy, especially Nena who started to thank me profusely. I knew her very well, and she was one of my best friends from my hometown. We accommodated the couple and their children, Pietro and Mariú, comfortably on the first floor, and my husband and I slept on the second floor. The next morning,

I called TIAA-CREF office and told my boss that I needed to take a few days off. It was okay with him because in case of necessity, he would call me at home. We took our Sicilian guests to Manhattan for some sightseeing only one time. They just preferred to stay home or to take a walk in our neighborhood. They had already done a cruise in the Caribbean, traveled in several parts of the United States, and now they just needed to rest.

One day, while we had the Sicilian friends at our place, I got a telephone call from TIAA-CREF, telling me to go to the office because my presence was needed immediately. There was a problem in the Immediate Annuity computer processing for the monthly payments. Because I was in charge of the system, it was my responsibility to resolve the problem as soon as possible. So, I left the guests at home, and went to the office in Manhattan where I found a lot of printouts in my cubicle. Without wasting any time, through the computer printouts, I located the source of the problem and made the appropriate fixes in the computer programs. Afterward, I stayed there for a while during the re-execution of the system, and then I went home. At home, I found dinner ready on the table. My friend, Nena, had prepared everything, and they were waiting for me to eat. It was the first time that I ate stuffed eggplants, an actual Sicilian specialty dish! Up to now, in every special occasion, I serve the stuffed eggplants, which are a first-class gourmet dish. This is what people tell me while they are savoring the eggplants. One day, the Cristandos, close friends of the Amorellis, invited all of us to their home on Long Island, New York, for dinner. I had met the Cristandos, Sofia and her husband, some year earlier on a ship and precisely when the Amorellis were returning to Italy at the end of their honeymoon in America. Anyway, the hosts were great, and dinner was super.

The Amorellis' two children were wonderful. Pietro was a little shy and a very polite boy, and Mariú was a beautiful girl with big, expressive black eyes and was a little naughty. One day, in front of our house, I don't remember why, but Mariú got very angry at my husband and started telling him, "You are puttana (whore)," and she repeated the same word many times. She was about three years old, and we all were surprise at her language, and at the same time, we could not stop laughing, recognizing that she didn't know the meaning of the word. After a pleasant stay with us, we brought the Amorellis family to the airport where they took the flight to Italy.

The Amorellis' overfriendly behavior was terrific. My husband and I enjoyed their stay at our place immensely because it was like having very close family members with us.

* * *

In the middle of 1979, Andrew lost his job at the European American Bank due to the reduction of personnel. My husband who had worked there on a temporary basis for over three years was one of the first to go. At the beginning, it was not so bad, but when the realization of what was ahead started to sink into my husband's mind, the uneasiness began again. As before, I became worried about him, and I had to come up with something to keep him occupied. It happened that for some time, we had thought about upgrading the outside of the house, and because we both had been busy with our jobs, we had delayed planning for this. With my husband at home and plenty of free time on his hands, it was just the right time for this project.

Therefore, Andrew soon got busy and called a few contractors to get the estimates for putting new siding on the walls of the second floor, redoing the driveway, and so forth. There was plenty of work to be done, and it was good that my husband could supervise. After the estimates and schedules were finalized, the work began. In those days when nobody showed up for the work, my husband went to the city for a break, and each time, he came to see me at my office where we had lunch together and afterward he went wherever he wished. When he was peaceful, I was happy. Because of several independent contractors and different schedules, it took a few months for the work to be completed.

During the time of our house's improvement project, Andrew's ex-wife, Magda, came back into the picture. She had lost her husband some years earlier and now suddenly started calling my husband at home. Magda completely ignored the fact that Andrew was married. For her, it was like he was a free man and she could have him at her disposal whenever she wanted. As a matter of fact, not only did she call him when she wanted to talk to somebody, she also asked him to take her to the cemetery and so forth. Of course, she also knew that my husband was not the kind of person to be disrespectful or to say no to a lady. Three or four times, he took Magda wherever she wanted to go to, and every time, he kept me informed of everything. I remember one day while coming home from work; I found her at my place. I didn't say a word, but I was very disappointed, though I was sure that there was nothing to be concerned about. Anyhow, after a while, Andrew got tired of her calls, and also, he hadn't forgotten their history, so he told her not to call him anymore.

* * *

At TIAA-CREF, one of the benefits that all the employees had was the free annual medical checkup. At the beginning of the year 1979, when I went to the doctor for my annual physical, he told me that there was an echocardiography machine, which could identify the causes of my heart murmur. In order for me to have that test, the doctor needed permission from my company, so he called the head of the personnel for the approval, and afterward, he made the arrangements for my test. In February, I went to the Lenox Hill Hospital where the test was to be performed. There they told me to lie down on the bed, and I remained in that position for more than two hours. At that time, because the apparatus was not well known yet, the test took some time to finish. The machine finally showed that two leaflets of my mitral valve were closing abnormally. In short, I was diagnosed to have mitral valve prolapse, and as a consequence, I am at high risk of bacterial infection of the heart. Therefore, the murmur was the problem with my heart when a cardiologist in Sicily in 1962 gave me six months to live!

1980 – OUR SECOND EUROPEAN TRIP INCLUDED A WALK ON MOUNT ETNA

The preparation for this second trip, in six years, was easy. I had a three weeks' vacation, and I got an extra week off from my boss. In the middle of September, we flew from New York to Rome and then to Palermo's airport where some of our relatives welcomed us, and afterward, we went to my hometown with my brother.

In Casteltermini, relatives and friends came to visit us at my brother's place. This time, we just accepted a few invitations because I had a specific itinerary in mind for my husband. I wanted him to see some interesting parts of Sicily. In fact, two days later my brother with his wife and children took us to Syracuse, Mount Etna, and Catania.

We stayed in Syracuse for three days. The city of Syracuse is impressive and has extraordinary archaeological sites, beautiful monuments, and excellent restaurants. We spent a wonderful time there. With respect to my nieces, Giuseppina and Alida, I do not know if they had good time or not, but for sure, they were happy to be with their uncle Andrew!

Mount Etna was our next stop. Mount Etna is the largest active volcano in Europe. The eruption of the volcano can occur from the summit or from the flanks, and the one from the flanks is the most dangerous because the lava flow that it generates destroys everything in its path. Mount Etna has a strange and mysterious volcanic landscape, and it is one of the greatest and most beautiful volcano adventure destinations.

Arriving at Rifugio Sapienza, a destination area for the tourists, we went to the tourist station where we got special clothing and boots. Afterward, we followed a tour guide. We started our trip up the mountain through smoldering cracks, walking on grey and reddish stones, and the incredible surroundings were immersed in a very bleak atmosphere. At a certain point, we felt like we were on the moon. To the extent our eyes could see, it was a completely mysterious world, and although we were walking on the warm cracks, the climate was cold. I enjoyed looking at my nieces holding the lava stones in their hands. Anyway, the tour lasted for about two hours, but the experience will remain with me a lifetime.

We stayed in Catania for two days. Located at the foot of Mount Etna, Catania is the second largest city in Sicily. It has been destroyed by catastrophic earthquakes and by several Mount Etna volcanic eruptions. Although it was my second visit here, this time, I enjoyed the stay even more because I was with my husband and my brother's family.

We returned to Casteltermini. The children went back to school. My brother went to work, and Andrew and I got under way with the invitations extended to us by friends and relatives before our excursion. Among the friends were Frank and Nena Amorelli. They had a grapevine, and Frank was growing a special type of grapes as a hobby and afterward giving the fruit to his friends. One day, they took us to their countryside, and there, with a lot of enthusiasm, Frank showed us his vineyard. Each plant had the largest grapes I had ever seen. They were really incredible and not to mention their delicious sweet taste. Before going back to my brother's place, he presented us with a full basket of those grapes. Another day, they invited us to their home for dinner. They lived in a large penthouse with a beautiful view of the town and its surrounding mountains and valleys. This building was not there at the time I was living in town. The apartment was furnished and decorated with the most modern style and accents.

The dinner was exceptionally good. On many occasions, people in my hometown like to serve domestic-bred rabbit as something special. The Amorellis told me that they were serving the rabbit, and I told them not to mention rabbit in front of my husband. I remembered when I told him how tasty the rabbit meat was many years back, and he said to me, "Rabbit meat! That is repulsive!" Anyway, we all ate the entire dinner, including Andrew who told me that the meat was very good. The following day, I told him that he had eaten the rabbit. He was surprised but didn't say anything. We spent a wonderful time with the Amorellis, and they treated us excessively well.

While in Casteltermini, my beloved uncle Peppino, besides inviting us at his home for supper, came to my brother's place with a basket full of special treats more than once in the morning. There were figs, Indian figs, and grapes, which were my favorite fruits. My brother and his wife did their best to make our stay at their place as pleasant and comfortable as possible. Their children were wonderful, and before leaving town, Vincenzo and Maria gave us a lot of goodies to take with us to America. Next, my brother drove us to the Palermo Airport where my Giudice cousins and other relatives were waiting for us to say good-bye. From there, we flew to Rome.

At Rome Airport, after waiting for more than six hours for the Malev Airline plane to arrive from Budapest, they announced that the plane was not coming until the next day because of mechanical difficulties. It was late evening, so we went to the nearest hotel for the night. The next day we returned to the airport, they announced that the Malev plane was not coming to Rome, so we took the Alitalia Airline for Zurich, Switzerland, and from there, we flew to Budapest. At that time under the communist regime, only the Hungarian Malev Airline was operating from Rome to Budapest and vice versa.

In Budapest we stayed for a few days. As soon as we went through the communist security inspection at the airport,

Andrew's relatives brought us to the city where the accommodation was not great and the atmosphere was depressing.

While in Budapest, we got together with the relatives at Aunt Maria's apartment every day, and then we all went to see some of the historic places. We visited the Hungarian Parliament Building, the largest and tallest building in Budapest; the Citadel, a former king's fortress, located upon the top of the hill in Buda, has a beautiful view of Budapest, divided by the Danube River; the Buda Castle, an impressive royal complex of the old Hungarian kings, we reached this complex by a funicular.

At the end of our brief sojourn, we flew from Budapest to Zurich with the Malev Airline and then to New York with Alitalia.

* * *

After returning from our second European trip, my husband again began to look for employment. Through the employment agencies, he went to several banks for interviews, and wherever he went, he got the usual answer that he was overqualified. After some time, discouraged and hopeless, he stopped looking for work. At this point, frankly speaking, I didn't care about the job because I was more concerned about his mental health than anything else.

Toward the end of 1980, Andrew came with the idea of writing business books in three languages—English, German, and French—and the theme would be based on the Letter of Credits in the banking business. I told him that, in my opinion, the subject was not interesting and recommended that he write his autobiography instead. He didn't like to reflect on his past. With the explosion of the computer industry, everything was continuously changing, and for sure, by the time his hard work was finished, his material would become obsolete. Nonetheless, because he liked the idea of doing something stimulating, he made up his mind and started to work on his new project. I was glad because this new undertaking was keeping him mentally and physically occupied and at the same time content.

It was in 1983 when Andrew suddenly got a call from an employment agency to go to a bank in New York for an interview. He went and got the job at Citibank in the international division. It was an interesting assignment, dealing with the US Government loans to foreign countries. The travel from our home to the end of Wall Street where Citibank was located was long, but he didn't mind. He was happy to go back to work.

* * *

During the summer of 1981, I got a severe irritation in my eyes. The redness and itching were unbearable, and I went to see my ophthalmologist. The doctor didn't say much. He just prescribed some drops to put in my eyes twice a day and wanted to see me in two weeks. Unfortunately, the effect of the drops was scary, and the problem with my eyes had become worse. When I went to the TIAA-CREF medical office, the nurse there immediately noticed that something was seriously wrong with my eyes, and without wasting anytime, she made an appointment for me with an eye specialist in Manhattan. Dr. Miller, the specialist, sent me to the hospital to have a biopsy of both my eyelids. Whatever test was done, there was nothing to be concerned. The drops previously prescribed for me were wrong. Dr. Miller gave me a new prescription, and in no time, my eyes improved.

ANDREW'S ADVANCED GLAUCOMA DISCOVERED BY CHANCE

After my bad experience with the old ophthalmologist, I persuaded Andrew to see Dr. Miller, and that was an excellent idea because it was Dr. Miller who diagnosed the advanced glaucoma. The previous doctor had never mentioned the glaucoma, and the bad news was shocking for Andrew and me. I remember how terrible we felt when Dr. Miller explained to us the seriousness of the glaucoma and that Andrew could lose his eye sight any day! The doctor prescribed some drops for his eyes and warned my husband to be careful when driving or doing other tasks. Afterward, Andrew went to Dr. Miller to have his glaucoma checked every three months. A few weeks later, we took a day trip to the historical Mystic town in Connecticut. It was a beautiful sunny day, and there we visited, among other places, the Maritime Museum. On our way back home in Queens, it was almost evening and becoming dark. I then started to think of Dr. Miller's warnings regarding my husband's eye sight, so I didn't want to travel any further. At that time, I didn't drive, and I was really worried that something could happen to Andrew, so I told him to stop at the nearest hotel for the night, but with his stubbornness, he continued driving home, luckily with no problems.

In 1982, TIAA-CREF started a new medical plan for its employees. With the new plan, all the employees with medical care had to go to the assigned health groups, which were given according to their residence area. It was no longer possible to choose a doctor outside the plan. My assigned medical group was at the Long Island Jewish Medical Center in Queens, which luckily happened to be one of the best in the borough. It was time for my annual physical and the first time to go to the new facility. Among the tests I had there, I requested an echocardiogram because I wanted to know more about my mitral valve prolapse. After the test, the cardiologist told me not to worry about it, just keep the dentist informed about your mitral valve prolapse.

For his annual physical, Andrew also went to the Long Island Jewish Medical Center where the ophthalmologist told him that he could have a laser trabeculoplasty. This laser procedure, to open the clogged drainage canals that cause the intraocular pressure and often blindness, would take a few minutes, one eye at the time. Up to now, no doctor had ever mentioned that there was laser treatment for the glaucoma, so Andrew and I were skeptical, and to be sure of the new procedure, we went back to the previous doctor in Manhattan for a second opinion. It was now that the doctor told us that eventually he would have suggested the surgery. We had no idea why this doctor kept us in the dark, and meantime, Andrew went to see him for a checkup every three months and paying the full fee each time because this doctor didn't belong to our medical group. It was unbelievable, and all this time, Andrew was living with anxiety, thinking of the blindness that could have occurred at any time! We left the doctor's office very disappointed, but at the same time, we were very encouraged with the knowledge there is a way to cope with the glaucoma problem. Subsequently, Andrew made the appointment at the Long Island Jewish Medical Center for the laser surgery. Thank God, it all went very well.

All my life, I was conscious of my bottom crooked teeth, and I didn't know what to do. In the late sixties, I remember when I told Andrew about my teeth, and he took me to his dentist in Manhattan. After the examination, the dentist told me that he could fix my mouth by pulling all of my bottom teeth and replacing them with dentures. I thought to myself, *It doesn't make any sense*, so I ignored him completely. Then a colleague of mine at ADP took me to her dentist in Brooklyn who, after assessing my mouth, advised me to keep my own crooked teeth because they were healthy and strong. I liked to hear that, but the awareness of my ugly teeth remained until, a few years later, I moved to Queens where I found a very good dentist who, after a consultation, told me that he could fix my teeth with no problem. I cannot describe how happy I was, having finally found this dentist.

1981 – THE RIGHT TIME TO FIX MY TEETH

Because of the heavy work load in the system division at TIAA-CREF and consequently no time for me to go away on extended vacations, I thought the timing was just right to take care of my teeth. The procedure would be long and expensive too, but at this point, I wasn't worried. I was ready and glad to get this under way. The process started with the pulling out of the four bottom overcrowded teeth and replacing them with a temporary bridge. Then the dentist sent me to an orthodontist who placed braces to straighten my top teeth. At the beginning, the braces were uncomfortable, but with time, the situation improved, except for the ugliness of the braces in my mouth. The braces remained for the duration of the procedure, which lasted for over a year. At my age, it seemed ridiculous to have the braces on, but I said to myself, "It is better late than never." And once the teeth were straightened out, I went back to my dentist to have the job finished. The end result was excellent, and until now, more than thirty years later, I am happy with that job.

SEPTEMBER 1983 – VISITED THE FIRST CASINO

Andrew and I went to Atlantic City for five days. I cannot describe how strange I felt when, for the first time in my life, I entered a casino called the Playboy. If my recollection is correct, the casino was decorated in black and white, and there were also plenty of mirrors all over the place. Then looking around and seeing the Playboy bunnies, the many people at the blackjack and baccarat tables, the noise of the slot machines, the clouds of smoke everywhere, without exaggeration, my sensation was of something diabolic. Once in town, we visited several casinos and noticed that, more or less, they were all the same. Each had some characteristic of their own. For example, the atmosphere at the Caesar Casino was more pleasant, maybe because it had a certain fake opulence of Ancient Rome. In all the casinos, there was a lot going on, and soon, I too started playing with the slot machine for fun. I tried the five- and ten-cent ones without luck. In the evening, we went to see some comedy shows. Outdoor, it was nice to walk on the boardwalk and enjoy the view of the Atlantic Ocean on one side and the Casinos on the other. I can say that at the beginning, it was strange, but all in all, I had great time in Atlantic City.

1985 – TRAVEL AROUND EUROPE ON THE ORIENTAL EXPRESS

For our September–October vacation, I wanted something exiting, completely different from the previous ones. In other words, besides visiting relatives, I wanted to spend some time with Andrew alone. The places that I wanted to visit were Budapest, Vienna, Salzburg, Innsbruck, Venice, Florence, Palermo, and Casteltermini. To execute my plan, I went to the German railroad tourist office, which was located just across the street from TIAA-CREF. There, I got the airline tickets and the one-way railroad tickets, which were valid for six months with the departure in Budapest and ending in Rome. The tickets included the cabin reservation aboard the Oriental Express train. I also got several hotel reservations from the same travel agency. Afterward, we flew from New York to Rome with Alitalia, and to Hungary, with the Malev Airline.

Our stay in Budapest lasted one week. This time at the airport, we found more relatives waiting for us. Cousin Lila had brought her two married children with their families from Prague, and among them were Helenka and Andrea, two beautiful and polite young girls. We went to Aunt Maria's apartment in Budapest, but everybody had to be very cautious not to talk about the communist regime in front of the girls because, going back to Prague, they would innocently pass on what they had heard in Budapest, causing trouble to their parents. At that time, Eastern Europe was full of spies, and everything said was taken seriously. While in Budapest, every day, all of the family members met at Maria's place, and then they decided what to do next.

We traveled from Budapest to Vienna on the Orient Express train. The morning of our departure, Andrew's relatives accompanied us to the railroad station where we boarded the famous train, and once aboard, in no time, we found the cabin with our names posted on the door. What a nice feeling we experienced because of the punctuality, organization, and atmosphere on the train. We also found our small cabin very comfortable. With no more stress by way of the Czech and Hungarian languages, especially for me, everything was now wonderful. At the Austrian frontier, the train made a stop for the Hungarian communist police to inspect the passports and other documents and also to search the cabins of all the passengers, and of course they looked at our cabin too.

We stayed in Vienna three days. At the railroad station, we just took a small suitcase with us and left the rest of our belongings there where, for a small fee, they were stored until we were ready to continue our trip. Then we went to the hotel located near the center of the city.

In Vienna we took a few guided and sightseeing tours. The places we visited are as follows: the Hofburg Palace, where some of the most powerful people in Austrian history lived. The St. Stephen's Cathedral is one of the most famous sights in Vienna. The Schönbrunn Palace, a former imperial summer residence in Vienna, is one of the most magnificent cultural monuments in Austria. The castle was built to rival the baroque French Versailles. With the guided tour, we got to see about forty rooms of the palace. The Belvedere, close to the center of Vienna, is an extensive complex consisting of two magnificent Baroque palaces. For sure, only with the tour guides would it have been possible to see so much in a short time.

Back at the railroad station, we picked up our suitcases and continued our trip to Salzburg. We were on the schedule, so the names were on our cabin door. The ride on the Orient Express was fantastic, and along the way, the view of the Alps and the houses on the mountains with their balconies adorned with flowers was very picturesque.

Note: From here to Rome, every time we left the train, we also left our luggage at the railroad station, as we did in Vienna.

We were in Salzburg for a three-day stay. Coming out of the station, Andrew was surprised because he didn't recognize this part of the city anymore. Since he had left Salzburg over thirty years earlier, the city had gone through many renovations, which had changed the appearance of the railroad station area completely. Our hotel was conveniently located at the center of the town. It was a lovely place, and it had good amenities too. I remember the morning's fabulous breakfasts. They were really exceptional, and I had never seen so many tasty food selections!

Andrew had already described the beauty of Salzburg, but it was quite an experience seeing it in person. It was a very picturesque Alpine town. There were many fortresses, castles, gardens, and more. We visited some of them, such as the Mirabel-Garden, the Cathedral, and by cable car, we went to the stately Hohensalzburg Castle on the hill overlooking the city. From the castle, which is the largest medieval fortress in Europe, we walked down the hill and on the way down we made a brief stop. Here Andrew enthusiastically showed me the apartment where he had lived for two years during his stay in Salzburg.

We saw a lot in this charming city by ourselves and also enjoyed strolling along the narrow streets of the old town where the stores full of Mozart souvenirs were very interesting. The chocolate boxes with Mozart's picture packed in several shapes were so attractive that we bought a few to bring to my Italian relatives as souvenirs. With a guided tour, we went to the location where the *Sound of Music* was filmed, including the church where the wedding took place.

At the end of our memorable stay in Salzburg, we went back to the railroad station to continue our trip to Innsbruck. The train ride from Salzburg to Innsbruck was breathtaking. It was the most beautiful scenery I had ever seen, and I really cannot describe it in words. While admiring the natural wonders of the Alps, Andrew and I suddenly decided to visit the Kitzbüel's Mountains. Our next station stop was in the town of Kitzbüel, and here we got off the train.

From Kitzbüel town we went by cable car to the ski area in the Kitzbüel Alps which is at an elevation of 5616 feet. It was not yet the ski season, consequently, the only people in the resort were some tourists like us and a few workers. It was a beautiful day; the blue sky, the calm weather, and the stillness made the view of the Alps and the greenery below more scenic. We were almost alone; at that altitude, we seemed to be flying into the sky. It was really a marvelous feeling. What enjoyable experience! Back to the railroad station we continued our trip to Innsbruck.

We stayed in Innsbruck three days. While in the city, one of Andrew's cousins, Janos, with his wife from Munich, Germany, came here to meet us. We all stayed at the same hotel, and during the day, Janos brought us around to visit some of Innsbruck's beautiful monuments. We spent almost two days together, and though they all spoke German and Hungarian, I had a pleasant time with them.

On the way to Venice, from the train, the view of the Austrian landscape sceneries was striking, and in addition, the crossing of the Brenner Pass, which is a mountain pass through the Alps along the border between Italy and Austria, was interesting.

We stayed in Venice three days. At Santa Lucia railroad station, I told Andrew that it was finally my turn to speak Italian. In Venice, we didn't have any hotel reservation because at the time of the booking, our New York travel agency was unable to find anything available. At the railroad station, there were many Italians asking the newcomers if they needed lodging, so we got one. By water bus, the man took us to the lodging, which was a bed and breakfast. The room was small, the price, which included breakfast and supper, was quite inexpensive, and the location was excellent. As a matter of fact, we were able to walk to the rail-road station to have the express coffee or the cappuccino, which Andrew liked very much.

The city of Venice is simply stunning, completely unique, and it is also one of the most popular cities in the world. The sight of the Venetian palaces, emerging from the water without pavement and the continuity of the peaceful sequence of façades reflecting on the Grand Canal, is really magical, especially at night when the city is illuminated.

We visited the Basilica of St. Mark and the Doge's Palace with a tour guide. We took a gondola, which went under the Bridge of Sighs (Ponte dei Sospiri). This is an enclosed white bridge that connects the old prison to the interrogation room in the Doge's Palace. According to the legend, the view from the Bridge of Sighs was the last view of Venice that convicts saw before their imprisonment. Getting around through the very narrow streets of Venice, full of stores, restaurants, and tourists was amusing, but everything was within walking distance. We enjoyed sitting at a café in San Marco's Square, savoring the espresso while looking at the ultra-busy and fascinating piazza.

After spending a wonderful time in Venice, we walked back to the Santa Lucia railroad station to continue our trip to Florence. On the way, at the Bologna railroad station, we changed trains from the Oriental Express to the German-Italian railroad and then continued for Florence.

We spent three days in Florence. We arrived here also with no hotel reservation. Upon leaving the train at Santa Maria Novella railroad station, we found many Italians looking for passengers in need of accommodations, so we went to a bed and breakfast. I do not know how the things are today, but in those days, getting lodging in this way was normal in Italy.

By the time we got to Florence, we were too tired of visiting famous attractions. From Salzburg to here, we had already seen so many monuments that we could not absorb anymore, so on our last day, we decided to take it easy. We went to some squares and strolled around while looking at some of the gorgeous building facades and elegant stores.Next at the railroad station we took the train for Rome, and from there we flew to Palermo.

At the airport in Palermo, among the relatives waiting for us were my brother and my nieces Giuseppina and Alida who, since our last visit, had become two beautiful teenagers. Afterward, my brother took us to Casteltermini where we spent six wonderful days.

In Palermo, we stayed three days at my Giudice cousins' home. There we found their son Giuseppe in bed and then saw him walking with crutches. He was lucky to be alive for he had survived an almost fatal motorcycle accident. Anyway, I was happy to see him but not in those conditions! Next, we met the rest of my cousins' children—Franca, Giovanni, and Tony. They were very happy to see us and appreciated enormously the Mozart's boxes of chocolates that we brought from Salzburg.

As I said before, I had many first cousins but was only close with a few of them. My cousins Franco and Adalgisa Martorana invited us and the Giudice's family to spend a day at their villa in Mondello. Here we met the Martorana's children, Fernando and Maria Gabriella, and Aunt Marietta with her husband and their children—Elio and Gino—with their families. The warmhearted atmosphere, the gourmet foods served, and most of all, the attention that Andrew received from everybody was really great.

In Palermo, we completed our memorable European vacation, and subsequently, we flew back home to New York City.

TROUBLESHOOTING AT TIAA-CREF

As soon as I went back to work, many of the employees were eager to see me, and I wondered why they were so interested! When I went to my cubicle, I found a huge mountain of computer printouts with a big sign "Welcome back Lina." While I was in Europe, the company could not produce the "Immediate Annuity" monthly payments because of an unexpected problem in one of the programs. I was told, some of the programmers and analysts in the systems division tried to find the cause of the problem without success. At that time, nobody knew the immediate annuity system as I did, so it was important for me to resolve the problem as soon as possible. Once I found the cause, I made a temporary fix to one of the computer programs in order to continue with the monthly processing. The cause of the current problem was that a retiree had reached the age of a hundred, which was a rare case, and the application software didn't have the provision for an age above ninety-nine. In order to resolve the problem once and for all, it required some system analytical work, programs to be modified, files to be changed, and much more. It was a big project.

The computer systems division personnel were always busy with the development and implementation of new systems, with the maintenance of the existing systems, and in keeping up with the continuous IBM updates or new releases. I liked my job very much; it was stimulating, and with new things to learn all the time, certainly there was no time to be bored. As a matter of fact, I often took some work home. Every project had its own timeline, and every time a big computer system was installed successfully, the system manager invited all the people involved in the implementation to a celebration, which was usually held at the TIAA-CREF executive restaurant. Sometimes, the successful implementation was celebrated with a party held at the Waldorf Astoria restaurant on Lexington Avenue. This was a special occasion to be dressed up, to go, and enjoy the party with drinks, good food, and a small gift. Once, we got a special pen with our names engraved on it. Because I was involved in the project 90 percent of the time, Andrew too was invited. Anyway, each celebration, whether big or small, was great. Also for the Christmas party, more than once, Mr. Jack Putney, the systems division manager, invited the entire division to his home in Upstate New York.

1986 – VINCENZO AND ENZA ARNONE GUESTS AT OUR HOME

They were newlyweds who had gone from Sicily to Florida for their Caribbean cruise, and after that, they were coming to New York City. Vincenzo was my cousin Lina's Fantauzzo Arnone's son. On their arrival, Andrew and I went to Kennedy Airport to welcome and bring them at our home where they would stay with us as long as they wanted to. In order to show the guests how to get around Manhattan, I took a few days off from work. Enza didn't speak any English, and Vincenzo had some knowledge of the language, so with the help of a dictionary and the map of New York City, they were able to get around by themselves.

I made a deal with them that if they desired to stay home, it was okay with Andrew and me, and if they wanted to go to the city during the week, they had to come with me up to the Fifth Avenue subway station in Manhattan in the morning, and afterward, they were on their own for the rest of the day until a specific time in the afternoon when we would meet at the same station for the ride home. The arrangement worked very well. On weekends, we took the guests around. Together, we visited some of the most important places in Manhattan. In Central Park, we spent an entire day. We went to the Loeb Boathouse, where we took a boat ride on a Venetian gondola and then went to have lunch at the restaurant there.

One Saturday, some of the honeymooners' Sicilian friends invited all of us to their home on Long Island for supper. They were Pietro and Giovanna D'Acquisto, both natives of Casteltermini and who had immigrated to the USA several years back. There were also Gino and Carmela Pellitteri. Andrew and I knew the D'Acquistos and the Pellitteris. They were our friends too, and they had already been at our house in Queens. We spent a very interesting afternoon in a warm atmosphere and animated talk on past recollections, and everybody had a great time.

Whenever the newlyweds stayed home by themselves, Enza prepared delicious dinners for all of us. I remember an unpleasant occurrence from which I was really disappointed, and most of all, I felt bad for our guests. One day, Enza made a lot of arangines, a Sicilian food specialty, and because they were so appetizing, I told her and Vincenzo to bring some to our neighbors whom I considered good friends. I thought they would be pleased to meet the young foreign couple. To my surprise, the couple came back without saying a word. I noticed certain displeasure in their faces, and after a while, I learned how badly they had been treated. In a few words, the neighbors didn't show any appreciation; they only said thank you and closed the door.

In conclusion, the newlyweds were a real lovely, affectionate, and wonderful couple to be with, and they made us very happy.

SEPTEMBER 1987–THE CALIFORNIA EXCURSION

This trip of eighteen days was very pleasant, because we saw some of the western parts of the USA. We traveled with the Domenico bus tour, which started in New York City, went to California on US Interstate 80, and came back through the US Interstate 70.

Along the way to San Francisco, we stopped in Chicago, Lincoln, Salt Lake City, Virginia City, and Reno; in some of the places we took a guided tour.

We spent five days in San Francisco. With a tour guide, we went sightseeing and visited many interesting landmarks. One evening, the leader took us to Chinatown for dinner. It would have been much easier going uphill by cable car than by bus for the driver had to do special maneuvers to move the bus forward on that very steep street. Anyhow, it was worth the effort for the food was excellent, and service was good too. On our free day, we took the cable car to Fisherman's Wharf where we had lunch and then walked to the boat that was transporting tourists to Alcatraz Island. In Alcatraz, we took a tour of the famous prison. A guide gave us the highlights of the place, and we saw the Al Capon cell. San Francisco is a very interesting city. Our stay there was nice, but I didn't appreciate the cool and foggy weather.

Driving down the Pacific Coast Highway, there was a long stretch of the way that scared the tourists on the bus, because the bus was going along the high roadway on the ocean side very close to the edge of the road.

We stayed in Los Angeles six days. It was late afternoon, so upon our arrival, we were left on our own for the rest of the day. We phoned Eileen and Scott, our friends from New York who were now living in Playa Del Ray. They knew of our trip, and they were waiting for our call. Scott came to the hotel to take us to their home where we met Eileen and their first baby girl. The present we brought for the baby was just right in size and color. We knew Eileen from the time when she leased our second floor apartment while she was attending law school at St. John University in Queens. She was a wonderful person, and to this day, she is a good friend of mine. We spent a lovely evening together, and afterward, Scott took us back to the hotel. The following days, we took some guided tours to a few landmarks of the city. We also went to the Universal Studios, where we took the forty-five-minute tour led by a studio guide. With the guide, we traveled around the area of attractions on a tram. At the end of our stay in Los Angeles, we resumed the trip to Nevada.

At Lake Mead, Nevada, we took a boat ride and enjoyed the spectacular view of the many fish and the different species in the lake's limpid water. Next at Hoover Dam, we took a tour of the power plant, and afterward, we just walked around, admiring the beauty of nature and the manmade majestic work.

At the Grand Canyon National Park, we stayed one night. It was late afternoon when we arrived, and we were just in time to witness the spectacular sunset view over the Canyon, which gave us a fantastic thrill. In the evening, as we were getting ready to go to have dinner, Andrew started shivering and said to me, "I want to go to bed." He was very hot and probably had a fever. I became very worried, and for a few hours, I kept watching him for any change, and then, thank God, he fell sound asleep and looked very comfortable. The following morning, he was in good shape and ready to continue the trip. We made brief stops in New Mexico and Oklahoma.

We arrived in St. Louis, Missouri, in the afternoon and stayed there for the night. My cousins who lived there knew of our arrival, so they came to meet us at the hotel and afterward took us to a restaurant for supper. I was not hungry, but I ate to please them. Then after a lovely evening, my cousins accompanied us to the hotel where I spent a terrible night. I felt sick, and I was also vomiting. It was Andrew's turn now; he became concerned about me and didn't know what to do, but we decided to wait until the morning. In the morning, I felt better and ready to continue the trip to Indianapolis where we stopped for lunch and afterward ended the trip in New York City.

SPRING OF 1988–THE FIRST SOUTHEAST COAST TRIP

For some time, Andrew and I were thinking about where to retire, and in some way, we had reached the conclusion that Florida would be a nice place because of the warm weather. Since we had moved to Queens, almost every year, we were dealing with big snow storms, which besides making traveling difficult, the snow shoveling in front and on the side of our home had become too much to endure. I remember once, because of the heavy snow prediction, Andrew and I had left our workplace earlier than usual to get home safe and sound. That winter evening, when we got out of the subway at the Kew Gardens Union Turnpike Station in

Queens, we found no transportation to take us home. The heavy snow conditions suddenly worsened with freezing temperatures so that everything became frozen. We were stuck at the bus stop for more than eight hours, and, believe me, standing on our feet in that freezing weather was really awful. There were no shelters for the long lines of people waiting for the buses to arrive, and the stores and coffee shops in the area were all closed. At a certain point, many travelers went home on foot, but we couldn't because our house was six miles away. Anyway, after midnight, the buses with chained wheels started to arrive, and then because of a small section of the Union Turnpike road, which is on a hill, the bus taking us home had some difficulty going up the iced hilly road. It was a real bad experience.

In the spring, I took some of my vacation time and travelled with Andrew along the Southeast Coast. We were planning to stop in the Chesapeake Bay area, in Virginia Beach, and in Myrtle Beach, and Florida was our final destination. In New Castle, Delaware, we took US Route 13 south, and along the way, we crossed the 17.6-mile-long Chesapeake Bay Bridge Tunnel, which seemed endless. Driving through, it was a great experience, and it was also astonishing looking at that outstanding human achievement! Then we stopped in Virginia Beach for two days. It was during the Ester holiday, and the town was full of tourists. At the beach, there was a nice sidewalk, and the weather was cold, but many people were getting into the water. Next, we continued our trip on US Route 17, which took us to Myrtle Beach in South Carolina.

It was early afternoon when we arrived in Myrtle Beach, and our first impression of the town was very favorable. We found mild weather, plenty of flowers everywhere, many palm trees, a nice beach, and friendly people. Altogether, it gave me the feeling of being in Sicily, and I really felt good. I suggested to Andrew that instead of going to Florida, we should stay here and see if we would like to retire in this area. Fortunately, I didn't have to convince him because he liked the town too. So, we remained in Myrtle Beach for the rest of our vacation and settled at a hotel near the beach and close to the Myrtle Square Mall, which, at that time, was the only mall in town. Afterward, we started becoming familiar with this part of South Carolina. We went to more than one real estate agency, and they showed us many single family homes and a few retirement communities. Frankly speaking, we didn't know what we were looking for, and whatever they showed us, we did not find attractive. One morning, while we were having breakfast at a nearby restaurant, we saw a brochure about Myrtle Trace by chance, and after reviewing it, we decided to visit it that same morning.

Myrtle Trace was a retirement community. Here, we went to the sales office to get some information, and Mr. Ralph Moore, the only agent available, showed us a few model homes and also took us around to get an idea of the area. At that time, the phases in development were from one to five, so if we were ready to move in, we had to select an available lot on which the house would be built. We were not ready for any commitment yet. We just visited the place out of curiosity, but what happened was that once we saw the place, we wanted to know more about the community. I liked the place very much. It was spring, and everywhere we looked, there were flowers, and each property was well kept. In all, everything looked wonderful. Andrew was not so sure. He thought that the people living there were too snobby. I was sure that he got that impression when the agent took us to the clubhouse where many residents, nicely dressed, were playing at the various tables. Anyway, we didn't make any decision. We had to think things over and be convinced that this was the right place for us. Then before returning to New York, we went to see other communities in Myrtle Beach.

1988 – GIUSEPPINA'S WEDDING

Toward the end of September we went to Europe for my niece's wedding. Giuseppina was my brother's daughter. From New York to Rome, Andrew and I flew together, then Andrew went to Budapest to visit his relatives, and I went to Sicily to be with mine. When I landed at Palermo, my suitcases were missing. Imagine how concerned I became, especially because I didn't have any clothes for the wedding. At the airline claim office, they told me that because my plane was full, the airline personnel had left my luggage behind for later forwarding. With my brother went to Casteltermini, and from there, every day, I kept calling the airline for further information. On the third day, my suitcases finally arrived, and with great relief, I returned to Palermo to claim them.

This was the first time I met my niece's fiancé, Pino Bartolomeo, and I liked him. He really gave me a nice impression. He was in the Italian police force (carabiniere) and was from San Biagio Platani, a town close to Casteltermini. Days before the wedding, I spent a lot of time with the couple to be, Giuseppina and Pino. They had a very busy schedule to complete final touches of their wedding, and I enjoyed going with them wherever they had to go. Because they were not married yet, they could not go out alone, so I was glad to be their chaperon. Then two days before the wedding, I went to the Palermo Airport with my brother to pick up Andrew. I was not just glad to see him, but I felt more relaxed and comfortable to be with him.

My niece's wedding took place on October 1. The religious ceremony was held at the Church of San Giuseppe in Casteltermini and the reception at the Hotel dei Pini in Agrigento. The groom, dressed in high uniform of the Carabiniere, which gave him a very distinct look, went to the church first, and he waited there for the bride to arrive. In her white wedding gown, the bride accompanied by her father, walked to the church, crossing the entire town's main street. She looked marvelous. At this point, I want you to imagine the townspeople standing on the sidewalks, looking at the bride! The religious ceremony was great. The church was packed with relatives and friends, and I cannot describe how happy and proud my brother- and sister-in-law were, and by just looking at them, I was happy too. The clear and mild weather conditions added more beauty to the event. Looking at the couple, followed by the guests descending the impressive stairway of the church of San Giuseppe and then continuing with their trip to Agrigento was fantastic. The road from Casteltermini to Agrigento is very steep, narrow, and full of curves. From the top looking down, the view of the cars going through the treacherous and winding road looked like a very picturesque scene in a movie. In Agrigento, the restaurant was nicely adorned, had excellent service, good food, romantic music, and in addition, it had a beautiful view of the Mediterranean Sea. With the happy occasion at the restaurant, I met all my relatives and friends. Andrew and I were delighted that we had been part of this very beautiful wedding. A few days later, we returned to the USA.

SEPTEMBER 1989–SECOND SOUTHEAST COAST TRIP AND THE HURRICANE HUGO

The purpose of this trip was to go to Florida and see what we could find there. Knowing the reason of my trip, a colleague of mine at TIAA-CREF suggested I go to visit some of his friends who were living in an assisted living or retirement community in Advance, North Carolina. So on my colleague's advice, our first stop was in the town of Advance where we registered at the hotel, and from there, we contacted the couple who were waiting for our call. That same evening, the old couple invited us to their place for supper, and we gladly accepted the invitation. They lived in a very luxurious complex. The majority of the residents were retired professionals. The couple we met, the husband was a retired lawyer. This retirement community had a first-class restaurant, and the food there was incredible good. The next day, we went back to the complex to get some information about the place. The community consisted of several two-story building apartments, a grandiose clubhouse, a huge swimming pool, an elegant restaurant, a convalescent section, and so on. The monthly payment plus extra expenses was extremely high, and the residents' average age was in the eighties. The day before leaving town, we invited the couple out for dinner, and they happily accepted. They were pleasant people and hoped that we would decide to retire in the same community. We were more than sure that the place was not for us.

The night of September 22 was the night of the Hurricane Hugo in South Carolina. We were at the hotel in Advance, North Carolina, and the impact of the hurricane was also felt there. During the night, the blustery weather, heavy rain, thunders, and lightning flashes made it the most dreadful night of our lives. We didn't know if we would make it to the next day. Fortunately, the following morning, everything was tranquil as if nothing had happened earlier, except for some damage that we saw in the surrounding area. We continued our trip on I-40 going east and then on I-95 south with the intention of going to Florida. On the way, we saw the sign for Myrtle Beach. Andrew and I looked at each other, and we both had the same idea—to make a stop there.

We arrived in Myrtle Beach on September 25. Three days had passed since Hurricane Hugo, and we found all the beach entrances blocked by the South Carolina national guards. Many rooftops were gone; trees were down, and the area was devastated. We settled at a hotel, which had very little damage and then went to the community of Myrtle Trace to see the situation there. After having seen the destructions in Myrtle Beach, we were amazed to find this place with just a few fallen trees, and the rest was intact. Instead of going to Florida, we again decided to remain in Myrtle Beach for the rest of our vacation.

We were not ready to buy a house yet. I was working, and I wanted to continue working for a while, but when we stopped at the sales office in Myrtle Trace just to say hello, Mr. Ralph Moore, one of the agents, approached us and started talking about the deals that were going on there. Soon after the hurricane, to attract new buyers, the real estate company was now offering some good deals. The agent succeeded in convincing us to take advantage of this occasion. At this point, we gave up our Florida idea, and with Ralph, we went to see some model homes and the lots available. We stopped at lot 45. Here Andrew stepped on a mound of fire ants, and in no time, he got infested. It was terrible. We were not familiar with these small but ferocious creatures! Andrew's discomfort lasted for some time.

In Myrtle Trace, we chose lot 45 in phase 5, picked the model of the house to be built, agreed with the basic price, and, all said, we closed the deal. Afterward, I asked for the home layout because I wanted to make some modifications to the interior and I also wanted to upgrade the basic fixtures that came with the house. As soon as we returned home in New York, I started studying the layout, and I came up with a few ideas to make the new house more comfortable. Then I showed Andrew the new plan and he loved my enhancements, and what he liked most was the study, which would become his favorite room. We sent the new plan to Ralph Moore and when the agreement on the extra cost was reached, they started the construction of our house.

MAY 1990 – VISITED CZECHOSLOVAKIA FOR THE FIRST TIME

With the fall of the communist regime, it became easier for the westerners to go to Eastern Europe, and Andrew could finally go back and see his native country. Andrew called the American embassy in Washington DC for information and was told that he didn't need any visa. He could visit Hungary and Czechoslovakia with just the American passport. For me, it was a different story because I was not an American citizen. With the fall of the communist regime, I could visit Hungary with my Italian passport, but for Czechoslovakia, I also needed the Czech visa until midnight of May 31, 1990.

On the twenty-eighth of May, we flew from New York to Rome, then to Budapest, where we remained for two days to visit Andrew's Hungarian relatives.

On the thirty-first of May, we flew from Budapest to Prague where we landed in midafternoon, and soon after, we went through the Czechoslovakian authority. Andrew was in order with his American passport, but I was not because I had arrived there before midnight without the Czech visa. The authority took me to a room where I was searched and questioned in English, and then they let me go but not before paying a small fee. Although the end of the regime was just a few hours away, the Czechoslovakian authority was inflexible. My ordeal with the authority lasted for more than one hour during which Andrew was waiting anxiously, concerned because he didn't know what was going on, and I didn't speak Czech, but this was not yet the end of it.

When we went to pick up our suitcases, the place was empty; the luggage was gone, and no office to go to reclaim them. Meanwhile, Andrew's relatives, Lila and Joska, were waiting at the airport for us without knowing what had happened until we met them. This was our first experience in Czechoslovakia. From the airport, Joska took us to his home in Prague where we found other family members waiting for our arrival. After many years, this was the first meeting together with the relatives. It was really a joyous occasion, and though they all spoke in Czech, which I didn't understand, it didn't matter; for me, it was fantastic to look at them having a good time. Because it was my first visit, I came here with a lot of enthusiasm to meet Andrew's family and friends, and for this special occasion, I had brought many elegant clothes for my husband and myself and gifts for the relatives; but with the disappearance of our suitcases, everything was gone, so we now had no clothing and no presents. That evening after supper, the Reznick family—Irena, Honza, and their daughter Andrea—took us to their apartment in another part of the city.

In Prague, we stayed at the Reznick's place from June 1–5. The apartment was very small, but the hosts did their best to make us feel as comfortable as possible. I would have preferred to go to the hotel, but Andrew wanted to stay with relatives. The second day in Prague, Lila, Irene, and Helena gave me some of their clothes to wear, but I could only use a few of Lila's skirts and nothing else. For Andrew, it was more difficult because Joska and Honza were taller and bigger than him. Then when we went shopping for clothes, there was not much of a selection in the stores, so we just got what we needed to get by until the end of our trip. In Prague, Andrew contacted some of his old friends that he wanted to see, and subsequently, they met, and their reunion was wonderful and full of nostalgia. From time to time, I noticed some sadness during their animated conversations. Many terrible events had happened over the years, especially to Andrew. Anyway, although the language was strange, I was pleased to see them enjoying the happy reunion.

Prague is a very charming city. With relatives and friends, we visited several beautiful and historic places, such as the Prague Castle, which is the largest castle complex in the world. The most recognizable landmark in the city is St. Vitus Cathedral, which is part of the castle complex that dominates the city skyline and is visible from far and wide.

From St. Vitus Cathedral, walking down the hill, we saw Shirley Temple who was leaving the embassy building and going toward a car. At that time, she was the American ambassador to Czechoslovakia, so there were many spectators waiting to get a glimpse of her. Then we walked to the picturesque Charles Bridge, which is the most important connection between Prague

Castle and the city's Old Town. In the center of the Old Town Square, there is the huge statue known as the Jan Hus Memorial, who was burned at the stake for his beliefs, and close to this square, there is the famous astronomical clock. With Lila and her family, we came here many times to have lunch or something else and enjoyed sitting at an outside table while looking at the townspeople passing by. It was great.

From Prague, we flew to Kosice where we stayed for a week. This was Andrew's birthplace and where he had spent his youth. Arriving at the airport, I felt heartbroken since no one was waiting for him at the airport. But I knew the reason no one was there. Andrew's family who used to live in Kosice had been killed along with the other Jews of the town during the German occupation of Czechoslovakia in World War II. After settling in at a hotel, we went for a walk.

Kosice is the second largest city in Slovakia. Andrew had described to me his hometown many times, and now, with a lot of enthusiasm, he was taking me to see the places that he remembered most. Among them were the house where he had lived with his father, the building where he went to school, the house where his cousin Lila used to live with her family, and so forth. I enjoyed strolling on Kosice's main street with Andrew and listening to his nostalgic and vivid recollections of his younger years. I enjoyed going to the department stores. They were not elegant, but the Czech crystal goods were inexpensive and fabulous. Every time we took the public transportation, it was impressive to see young people giving their seats to any older person. They were very polite. In Kosice, Andrew contacted two of his old friends that he wanted to see. Forty years had passed since they saw each other, and their meeting was very emotional. Although everybody had changed physically, they had one thing in common—the memories of the good and bad old days. I liked the city of Kosice very much. People were friendly and polite, and the time spent alone with Andrew was fantastic.

From Kosice, we flew back to Prague where we stayed for another five days at Joska's home. During our sojourn, Cousin Lila came to her son's place every day to be with us, and her son also took some time off from work to take us all over the place while the rest of the family went to work or to school. The things mother and son did for us was incredible, and I will never forget that. All in all, the warm feelings that I experienced in Prague and Kosice were wonderful. From Prague, we flew to Switzerland and then to New York.

AUGUST 1990 – BOUGHT A NEW HOME IN SOUTH CAROLINA

At the end of July, Andrew and I drove to Myrtle Beach for the final arrangements of our new house. The closing took place on August 1 in the Myrtle Trace office, and soon after we got the key, we went to our new house to look around. Entering the premise, we were very enthusiastic because everything was new and all had started from scratch. Then with a great disappointment, we noticed that the tiles on the kitchen floor had a different color tint from the other areas, so we went back to Hall Development office to report the problem. Soon after, they came to verify the tiles and promised to have the problem fixed immediately. We left Myrtle Trace with no concerns because in our opinion, Hall Development was a reliable company, which would replace the tiles in the kitchen as promised. In addition, there was Ralph Moore, our real estate agent who would make sure that the job was done properly.

Since we were not ready to move in, Ralph also would take care of the house by renting and supervising the place until further notice. The people we met at Myrtle Trace were Bob and Helen Ridgeway and their daughter, Christine. They were our neighbors across the street, and they were very friendly.

Then on our way home in Queens, we stopped in Atlantic City for two days. There we went to see a few shows, and I also had some fun playing the slot machines. Andrew didn't like to play and didn't mind seeing me playing. In fact, he was providing the change for me to play.

1991 – SERENA AND MAURIZIO BIONDOLILLO IN NEW YORK CITY

During the month of July, on their honeymoon in the USA, Serena and Maurizio had a short stop in New York City. Serena was my cousins Lina and Enzo Arnone's daughter, and once she was in NYC, I wanted to see her, so I postponed my trip to Sicily for my niece Alida's wedding for a few days.

Andrew flew from New York to Budapest around the fifteenth of July, and as soon as he arrived there, the first thing he had in his mind was to send me a telegram to let me know that he already missed me. Frankly speaking, I liked to be made aware of that because in writing, it gave me a much warmer feeling.

On July 20· I got a call from the newlyweds to let me know they had arrived in New York City that afternoon and gave me the name of the hotel where they were staying. The following day, I went to meet Serena and her husband for the first time at the hotel near Central Park South. Subsequently, without wasting any time, I took them downtown to Battery Park to take the ferry to the Statue of Liberty. Unluckily, we had to give up the visit to the island because the lines were long and the honeymooners didn't have time to spare. Next I took them to the Empire State Building where the wait was also long but not too bad. It was a beautiful and clear day, and the view from the observation deck was wonderful. The couple enjoyed the sight of Manhattan and its surroundings very much. Then we had lunch at Rockefeller Plaza, and afterward, we took a walk on Fifth Avenue where Serena was interested to see some of the luxurious stores on the avenue.

There was no time to bring them to my place in Queens because it was almost dark and the following morning they were flying to California for the continuation of their honeymoon. Anyway, although short, we spent a lovely day together.

AUGUST 1991, ALIDA'S WEDDING

On July 23, I flew from New York to Rome then to Palermo for Alida's wedding. With my brother I went from the airport to Casteltermini where, for the first time, I met Alida's fiancé, Nino Iaria, and his family—all from Reggio Calabria. A few days later, I returned to Palermo for the arrival of my husband from Prague.

The ceremony took place on August 1 in Casteltermini. That morning at my brother's home, there was plenty of confusion with the arrangement of the bride Then the bride, accompanied by her proud father, followed by her radiant mother and guests, left the house, crossed the town main street on foot up to the stairway leading to San Giuseppe's church, and afterward to the altar. The religious ceremony was great, the bride looked fabulous, and so did the groom. After the church ceremony, all the guests drove to Agrigento for the reception. The reception at the restaurant was great. The atmosphere among relatives and friends was very joyous, and all together, it was a beautiful wedding.

At my brother's place, I also met my niece Giuseppina's first son, Giovanni, who was about two years old. He was an unbelievably quiet and beautiful boy. I never saw a child of his age behave like him. He was a very happy boy and a joy to look at.

While in town, our friends the Amorellis, Pietro and his mother Nena, took us to a restaurant on the outskirts of the town. This was a newly constructed and very attractive place, and because of the delicious food and warm ambiance, it was packed with customers. At the restaurant, we met my nephew Giuseppe Giudice, his wife, and, for the first time, their two adorable little children, Marco and Giuliana. The friendly spontaneity of the children toward us took Andrew by surprise, and he was so pleased! Anyway, we spent a nice evening with our friends.

After a few days in Casteltermini, we left for Palermo where we took the flight back to the USA.

With Frances Diamond, the old acquaintance I met by chance in New York City.
Here we were in front of City Hall after her civil marriage

My husband, Andrew Janovitz

1972 – Our first home in Hollis Hills, Queens, NY

In Casteltermini 1974 - With uncle Peppino
Fantauzzo at his country house.

In Agrigento - With my brother Vincenzo and his wife Maria
Their little daughter Alida was looking at us

With aunt Marietta and uncle Enzo Ricotta
in front of Palermo's Cathedral

With cousins Giudice and their son Tony in
front of the Chinese Palace in Palermo

1974 - In Budapest with Andrew's relatives.

1980 – In Sicily on Mt Etna with my brother's family

1985 - In Mondello at my cousins Martorana' summer home
It was a reunion in occasion of our visit

At my cousins Giudice' home in Palermo

1988 – In Casteltermini at the wedding of
Giuseppina and Pino Bartolomeo

1986 – With my relatives, Vincenzo and Enza
Arnone at the Statue of Liberty

1991 – In Casteltermini at the wedding of Alida and Nino Iaria

GIVING UP WORK

1993 – DECIDED TO STOP WORKING

My last twenty-two working years at TIAA-CREF had been pretty good and rewarding too. Being in the computer field, my job had been interesting and had also given me a sense of accomplishment and satisfaction. Of course, things were not always rosy for me. There were periods when I felt that I was treated unfairly because, in my opinion, I was a foreigner and plus I had a heavy foreign accent; consequently, I had to prove my capability more than anybody else.

I could not believe that, for the first time in my life, I didn't need to work any longer! Was this real? I had already reached the point that I had everything I desired and thought to enjoy the rest of my life with my loving husband. Therefore, in September, we put our house in Queens on the market with the hope that in six months it would be sold. Instead, it was sold in three weeks. We didn't expect that the house would go so fast, and we were not ready to leave yet. I was still working, and our home in South Carolina was rented. We told the new buyers that if they wanted the house, they had to let us stay in our house until the end of the April 1994, and they agreed to wait.

The closing of the house took place in November, and as compensation for the extra months granted, we were leaving all our furniture and more in the house. It was a good deal for us but most of all, for them because instead of starting from scratch, they had a furnished place ready to move in. The buyers were a very young oriental couple who fell in love with our home from the moment they saw it. Their excitement was contagious. They were telling us their future plans, and looking at them, I became so enthusiastic to the point that I agreed with the price they offered, while we could have gotten a better deal from other two couples who were also interested in buying. Andrew was very disappointed with my behavior, and he was 100 percent right because I reacted from emotion and not with my head. Subsequently, Andrew sent a letter to Ralph Moore, the Myrtle Trace's real estate agent, letting him know that he had to inform the people who were renting our house to vacate the premise as of April 1, 1994. At home, we started to get rid of all the useless things accumulated over the years and put aside what we were planning to take with us to South Carolina.

In January 1994, I told my manager that I was resigning as of May 1, so that he had four months to find someone to take my place. I also told him that I was going to take my accumulated vacation prior to my last day on the job. I needed that time off to go to South Carolina with Andrew in order to inspect our house before moving in. Subsequently, my husband and I began to be busy with our relocation and by March 31, everything was done.

In New York City, it had been a very snowy winter, and it looked like there was no end to it. Our home had a detached garage on a hill, and when we were shoveling the snow, there was no room on both sides of the house to put it so that we had to bring the snow all the way down to the street. Believe me, it was a very hard work for both of us, especially since we were not so young anymore! The evening before our trip to South Carolina, we cleaned our driveway to make it passable the next morning. However, the morning of April 1, the driveway was again covered with more than eight inches of snow, and we did the cleanup all over again.

On April 2, we arrived in Myrtle Beach where we found blue skies and mild temperatures. It was a perfect day. As soon as we got settled at the hotel, we went to our house in Myrtle Trace. There we started looking around and came up with a list of things that had to be done immediately. In four years, three different couples had lived in the house; the first two had been careful, but not the last tenant who had a dog. We found the empty house with a lot of dog's marks all over the floors, dirty and stinky. We contacted the Hall Development people, and through them, we got some contractors to do whatever work was needed. Every day, we went from Myrtle Beach to Myrtle Trace to check on what was going on with the maintenance. Everything was done on time, and the house was ready for us to move in on the scheduled day.

On April 26, we returned to New York. I went back to work, and Andrew contacted the moving company to come to our home for the pickup of whatever had to go to Myrtle Trace in South Carolina. Then on the April 30, which was my last day at TIAA-CREF, I received a gift certificate from the company, and from my colleagues, I received cards and a good-bye party. The morning of May 1, the new owners came to pick up the house key. They also brought some food in order to have breakfast together. They were really nice people. To conclude, with regret, we left the lovely house behind, and with pleasure, we left the cold weather and our Queens neighbors. Finally, we were on our way to our new life in South Carolina.

MAY 1994 – MOVED TO SOUTH CAROLINA

Myrtle Trace was a beautiful retirement community on the outskirts of the town of Conway, South Carolina. On the same day, the moving truck arrived, bringing a pair of twin beds, clothing, and so forth. Next, the Myrtle Trace Association representatives came to our house to welcome us to the community, and then our new neighbors Helen and Bob Ridgeway, Harry and Helen Moritz, Frank and Vinnie Petrucelli, and Jack and Peggy Rodgers came to our place and introduced themselves. To conclude the welcome, the Rodgers invited us for supper. Honestly, we didn't expect to receive such a nice reception, and for that, we were more than pleased. What a huge difference between our new neighbors and those cold ones left behind in Queens!

In no time, we started taking part in the activities that the community offered. There were the weekly line dances, evening bingo, daily trips, summer pool exercises, and a lot more going on at the clubhouse and at residents' homes. Everybody and everything appeared to be wonderful; we were really impressed. The warm feeling we got made us believe that it was the right place to start a new life! For the newcomers, the Myrtle Trace activity committee organizes a monthly dinner at a nice restaurant, and the invitation is only extended to the new residents for the first two years. It is a pleasant evening designed to get to know each other in the community.

Our home was practically empty because we had left most of the furniture in Queens, so we soon started looking at some furniture stores. Elisabeth Yorshaw, a neighbor, took us to the Stuckey Brothers Furniture store in Hemingway, a town not far from Conway. It was a huge place with a very good selection, and there we bought the furniture we needed. It was not so pleasant going around for the furniture because, between my husband and me, there were some disputes. Andrew wanted to bring the furniture that we left behind in New York, and I didn't like what we had there. With the new house, I wanted to have everything new. Anyway, later on, we bought the rest to finish the interior decorating, and we also hired some people to make the window treatments.

In New York, Andrew had his own study, and here he wanted to have one with built-in bookcases. For that, we got a carpenter to do the job.

Being on one-level floor, we felt too exposed to the outside world. We were not accustomed to this situation, which, for us, was awkward. We hired a service provider to install the LLumar Solar Control Window Film. The end result was very successful. From inside, we can see the outside people going by, but from outside, nobody can see inside the house, except in the evening when the lights are on. This film is also good for the protection of the furniture from the sun, and moreover, it reduces the broken glass fragments. By the way, the glass on the outside looks like mirror, and after the Llumar installation, every morning, we were awakened by noises on the glass of our bedroom windows, and that was not fun at all. At first, we didn't know what the noise was about, but then we discovered that the birds were pecking at their own reflections. In the back of the house, there were also glass doors, and here too the squirrels had the same reaction; they were not pecking, just looking at and touching the glass. Once, there were two snakes against the glass door, looking at their reflections too. This time, I called Bob Ridgeway, our neighbor across the street, and he immediately came to kill the snakes, but when he saw them, he said not to worry because they were not poisonous. The situation with the pecking on the windows lasted for quite some time. Fortunately, it now happens only once in a while.

In early October, 1994, our next-door neighbors, the Rodgers, were approaching their fiftieth wedding anniversary, and for the special occasion, the neighborhood gave a surprise party. Each one of us contributed something, and I offered to make a fifty-dollar tree. Andrew went to the bank and got fifty new dollar bills. I bought a vase for the tree to be built. Then somebody in the vicinity showed me some samples, and afterward, with Andrew's help, I made an interesting dollar tree.

The first Christmas celebration at Myrtle Trace was great. The dinner party for the residences took place in the middle of December and was held at a nice restaurant in Myrtle Beach. The year's end was celebrated at the community clubhouse where everybody was cheerful, had fun playing bingo, drinking, and so forth until midnight.

* * *

All the years we lived in New York, we were busy with our jobs and also could not afford to invite some of the relatives to visit us. Several times, we had guests from Italy, but they came at their own expense. It was different now because we had plenty of time, and economically, we were okay too, so we decided to invite a few close family members from Europe to the USA for a visit, with a fully paid trip and nothing for the guests to worry about. Subsequently, we planned to bring them here in two separate groups for a month each. My Italian relatives would be the first group to come in the spring, and Andrew's family would come in the fall. I wrote to my brother, asking if he and his wife would like to take a trip to America, while Andrew wrote to his cousin Lila in Czechoslovakia and to his aunt Maria in Hungary. They all happily answered positively, and we sent them the round-trip tickets from their various cities to New York City.

MAY 1995 – GUESTS FROM ITALY

We drove from Myrtle Trace to Long Island, New York, for the arrival of my relatives. The following day in New York, we went to Kennedy Airport to welcome my brother and his wife who were exceedingly happy, and when they saw us, they were thrilled to be in America. Afterward, we took the guests to the Holiday Inn Hotel in Long Island where we had already reserved two rooms for three days. That evening, my relatives were so enthusiastic that they could not stop talking! Every day we traveled to

Manhattan. We took them to the Empire State Building, to the Rockefeller Center, to the Statue of Liberty, and to other places, and they were very impressed.

On our last evening in New York City, our friend Irene Hallaka invited the four of us for dinner at her mother's home in Queens. Alice, Irene's mother, prepared some Egyptian and American meals, and everything was delicious. The warm welcome that mother and daughter gave the guests was incredible. In fact, to this day, my brother remembers their hospitality.

When we left New York City for South Carolina, on the way south, we decided to stop in Atlantic City for the rest of the day to show the place to my folks. Here we started visiting some of the casinos. My brother was familiar with the gambling places, but for my sister-in-law, it was something new. Except for Andrew, the three of us had fun playing the slot machines. The Next morning, we continued our trip by way of the Chesapeake Bay Bridge Tunnel where we made a short stop for Vincenzo, who wanted to take a few pictures of the bridge. Later on, we arrived in Virginia Beach where we spent two nights. Our guests liked the place very much.

We finally arrived at our home in Myrtle Trace. How good it was to get comfortable and relaxed for the remainder of the day and especially for Andrew who was exhausted as he had done all the driving without any complaints. I was sure that he was bored to death because he could not communicate fluently with my relatives.

The day after their arrival, we took the guests around Myrtle Trace to show them our beautiful and peaceful community, its surroundings, and the many advantages in the neighborhood. My brother was disappointed with the construction of the houses in the community; he had never seen wooden homes with shingled roofs. At that time, where he was living in Sicily, there was no such construction. He was now asking us, "What about fire?" On that aspect, he was right because we also worried sometimes.

We soon started entertaining my relatives by visiting some places in Myrtle Beach. There they enjoyed walking on the beach, or strolling on Ocean Boulevard. Of course, everybody likes shopping, so we took the guests to the Waccamaw Factory Shoppes where they bought a lot of clothes for them and for their children and were surprised to see the good merchandise at very reasonable prices. This place is now closed, but when it was open, it was a big attraction for the tourists and for the locals too. Andrew and I often went there to spend some time while we enjoyed looking for bargains. It was really a nice place to visit.

One time, we took our guests to see a matinee show, thinking that they would have enjoyed the theater; instead, it was a waste of time and money because they didn't understand anything. At this point, it was silly to remain at the theater while our company was uninterested, so we all left before the end of the performance. One day, we took our guests to Barefoot Landing in North Myrtle Beach. They enjoyed the walk around the shopping complex and the ride aboard the Barefoot Princess boat crossing the Intracoastal Waterway even though it was just a nice ride and nothing else.

My folks had brought a lot of sweets from Sicily, so with this special occasion, we invited the close neighbors to our home to meet them. Soon after the introductions, we served all the Sicilian confections and drinks. While eating, everybody was complimenting Maria, my sister-in-law, for the sweets, and that made her very proud.

Once in America, my brother wanted to meet our cousins, Rose and Lilly Fantauzzo, who lived in St. Louis, Missouri, for the first time. I wrote Rosa about our relatives from Sicily, and she answered, saying that the entire family wished to meet them. Marie and her husband, David Driver, invited the four of us to stay at their house. Marie was one of Rosa's daughters.

We started our trip for St. Louis, about eight hundred miles from Myrtle Beach, and on the way, we stopped for an overnight stay at a motel. The following day, when we were approaching the city of St. Louis, we suddenly came upon a violent hailstorm accompanied by lightning and thunder. All the traffic came to a stop. It was impossible to continue for at least an hour until the storm calmed down. I remember how dreadful it was, especially for Maria who got terribly frightened!

We stayed with the Drivers in St. Louis for three days. Upon our arrival, Maria Driver took us to our rooms to relax for a while. That same evening, Cousin Rosa with her children and their families and Cousin Lilly with her husband came to meet my brother and his wife. Then after the introductions, the cousins immediately started to converse with the guests in the Sicilian, not knowing that my sister-in-law didn't understand a word for she was not Sicilian. Anyway, we all got an extraordinary warm welcome. The Drivers took us to the Gateway Arch where David and my brother took the ride to the top. Then we visited the Cathedral of St. Louis and many other interesting parts of the city. We also went to the Budweiser factory where we toured the brewery and afterward went to the guests' room to taste the beer served with nuts. More than once, Rosa and Lilly, with their families, took us to nice Italian restaurants. In addition, during our stay, Jim and Jennifer Pona invited us to their home for an afternoon get-together. The atmosphere there was very cheerful, and everybody enjoyed the company and the tasty Italian pizzas.

We stayed with the Browns in Perryville, near St. Louis, for three days. On Friday evening, David Driver drove Rosa and the four of us to Joan and Charlie Brown's home, located on the outskirts of the town of Perryville. Joan was my Cousin Rosa's oldest daughter. The following day, the Browns showed us their big country house with its surroundings; it was a lovely place on a hill, and at the base of the hill was a nice-sized area of green land with an area to play bocce, lakes containing fishes, and much more. In occasion of our visit, many relatives had also been invited at the Browns' home for a get-together party. Among the relatives, we met the Browns' children, Mark and Nancy, who were in their late teens. Here most of the cooking was done in the open, and there was plenty to eat and drink. The place had something for everybody to enjoy, and my brother liked fishing and playing with the bocce. Though nobody understood my sister-in-law, she was constantly talking in Italian with everybody and with a lot of exuberance. It was incredible how full of life she was! I did my best to translate her words, but it didn't matter because the relatives loved her simplicity very much. Andrew and I took some pleasant walks and enjoyed watching the folks involved in the diverse activities. The following Monday, we left the Browns' house and began the two-day trip back to Myrtle Trace in South Carolina. This St. Louis trip was very successful, and I was especially pleased for my brother and his wife who enjoyed their stay there tremendously, and I was also impressed with the way the cousins treated us all.

Regarding Myrtle Trace, this is a wonderful place to live, but only for those people who prefer serenity to the bustling lifestyle. The landscape of this residential community is beautiful; there are many trees, plenty of green grassy areas, flowers, lakes with some fish, turtles, and ducks. However, what makes the place more attractive are the well-kept single home properties and the common areas. On calm days, the surroundings reflect on the lakes, giving a sense of tranquility that is delightful to look at as we walk along the streets of the community.

After returning from our St. Louis excursion, my relatives still had some remaining time at our place so that when for some reason Andrew and I could not go out, they enjoyed watching some of the Italian movies that we had bought before their arrival. They also enjoyed taking walks in the Myrtle Trace areas, but soon, that became boring for my brother who liked the city's activities more than the tranquility of our community. Therefore, from time to time, the situation was a little challenging for everyone. The fact that the guests didn't speak English, Andrew didn't speak Italian, and me in the middle, required a lot of patience and understanding! To have guests for more than four weeks, at some point, became hard, not just because of the language barrier, but also for the lack of public transportation to go around on your own; and this was the case with my brother. Anyway, we really did our best to make their stay as pleasant as possible. Vincenzo and Maria were often arguing, and sometimes, the friction between them seemed to become very serious to the point that, that was making me concerned. A few times, I inquired what their problem was. On their return to Sicily, my brother wanted to move to his wife's hometown, Condofori Marina in Reggio Calabria, and he was trying to convince her of his idea, while his wife wanted to remain in his hometown, Casteltermini, where everybody knew, respected, and loved her. This was something that they had to resolve by themselves, and when they asked my opinion, I remained neutral.

The time for the guests to return to Italy had arrived so that in the middle of June, we began the two-day trip back to Long Island, New York. Next day, we accompanied my folks to Kennedy Airport for their flight back home, and the following morning, we departed for South Carolina. At the end, we were pleased that Vincenzo and Maria had a wonderful and memorable sojourn in America. It is everybody's dream to come to the USA, whether it is for a short or a long stay.

JUNE 22, 1995 – BECAME AN AMERICAN CITIZEN

Prior to August 15, 1992, I had a choice to make—remain an Italian citizen or become an American naturalized citizen. It was a difficult decision to make because I didn't want to renounce my native country even though I considered America my country too. After August 15, 1992, it became permissible for the Italians to have a dual citizenship, so I applied to the Immigration and Naturalization for the American citizenship. While I was in waiting to receive a reply from the immigration, several months had already passed. We decided to go to Europe for a vacation. Returning from the trip, I found a notification from the immigration to present myself on a specific date and time at their office in downtown Manhattan. The date had already expired, so I went to their office to explain why I was not present at the meeting. To come to the point, I had to start the procedures all over again, and I was not ready for that.

It was at the beginning of January 1995 when I decided to restart the US Naturalization procedures, and by this time, living in South Carolina, the whole thing was very simple. In fact, as soon as the immigration bureau in Charleston received my application forms with my fingerprints done at the police station in Conway, they sent me a notification letter informing me of an interview by an immigration officer at the end of January. The meeting with the officer in Charleston was quite pleasant. A few months later, I received another notification letter, saying that I had to present myself for the final US naturalization.

On June 22, I took the oath at the Charleston's courthouse. The court was a big room adorned with finely accented wooden work and fine furniture, and that day, it was packed with people and their families to be naturalized. The jubilant atmosphere looked like a nice movie setting. We were called one by one for the oath of allegiance, and the whole ceremony was wonderful. Afterward, we remained in Charleston for the rest of the day to celebrate the special event.

SEPTEMBER 1995 – GUESTS FROM CZECHOSLOVAKIA AND HUNGARY

Andrew and I drove to New York for the arrival of Cousin Lila and Aunt Maria from Europe. For Andrew's relatives, we repeated all the things we did for my Italian relatives.

The trip from New York to Myrtle Trace had been long and exhausting, and not just for Andrew who had done the driving, but also for the guests who were not young anymore. Anyhow, once arrived home, everybody was in high spirits and made themselves comfortable. Lila and Maria were pleasant and had good manners too. They were impressed with our home and our community. They enjoyed taking long walks in Myrtle Trace and in the surrounding area and enjoyed playing cards in the backyard or at the kitchen table. A few times, Lila and Maria liked doing some of their home traditional baking, and twice, we invited a few of our neighbors for coffee and baked goods prepared by our relatives. As often as possible, we took our guests out to Myrtle Beach, where they loved to go to the beach for a walk, and to the Waccamaw Pottery shopping center, where they bought what they needed for themselves and for their families; this was their favorite place.

After a while, Aunt Maria started to feel restless and complained that their stay in the USA was too long, and she was right. We didn't realize it beforehand. There was not so much we could do to keep our guests busy; Myrtle Beach was not developed like it is today, and the television was in English, which both of them didn't understand. Also, for us, the situation became a little hard because I didn't speak their language, and Andrew had to do the translation back and forth. Anyway, given the circumstances, we managed the situation very well and did our best to make their stay at our home as pleasant as possible. Thereafter, for their departure in the middle of October, we drove our relatives back to Long Island, New York. There we spent a night before their next day flight to Czechoslovakia.

* * *

The year 1995 was the busiest year of my life. Taking into account the times we drove to New York, to Charleston, and to St. Louis and all the driving done by Andrew and, in addition, to have had guests for weeks and weeks and not speaking the same language sometimes took a lot from us. Anyway, in spite of all the above and the many disagreements along the way, we were really glad that we had invited our relatives to our home in America. We thank God it was over and it all ended successfully.

ADJUSTMENT TO MY LIFE AS A RETIREE

It was not as easy as it seemed. Ever since I retired and moved to Myrtle Trace, I hadn't had any time to reflect on my new status as a retiree because I had been so busy with several unique events. It was now, the end of 1995, when I started to realize that something was missing in my daily life. I remember getting up in the morning feeling very restless because there was a sense of emptiness since my day ahead had no purpose, and when evening came, I also started to have problems with sleeping. Before long, I began to be concerned about my frame of mind, so I went to see the doctor who prescribed a tranquillizer, which only helped my sleep.

From my very early years to my retirement, I had always worked, with the exception of two short periods in which I was busy looking for employment. Later, when I came to be extremely busy with school, work, and worries, and consequently fully engaged mentally and physically, I felt rather content, though the worries were not at all pleasant. Now I felt so strange! I had everything I needed, and yet it was not enough to help my inner feelings of the sudden changes that brought a stop to my old lifestyle. I was not accustomed to a luxurious and carefree existence because I had never had the opportunity to experience that lifestyle. By this time, we had reduced our participation in some of the social events in the Myrtle Trace community. We dropped those that we didn't find interesting. Having not much to do at home, I had plenty of free time on my hands, and in order to adjust to my new lifestyle, I needed to do something stimulating to occupy my mind and my time. I didn't tell Andrew how miserable I was. I kept all my feelings to myself, and at this particular time, I was not ready to do any volunteer work.

After some meditation, I started to share my feelings with Andrew, and that helped me a little. Before long, we started a three-mile daily walk in the community, which became a pleasant routine of the day. Then Andrew wanted me to go with him to take some music lessons at the musical instrument shop in Myrtle Beach, but I told him to go alone and then he would explain the lesson to me. At the music studio, he bought a small piano, and afterward, we both started learning and playing the piano. He was good, but his music interest only lasted for a few weeks. I tried, but I didn't have the talent to go any further.

Next, I thought that getting busy with a personal computer would be an excellent way to keep my mind occupied. My past experience in the computer field had only been with the IBM mainframe computer. I had no knowledge of the new small PC. I enrolled at the Horry Georgetown Technical College in Conway to learn the basics of the personal computer. I also bought the book there, paid for the course, and started attending. However, I made a mistake for not asking the details of the course in advance. The school was teaching how to load and unload the floppy disk and practice typing business correspondence. That was not what I needed to know so that three days later, I quit. Next, I bought an IBM desktop PC with Microsoft Windows 95 and also bought a book to help me navigate my new PC. I started reading the book, and I could not believe how easy it was. The basic principles of the PC had some similarity to those of the big computer so that right away, I learned how to use it and was amazed of the great discoveries on the internet. Once I got familiar with it, I wanted Andrew to try to learn to use the PC, at least for the e-mails. He tried, but he was not fond of the mouse. In reality, he didn't care about the PC.

Knowing that Andrew was an avid reader, I started downloading and printing a lot of international news—from the Czech Republic, Hungary, France, Germany, and more—from the internet. Later, I was spending a lot of interesting time on the internet, and among the many articles, I enjoyed downloading paintings of famous Italian artists and showed them to Andrew who became very captivated and wanted to do something with the pictures. In fact, Andrew decided to take a course at the Horry Georgetown Technical College to learn how to make frames and mats for the pictures. He bought the tools necessary for the matting at the school, and regarding the framing, he realized that there were discount stores selling attractive frames at a very reasonable price. Once the course was over, Andrew bought some nice frames and started working on his new project with great joy. Afterward, seeing the results of his work, he was so enthusiastic that nobody could slow him down. As a matter of fact, for a while, it became his hobby, and I was glad for that although he often asked me to help him with the matting. Before long, we had loads of really nice framed pictures, and we had no place to hang them for the walls of our home were already filled with real paintings. Then we decided to bring some to our relatives in Europe, and so we did.

Andrew's new hobby was the art postage stamps, and as with the matting, he was keeping me busy too. Over the years, he had accumulated a large number of stamps from all over the world and preserved them in boxes. He now decided to separate them by country and then organize them in books. This was a huge task, and it required a lot of patience, which, when he liked something, he had plenty of it. The end result was so interesting that every time we invited people to our home, he showed them his stamp books with a lot of enthusiasm.

From the first year we moved to Myrtle Trace, we bought the season tickets for the Symphony Orchestra played at the Myrtle Beach High School auditorium. Most of the times, I enjoyed the concert, but occasionally, the music made me fall asleep. It was different for Andrew, who loved music, and many times, I went to the theater just to please him. In early 1996, while I was looking at the program, I read that the Symphony Orchestra was from Kosice, Czechoslovakia. With great surprise, I showed Andrew what I had just read, and he could not believe that the orchestra from his hometown had come to South Carolina. We both were thrilled. After the performance, he went on stage and introduced himself to the conductor of the orchestra. Both men spent a few minutes talking about Kosice and then exchanged their telephone numbers. For my husband, it had been an exciting and happy evening.

THE FRENCH CLUB

In 1996, through a local newspaper, Andrew found out that there was a French Club in Myrtle Beach. Immediately, he became interested and soon joined the group. All the club's members were French born with a dual citizenship, and once a week, they were meeting at Barnes & Noble. At the club, they all spoke French, and my husband didn't have any problem for he too spoke French well. At the beginning, I also went there with him, sat at the table with the others, and listened to their French conversation. I understood a lot, but I could only say a few words, and most of the time, I spoke in English.

I met Francine (the leader of the group), the Blackburn couple—Marvis and Jim—who were both professors at Coast Carolina University, and many others. They all were professionals and very interesting people. At the club, we soon made some friends, and subsequently, we often got together at our homes or at some restaurant. It was very enjoyable.

Once, we invited Francine and her parents for dinner at our place. The parents were from France and were in the USA for a visit. In meeting Francine's father, I became very excited because it was like seeing my dear uncle Peppino Fantauzzo. The resemblance was incredible! They had the same facial characteristics, the same stature, and the same smiles! The meal that I had prepared for our guests was Sicilian specialties, without knowing that it was Francine's father's favorites. In fact, when I put the food on the dining table, Francine's father smiled at the sight of the meal because he remembered his mother's cooking. That evening, Francine's father was the center of attention. He was wonderful and made everybody feel warm, not to mention my great pleasure to have had him at my place.

After a while, the French Club was too much for me, so I decided to accompany Andrew there and then to go around the store where there was a lot to see and learn. I liked spending time going through books on different subjects, but mostly, I was looking at books that were PC related. Many times I got so involved with my reading that I forgot the time. In the meantime, the group's meeting had ended, and Andrew had to look for me all over the store. He didn't mind because he enjoyed looking around too.

From time to time, the club members got together to watch French movies, which had been rented for the group, and we always joined them. Once a year, the club held a dinner party for the members and their families at one of the best restaurant in Myrtle Beach. The last party took place around January 1999 and was held at the Dunes Restaurant. It was an enjoyable evening, and the restaurant was decorated with the French colors for that occasion. The food was French gourmet, and the music was French too.

Some years later, I remember when we took my brother to the French club while he was in the USA for a visit and how he amazed everybody there. After his introduction, he started singing the French national anthem without missing a note, and all the members immediately joined him. It was delightful to see so much enthusiasm among the group, but most of all, it was great to see my brother very proud in the middle of the French-speaking people, and he got lots of applauses.

For Andrew, the weekly meetings at the French club were very appealing, and he enjoyed every moment. Most of the members were women, and he was often the only man amid the ladies. From his behavior, I thought he liked that situation. The atmosphere at the club was always pleasant; everybody had some interesting topic to talk about, and they also brought photos and postcards to show and to share memories with the members. Unfortunately, a few years later, the French club came to an end. Francine, the leader, returned to France for good. Afterward, Jacqueline, one of the members, took over the responsibility of the club. Then some people left Myrtle Beach, and my husband stopped attending for health reasons. The number of the attendees became so small that, little by little, the club faded away.

* * *

Even though I was now leading an almost full active life, between the use of the personal computer, which I loved, and my involvement in several other pleasant activities, I was not completely satisfied yet. I still felt the need of doing something much different than the usual. I needed an interesting agenda to look forward to. Thank God, Andrew and I were healthy, economically sound, and had some free time available. I started thinking that my upcoming plans should include voyages by land and sea. To change the daily scene and see some new parts of the world, it seemed like a dream come true. In my school years, besides mathematics, history was my favorite subject, and traveling was now a great opportunity to visit some of those interesting ancient places. With a lot of enthusiasm, I told my husband about my new traveling ideas, and he liked that enormously so that with eagerness, I began to work on our next trip. My calendar started to fill up with interesting undertakings, and that made me feel wonderful. I really believed that I was going to enjoy a carefree lifestyle.

MARCH 1996 – OUR FIRST CRUISE

This was a seven-day Caribbean Sea Cruise. In the month of January, I applied for and got my first American passport, and soon after, I started getting ready for the trip. I had no idea what we needed for this first cruise, anyway, I did my best. In the following month of March, we drove to Tampa, Florida, where we boarded the Holland America *Noordam* ship. Our cabin was not first class so that when we entered it, we felt like being in a cage. Prior to our departure, all the passengers attended the mandatory lifeboat drill emergency procedure. Once the drill was over, with a great enthusiasm, we started walking around and could not believe how beautiful the ship was and the many amenities it had. We soon realized that there were plenty of activities going on all day long for everybody to choose from. It was really a nice surprise and amusing at the same time. It seemed like we were on a floating little city in an immense ocean. We were assigned to a dinner table with two other couples—one from California and the other from Maryland. They were friendly and warm people, and we enjoyed their company. The food was excellent, whether it was served at the restaurant or at the self-serve buffet.

There were four ports of call, and for each one, there were paid organized tours for the passengers to choose from, and since it was our first cruise, we took all of the tours. The stops were: in Key West, Florida; in Ocho Rios Jamaica; in George Town, Cayman Island; and in Cozumel, Mexico. In Cozumel, we visited some small shops where I bought a few very inexpensive and beautiful silver jewels. The cruising from Cozumel back to Tampa was the longest navigation time, and when we reached Tampa in the early morning, we disembarked.

My first cruise experience was wonderful, and what I also liked was the fact that there was no packing and unpacking to do; it felt like traveling within a hotel. Next, we returned to South Carolina.

THE CAREFREE YEARS

The following are some of the wonderful trips that I never imagined in my life that I'd be able to take with the man who, by now, had filled my life with contentment.

MAY 1997 – TRIP TO SEVEN EUROPEAN CITIES, FROM PARIS TO PALERMO

It started in Paris, followed by Prague, Kosice, Budapest, Salzburg, Munich, Pisa, Palermo, and ended in Reggio Calabria. From Kennedy Airport we flew to Paris, France.

In Paris we stayed at a comfortable American hotel close to the center of the city. Some of the sightseeing tours that we took had brief stops to the most beautiful monuments and historical places of the city, such as Les Invalides, which is the largest single complex of buildings in Paris. We visited the Basilique du Sacré Cœur, which has an imposing beautiful structure. The Musée du Louvre was Andrew's favorite place. We had lunch at the top of the Eiffel Tower, and at the foot of the Tower we embarked for the Seine River cruise. We enjoyed walking along the Champs-Elysées, doing window shopping, and stopping at some of the stores and souvenir shops as well. Though the stay in Paris was short, it certainly gave us a marvelous impression. Next, from the Charles De Gaulle Airport, we flew to Prague.

In Prague, we were warmly welcomed by Cousin Lila and her son Joska. They took us to his apartment in the city where we stayed for five days. Though it was my second visit, it was nice to see Prague again. From Prague, we flew to Kosice.

We stayed in Kosice three days. Since our last visit in 1990, the city had changed tremendously. As a matter of fact, when we returned to some places and looked for certain stores that we visited before, they were no longer there. Our first visit was one week after the fall of communism, and now, just seven years later, we found that things had changed significantly. Andrew was very glad to revisit his hometown where he met some of his old friends. One day we went to see the conductor of the Kosice State Philharmonic. He had come to South Carolina with the orchestra the year before and performed at the Myrtle Beach High School auditorium. He remembered Andrew and was pleased to see him again. From Kosice, we flew to Budapest.

This time in Budapest, we stayed at Aunt Maria's apartment for three days. Then we left Budapest for Salzburg by train.

We spent two days in Salzburg. Here, too, we found some changes. According to Andrew, the old Austrian traditional pastries were gone, and now the taste of the sweets seemed to be similar to those prepared in America. On the morning of the third day, my husband's cousin, Janos, came to Salzburg to drive us to Munich. On the way to Munich, we were stopped and fined by the German highway police because I was in the back seat and didn't have the seat belt on.

In Munich for three days, we stayed at Janos's apartment. There we met his wife Margit and their two children. Among the places we visited with Janos was the Dachau concentration camp, which was the first Nazi concentration camp opened in Germany. Visiting the Dachau camp and reflecting on the many atrocities that had been inflicted to human beings in that camp was very depressing. Imagine how Andrew felt! He had lost his family in other camps. We left the place without saying a word. Anyway, Munich is a beautiful and interesting city and we had a great time with Janos and his family. From Munich, we flew to Milan, then to Florence.

At the airport in Florence, we found my nephew Pino Bartolomeo waiting to take us to Pisa where he lived with his family.

We stayed in Pisa for five days with my relatives. At home we met my niece Giuseppina and her two children—Giovanni, who we already knew, and Irene, who we met for the first time. Irene was less than two years old and very delicate, while Giovanni hadn't changed, except he had grown a lot. This was our first time in Pisa, and, in order to show us the city, Pino took a week off from his job.

In Pisa, we visited Piazza del Duomo, where the Duomo, the Leaning Tower, the Baptistery, and the Camposanto are located. While in Pisa, with my nephew, we went to Lucca, Tuscany. There we spent a delightful day visiting a few of the most interesting places.

We flew from Pisa to Palermo, and my cousins Rosetta and Agostino took us to their home in the city where we stayed for three days. We soon learned that their three-week-old grandson Lorenzo was in the hospital, fighting for his life. Lorenzo was Giuseppe's youngest son. Thank God that during our stay, the little baby started to improve, and because of his condition, it was not wise for us to go to the hospital to meet the baby for the first time. With all his worries, on our last day in the city, Giuseppe took us to visit a few of the historic places in Palermo. At home, as always, my cousins' hospitality was warm and wonderful.

With my brother, we left Palermo for Reggio Calabria. Before taking the ferryboat to cross the Strait of Messina, we stopped in Messina. This is the third largest city in Sicily, and though its history goes back many centuries, there are few remnants left of the ancient world.

The Strait of Messina is the narrow passage between the eastern tip of Sicily and the southern tip of Italy. Connections between Messina and Villa San Giovanni are the ferryboats for passengers, cars, and trains, and the hydrofoil. In the late afternoon, we boarded the ferryboat with the car, then left the car on the main floor and went upstairs to watch. The crossing of the strait was slow, but the scenery was spectacular. The view of Sicily and Calabria so close to each other was really fantastic. After a one-hour ride, we arrived at Villa San Giovanni in Reggio Calabria, and afterward, we continued for Condofuri Marina, which is also in Reggio Calabria.

In Condofuri Marina, we stayed for eight days at my brother's lovely apartment near the beach. This was our first time there. At home, we met my sister-in-law, Maria, my niece, Alida, and her husband Nino, and also for the first time, their son, Stefano, who was about eighteen months old.

Condofuri Marina is a small town on the Ionian Sea coast with not much life, except during the summer months. In 1996, my brother and his wife moved from Casteltermini to Condofuri Marina to be close to the beach and to their daughter, Alida, who had settled here. However, the person who was really happy of the new location was my brother because he loved the beach, but it took Maria a little time to get used to the new location. Even though Condofuri Marina was Maria's birthplace, she was not fond of her hometown. She liked living in Casteltermini very much. To make it short, there is no comparison between Condofuri Marina and Casteltermini. Though Casteltermini has lost a great deal of its once-vibrant life, on a small scale, it has everything, including many friendly people.

With my brother and his family we visited some of Reggio Calabria interesting places. Toward the end of our wonderful stay, Alida and Nino gave us two small Riace bronzes statuettes from the Reggio's museum, and from Maria, we received some homemade sweets to take with us to America.

From the airport in Reggio, we flew to Rome and then back to New York. Afterward, we returned to South Carolina. What a wonderful experience the month long European trip had been for us!

APRIL 1998 – THE EASTERN MEDITERRANEAN CRUISE, FROM ATHENS TO ISTANBUL

This was an extraordinary voyage of fourteen days. The nine ports of call were in Athens-Greece, in Heraklion-Greece, in Ashdod-Israel, in Haifa-Israel, in Limassol-Cyprus/Greece, in Rhodes-Rhodes, in Kusadasi-Turkey, in Mytilene-Greece, and in Istanbul-Turkey. In addition to the cruise, we stayed two days in Athens before the cruise and two days in Istanbul after the cruise. From Kennedy Airport we flew to Athens aboard the Olympic Airways.

In Athens, we found the cruise organizers at the airport waiting to take us to the Divani Caravel Hotel. In no time, we started taking tours. We wanted to see as much as possible of the ancient historical remains, which are scattered all over the city. With a guide, we visited the Acropolis. Among the many famous buildings erected here are the Parthenon, a temple dedicated to goddess Athena; the Porch of the Maidens, a large porch with six draped female figures as supporting columns; and many more incredible ruins full of mythology—the Library of Hadrian, the Sanctuary of Apollo, the Temple Delphi, and others. On our own, we went to the Agora, which is the main shopping center in the city and the place where many attractive souvenirs can be found. The sojourn here was brief but amazing.

After two days in Athens, the cruise organizers came to the hotel to take us to the port of Piraeus where we boarded the *Renaissance Aegean* ship, and the sailing started at 5 p.m. The cruising was done at night, and by 7 a.m., the ship was anchored at a new port, and by 8 a.m., the bus tours were ready to leave for their various destinations.

In Heraklion, in Limassol, in Rhodes, and in Mytilene we only took sightseeing bus tours. The city of Rhodes was outstanding.

In Ashdod, the stop was for two days. This is a port city where we also started the daily guided tours.

On day 1, we went to Tel Aviv, got a general view of the city and met Frances and Haim Glasner, my friends from New York, who had moved to Israel a few years back. Although Haim was very sick with cancer, they insisted on taking us to their home. There we had lunch together, talked for a while, and later that afternoon, they brought us to the bus stop where we took the transportation back to the port of Ashdod.

On day 2, we went to Jerusalem and Bethlehem. We visited the Church of All Nations located on the Mount of Olives, which enshrines a section of bedrock where Jesus is said to have prayed before his arrest. Then our walking tour of the Old City took us to the Wailing Wall, which is considered as the holiest site by the Jews. The Dome of Rock is the oldest existing Islamic building in the world. Next, from the Church of the Holy Sepulcher, we walked through the Via Dolorosa. In Bethlehem, five miles from Jerusalem, we visited the Church of the Nativity. This day was for me the experience of a lifetime.

In Haifa, the stop was for one day. This is Israel's largest seaport, and it is also the world center of the Holy City of the BAHAI faith. The BAHAI Shrine, surrounded by terraced gardens, is one of the most striking landmarks in Haifa. We saw this impressive monumental place from the sightseeing bus tour. From Haifa, we went into the hills toward the Sea of Galilee, Nazareth, Capernaum, and the Jordan River. In Nazareth, we visited the Basilica of the Annunciation. From Nazareth on the road to Tiberias, the tour bus made stops in some of the ancient biblical places. What wonderful places we saw!

Next, from Kusadasi we went nine miles to Ephesus.

Ephesus, considered one of the greatest outdoor museums in Turkey and maybe in the world, was an ancient Greek city and later a major Roman city on the west coast of Asia Minor. With an excellent Turkish guide, we visited some of the ancient sites, such as the tomb of John the Apostle and the house of the Virgin Mary. Ephesus is really an unimaginable outdoor museum. The people involved in the excavation of the old ruins have done a fabulous work and have brought to life so many evidences of the city's glorious past! I cannot describe the pleasant experience at Ephesus. For sure, I will never forget it. What a great place to visit!

Back in Kusadasi, the tour guide took us to a carpet store where we found ourselves in a big room with many salesmen. First, they offered us the strong Turkish coffee and afterward showed us a large selection of the most beautiful Turkish carpets. Next, we walked to town where we visited some of the shops. In many stores, we found very attractive souvenirs not seen in any other place. We saw the unique Turkish miniature carpets. We bought a few to bring back home and give as souvenirs.

Next, we stayed in Istanbul two days. After leaving the ship, the cruise organizers brought us to the Conrad Hilton Hotel, located on the European side of Istanbul.

In Istanbul, we took sightseeing bus tours and walking tours. The most striking monument in the city was the Blue Mosque. From the entrance door, we only saw the inside of the Blue Mosque, whose walls were adorned with blue tiles, making the place unique. The Hagia Sophia, once a Christian cathedral, later a Mosque, and today a museum, is a very interesting place to visit. What a church this must have been at different times in its history! When we visited the Bazaar, it seemed that there was no end to it. It was very fascinating to look at the stores full of goods of all kinds and the shopkeepers trying to sell their merchandise.

In addition, while in Istanbul, Andrew contacted a friend by the name Melika. She came to our hotel and then took us to a restaurant frequented by the diplomatic corps. There we ordered Turkish dishes for lunch. The following day, we invited Melika to a restaurant serving Mediterranean meals. The food was excellent, and the setting of the place overlooking the city of Istanbul was beautiful. Next, after lunch, Melika took us to see a few sites on the Asian side.

At the end, we flew from Istanbul to New York City.

*   *   *

Back from Istanbul, we decided to stay in New York City for three days. One day, while strolling on Broadway, we saw a beautiful painting in a gallery store window, and Andrew fell in love with it at first sight. He looked at me, and I looked at him without saying a word, but I imagined what he had in his mind. In fact, the following day, when we went to Barnes & Noble, he was very busy going through some of the art books and soon came across the painting just seen the day before with the full explanation—"The Storm" by Pierre Auguste Cot. He instantly bought that book, and together, we went back to the gallery and purchased the painting. Next, I called Dina Horowitz, a dear friend of mine, to know if she had some free time to meet us. That day, though occupied at the office, she invited us for lunch at a vegetarian restaurant in mid-Manhattan. Years had passed since the time we had seen each other, so we both were glad to get together and talk about the old days at TIAA-CREF. Overall, we had a good lunch and a pleasant time together.

Returning home to South Carolina, the first thing Andrew did was to hang the painting on our living room wall, and afterward, he called some of our neighbors to come and see "The Storm." He was so happy!

As soon as one trip was completed, I started planning for the next one. It was wonderful that both Andrew and I enjoyed touring greatly, and it also seemed that scheduling trips had become my hobby.

APRIL 1999 - THE PANAMA CANAL CRUISE, FROM FORT LAUDERDALE TO VANCOUVER

This was a twenty-day voyage aboard the Holland American Line, the *Ryndam*, which started in Fort Lauderdale, Florida, and ended in Vancouver, Canada. The eight ports of call were Half Moon Cay, Curacao, Panama Canal, Costa Rica, Acapulco, Puerto Vallarta, San Diego, and Vancouver. We flew from Myrtle Beach to Fort Lauderdale for the afternoon boarding. Our cabin, located on a high floor, had a big window from which the view of the morning sunrise was wonderful. The arrival to the various ports was always in the morning, and, at each port, there were sightseeing bus tours ready to leave.

One morning while we were having breakfast, a couple behind us was speaking in Italian. I turned around and asked them if they were Italians, and their answer was yes. Afterward, we all introduced ourselves. Anselmo and Angela Cirio, husband and wife, were Italian born. They had immigrated to Canada and for many years were living in Vancouver. After a warm conversation in Italian and in English, we got to know each other, and consequently, we spent pleasant times together for the rest of the cruise.

The Panama Canal, which joins the Atlantic and the Pacific Oceans, is a great manmade accomplishment. The sailing on the Panama Canal was really slow, the process was much elaborated, and the sight was very impressive. For us going through the canal was a great experience.

In Vancouver, we stayed for a day. After the disembarkation, around 1 p.m., before going to the hotel, we took a sightseeing bus tour, which left us really impressed with the beauty of the city. Our Canadian friends invited us to their house for supper, so close to 8 p.m. Anselmo came to the hotel to take us to his home where we spent a lovely evening together.

Early the next morning, we flew from Vancouver to Seattle. Due to the bad weather in Georgia, the airplane from Atlanta arrived at the Seattle airport six hours later, so when we got to Atlanta, we had to wait four more hours before taking the flight to Myrtle Beach. In conclusion, the Panama Canal cruise was a very successful experience, except for the flights coming back home, which took almost twenty-two hours.

APRIL 2001 – THE WESTERN MEDITERRANEAN CRUISE AND MEETING ITALIAN RELATIVES

This was one of the most enjoyable trips due to some of its stops in Italy and Sicily, where I planned to meet some of my relatives. It was a fourteen-day voyage consisting of twelve days at sea and two days in Barcelona. Cruising with the Renaissance Line, there were ten ports of call in Barcelona, Palma de Mallorca, Villefranche, Livorno, Civitavecchia, Napoli, Palermo, Valletta, La Goulette, and Mahon.

We flew to Barcelona, Spain, from Kennedy Airport.

At the Barcelona airport, we were met by the cruise organizers who took us to a waiting bus for the city highlight tour, and then brought us to the port where we soon boarded the ship. Our cabin, located on a high-level floor, was large and had a bathtub and balcony. It was really a nice cabin, and we were more than pleased when we saw it. At 5 p.m., the cruise ship left the port of Barcelona for Palma de Mallorca, Spain.

The Palma de Mallorca stop was for six hours. It is a beautiful town, rich of history and has many very impressive churches, monuments, and museums. Here, we enjoyed a bus sightseeing and a walking tour.

In Villefranche, France, the ship stopped for a day. Here we took the bus highlights tour along the French Riviera with some stops in Nice, Cannes, Grasse, and Saint Paul de Vance.

Nice is the largest city in Southern France, and everywhere, there are beautiful palaces, boulevards, squares, avenues, and statues. Cannes is the city best known for its annual film festival.

Grasse is the center of the French perfume industry. In Grasse we visited the Fragonard perfume factory where we received samples and bought some soap. To this day, I keep soap in a drawer for its fantastic fragrance and also as a souvenir. Saint Paul de Vence is a charming hilltop fortified village filled with art galleries, boutiques, and sidewalk cafes. In Saint Paul de Vance, we had lunch at a nice restaurant with a magnificent view. Late afternoon we went back to Villefranche for the embarkation and sailing to Italy.

The ship stopped for one day in Livorno, Italy. Livorno is surrounded by fortified walls, and its big port is overlooked by towers and fortresses leading to the center of the town. Here, the district of Venice is called so because of the characteristic architectural features, similar to those found in the famous city of Venice. At the Port of Livorno, we met my niece Giuseppina and her family who had come here from Pisa to welcome us. They took us around to see the most important parts of the city and then took us to a fine restaurant serving Tuscan meals. It was the first time that their children, Giovanni and Irene, were seeing a cruise ship. They were enchanted at the view and wanted to go aboard. Before our departure, we all went aboard the ship—but just at the entrance—to take pictures. Afterward, my relatives remained at the port, waiving to us until the cruise ship left the shore.

In Civitavecchia, Italy, the cruise ship stayed at the port for two days. Civitavecchia is a town where the main port of Rome is located. We arrived at the port and found my nephew Vincenzo Arnone waiting to take us to Rome.

Day 1 in Civitavecchia: Vincenzo took us to his place where we met his wife, Enza, and their children—Adriano, Rita, and Daniela. After many years, I almost didn't recognize the children. They were now three beautiful grown-up teenagers who warmly welcomed us. The Arnone family had just moved into this apartment located near the center of Rome, and they were in the process of remodeling their place. While Vincenzo had been busy bringing us here from the port, Enza too had been occupied in her kitchen. In fact, entering their apartment, the cooking smell was so good that our months watered, and afterward, we ate the delicious lunch with a great appetite. In the afternoon, Vincenzo took us and his family to see some parts of the city, and then in the vicinity of the coliseum, we stopped at a bar to have express coffee and pastries. While sitting at an outside table, the view of the historic area was very pleasant. Around 8 p.m., Vincenzo drove us back to the port.

Day 2 in Civitavecchia: My relatives wanted us to come back to Rome, but with appreciation and regret, we bypassed the second invitation because that day, I felt sick and spent the entire day in bed. Andrew was wonderful. He really took care of me on the ship.

We spent one day in Napoli, Italy. Upon our arrival at the port we didn't have any time to visit Napoli because by this time we had chosen the guided tour of Pompeii.

Pompeii is about eight kilometers (five miles) away from Mount Vesuvius, and the entrance to the excavations is a short but steep hill to the flat plateau at the top. Going up, Andrew and I felt a little weak maybe because of the strenuous slope, but thank God, once we arrived at the top, we were fine.

The city of Pompeii was destroyed and completely buried during a long catastrophic eruption of the volcano Mount Vesuvius, which lasted two days. The excavated town offers a snapshot of the Roman life frozen at the moment it was buried on August 24, 79 AD. Our tour guide was excellent; his explanation of the historic and tragic events of the town was lifelike. Just to make it brief, our visit here was really extraordinary. Then from Pompeii, we went to Sorrento.

Sorrento is a small town in the province of Naples. We took a sightseeing tour, and among the various points of interest, the best were the sight of the city of Naples, Mount Vesuvius, and the Isle of Capri. Sorrento is famous for the production of limoncello, a digestive made from lemon rinds, alcohol, water, and sugar. After lunch, we took a stroll around the town where the streets were narrow and congested. Later afternoon, we returned to the port of Napoli for the embarkation and sailing to Sicily.

In Palermo, the stop was just for a few hours. At the port, which is right by the city, my nephew Giuseppe Giudice was waiting to take us to his parents' home. After meeting Giuseppe, we remained at the port for a while, waiting for my brother and his wife to arrive. My brother and his wife had left their home early to meet us at the port. Unfortunately, they got mixed up with the directions, and consequently, they missed us. Finally, Vincenzo and Maria arrived at our cousins Rosetta and Agostino Guidice's home, where a happy reunion soon took place with the relatives, followed by a delicious lunch that Rosetta had already prepared for all of us and the sweets (the so-called pignulata) that my sister-in-law had brought to the Giudice family. Although the stay at my cousins' place was short, due to the scheduled time of the cruise, the few hours spent with them all were wonderful. At the end, Giuseppe, Vincenzo, and Maria accompanied us to the port where they remained until the ship left Palermo at 5 p.m. for Valletta. Sad to say, this was the last time I saw Maria, my wonderful sister-in-law.

In Valletta, the stop was for a day. This is the capital of Malta and is situated in the center of the Mediterranean Sea, ninety-three kilometers south of Sicily.

Looking from the cruise ship, we thought that we could not make the short and steep hill from the port to the center of Valletta, but we made it. We spent an entire day there. Our day, there just happened to be when the town does the reenactment of the sixteenth-century military drills conducted by the knights. It was nice to watch the festivities. Later that afternoon, we returned to the port for the embarkation, and soon after, the ship left for La Goulette in Tunisia.

Instead of reaching the port of La Goulette, we ended up in Sicily again. When we left Valletta, the weather seemed fine. It was calm, and there were just a few clouds in the sky. However, during the night en route to La Goulette, the weather turned really nasty. Because of the heavy hailstorm and strong winds that buffered the ship, the captain addressed the passengers on the intercom, informing that due to the "threatening weather and the bleak forecast," he was compelled to change course and seek a safe haven for the safety of the passengers, the crew, and the vessel. I remember the instability of the ship, the ice balls on our balcony, and how cold our cabin became. It was also getting water from the cracks in the balcony. It was indeed a scary night! The only harbor that the captain was able to find in the vicinities was a docking space in a small Sicilian town. Subsequently, all the maneuvers were done during the night, and in order to bring the cruise ship to the docking place, the captain had to circumnavigate Sicily via the Strait of Messina. The following morning, we were in Milazzo safe and sound.

Milazzo, Sicily, is a small fishing town with friendly and warm people. At our arrival, the town's mayor offered the cruise passengers a free bus ride to get around the charming town where we spent a pleasant day. Afterward, we went aboard the ship and sailed for Mahon, Spain, where we spent a nice day.

We stayed two days in Barcellona. Here we took a five-hour guided walking city tour, and the rest of our stay was spent on our own, and the ship was our hotel. The cruise terminals were conveniently located at the foot of La Rambla, which is Barcelona's most famous boulevard that runs through the heart of the city center. In Barcellona, in spite of the impressive works from the Romanesque and Renaissance periods, it is Gaudi's works that attract millions of visitors to Barcelona. His architecture is strange and unique. The combination of design, interestingly shaped stonework, and vibrant colors give the viewer a truly breathtaking visual experience. After two fabulous days in Barcelona, we disembarked the ship, and went to the airport where we took the flight to New York.

In New York City, we stayed for five days. While in the city, we met many old friends, including Dina and Leo Horowitz who invited us for lunch at a kosher restaurant in mid-Manhattan. I remember the tasty soup with big matzo balls and the huge pastrami sandwich. They were really good. We visited the Metropolitan Museum, went to our favorite stores, and also went to the eastside to buy some Hungarian delicacies. At the end, we drove back home to South Carolina.

* * *

The night of July 28, 2001, I got a phone call from Sicily. It was from one of my nieces, Giuseppina or Alida, to inform me that her mother had suddenly passed way. At the bad news, I momentary remained shocked for I had seen Maria with my brother just three months earlier in Palermo, and at that time, she seemed to be in good health. The following morning, when I called my brother, I didn't know what to say to him. He was so devastated that he was unable to speak to me. I only could give him some words of comfort. I was really worried for Vincenzo.

Just that evening the entire family, Maria included, went to a restaurant to celebrate Giovanni's birthday. Giovanni was Vincenzo and Maria's grandson. Soon after everybody returned home, Maria felt terribly sick, and in no time, she passed away.

It was really a great tragedy for all of them! At that time, I knew that the death was a terrible happening for the immediate family, but I didn't have any real understanding of what my brother and his daughters were going through. I didn't have any experience of that kind because when both my parents died, I was too young to comprehend the great loss, and later, when some of my very close relatives passed away, I had already been away from them for many years. Anyway, at that time, I was a little naïve to understand what the death of a spouse or parent really meant!

2002 – VISIT WITH OUR FAMILIES IN EUROPE AND OUR BALTIC SEA CRUISE

It was a thirty-one-day trip, which had two purposes—the first part in May, to visit relatives in Italy, Hungary, and the Czech Republic; and the second part in June, a cruise in the Baltic Sea. In May, we flew from Myrtle Beach to Atlanta and via Rome to Reggio Airport where my brother and his son-in-law were waiting to bring us home.

In Condofuri Marina, we stayed with my brother for eight days. Because this was our first visit since the death of my sister-in-law, as soon as we entered the house, we immediately noticed the gloomy atmosphere everywhere. Without Maria's vibrant voice and warm smile, the house was empty and cold. We missed the presence of Maria very much, and I imagined what Vincenzo was going through without his wife! After two days there, we decided to go to Casteltermini to visit relatives and, at the same time, to give a break to my brother.

In Casteltermini, we stayed at a hotel on the outskirt of the town. Knowing of our visit, some of the relatives had invited us to their home for lunch or dinner before coming to town. We went to the Giudices' country house where we met other family members, and afterward, we ate my favorite Sicilian foods that Rosetta had prepared in Palermo and brought there. The location of the country house at Santa Croce was one of Andrew's favorite places due to its beautiful scenery. In the evening, for dinner, we went to Dr. Pietro Amoreli's home where we met his family. The visit to my hometown coincided with the celebration of the Sacra Della Croce, which, as I described before, is the most important traditional festivity of Casteltermini, but this time, we were not up to enjoying the feast. After two days, we left town at daybreak to return to Condofuri Marina.

On the way to the Strait of Messina to reach our destination, I asked my brother if he would like to make a detour in order to visit Piazza Armerina.

Piazza Armerina is an interesting town located on a high plateau in central Sicily. It is an attractive town with a historic center clustered around its baroque cathedral. In common with many of the Sicilian towns, the remaining medieval and baroque architectural highlights are the churches and the palaces scattered around the town. After visiting Piazza Armerina, where we bought some fantastic souvenirs, we went to Villa Romana del Casale, which is about a five-kilometer far.

The Villa Romana del Casale is one of the most luxurious of its kind in the Roman world. The ancient village of Casale and the Villa Romana were completely destroyed by cataclysms and forgotten for centuries until official archaeological excavations were carried out and subsequently, the Villa del Casale was completely uncovered. Today, the Villa Roman del Casale is famous all over the world for the over 4200 square yards of well-preserved and highly refined mosaic floors. We all enjoyed walking inside and outside the villa, which is really an amazing Sicilian treasure. I had never seen such beautiful artwork so well preserved; by just looking at it, I could not get enough.

Later, exhausted but satisfied, we left the Piazza Armerina area for Condofuri Marina, and on the way home, we stopped for dinner at a fish restaurant. Among the selections, the restaurant served us huge shrimps. Andrew made some comments about their size, and I remember how funny the comments were that we could not stop laughing. Anyway, the meal was very good.

Back to Condofuri Marina, we went to the cemetery to visit Maria's grave and then to Reggio to see Maria's sister. The week spent with my brother brought a little relief to his lonely life, and I was glad for that. Fortunately, his daughter Alida was taking care of him. At the end, we flew from Reggio to Rome and then to Budapest

We stayed three days in Budapest to visit Andrew's relatives, and afterward, we flew to Prague where other relatives were waiting for us.

We arrived in Prague on June 2, and we stayed at Joska's place for five days. The first day was a reunion with Andrew's relatives, and after that, Joska took us and his family to visit a few places in the Czech Republic. Next, we flew from the Prague Airport to Copenhagen.

We stayed in Copenhagen, Denmark, on the seventh and eighth of June 2002, which was before the cruise. At our morning arrival, the cruise organizers took us from the airport to the hotel located at the center of the city.

On our first day, to get a glance of the city, we enjoyed exploring the city on foot, and taking public transportation one after another. The first evening in Copenhagen it was very amusing. Though we knew of the long summer days, we still found it interesting when we went to bed after 10 p.m. and saw daylight outside the window.

On our second day, with a guided tour, we visited some of the city historical places. Everything was very interesting.

At the end of our stay in Copenhagen, a cruise organizer drove us from the hotel to the port for the embarkation, and subsequently, the sailing started at 5 p.m.

* * *

The ten-day cruise in the Baltic Sea began on June 9, aboard the Holland American line. The eight ports of call were in Copenhagen, Tallinn, St. Petersburg, Helsinki, Stockholm, Kalmar, Warnemunde, and Aarhus.

In Tallinn, Estonia, our stop was for five hours. Here, the most impressive architectural masterpiece is the Alexander Nevsky Cathedral. This is a richly decorated Orthodox Church, which was built when Estonia was part of the Russian tsarist empire. By 5 p.m., we were back on the ship.

We stayed in St. Petersburg for two days. Here we arrived at 7 a.m., then, before the disembarkation, we waited for the Russian authority to come aboard the ship for the control. There were two tours—one for Moscow and the other for St. Petersburg. Everybody knew which one to take because the choice had already been made the day before. Since Moscow was more than three hundred miles away, which was not going to allow us enough time to visit the city, we chose the tour of Saint Petersburg.

St. Petersburg is a magnificent city. The grandeur of the past has faded, but the historic architecture of the city center, its wide avenues, romantic waterways, beautiful cathedrals, and row upon row of white palaces are just breathtaking.

On our first day in St. Petersburg we visited the Hermitage Museum with an excellent Russian guide. The museum is spectacular, and it is difficult to describe Andrew's enthusiasm and admiration during our visit. He was so immersed in his observations that, on several occasions, he forgot that we had to follow the tour guide, and I had to make sure not to get lost in that huge museum. After spending five extraordinary hours there, we returned to the ship, and the rest of the afternoon at our leisure.

On our second day in St. Petersburg, in the morning, we took a bus tour for the highlights of the city. The endless beautiful sights were just incredible. Afterward, the tour guide took us to a souvenir shop, which was a disappointment. We spent the afternoon aboard the ship because we were not allowed to go out without a Russian guide. All in all, our experience in St. Petersburg was wonderful.

In Helsinki, Finland, from the port we walked to the market square, and then went to the center of the city where the Senate Square and the Lutheran Cathedral are located. The Lutheran Cathedral standing on a hill in the center of Helsinki is just magnificent. On account of the steep steps, I went to the church alone; Andrew, who had refused to come along, was right because when I reached the top, I was really exhausted. Next, we went to another landmark of Finland with a guided tour.

The Temppeliaukio Church is a Lutheran church in the vicinity of Helsinki. It is called Church of the Rock because it is built into excavated bedrock, rising some twelve meters (40 feet) above street level. Only the domed copper roof is visible from the outside, no signs of a church inside and no bells. We were very impressed and could not stop wondering how the artists carved and structured it. It seemed something extraterrestrial, really spectacular. Then later that afternoon, we returned to the ship to continue the cruise toward the Stockholm Archipelago in Sweden.

The scenery of the Stockholm Archipelago, with so many islands close to each other, was very impressive, but the ultra-slow crossing of the islands to reach the city of Stockholm was a very long stretch. The very unique city consists of fourteen islands connected by fifty-seven bridges.

We were in Stockholm for a day. We took a bus tour for the highlights of the city, and then we went to Gamla Stan. This is the oldest town in central Stockholm, is very picturesque and contains several old buildings, which reflect the historic part of the city. Here there is the Stockholm Cathedral, the Sweden's royal palace, the Swedish academy, the Nobel Library, and the Nobel Museum.

The next stops were in Kalmar, Sweden; in Warnemunde, Germany; in Aarhus, Denmark. The cruise terminated in Copenhagen. After the disembarkation, we went to the airport where we took the flight to Paris, then to Atlanta, and finally to Myrtle Beach.

What an interesting and wonderful month long this journey had been!

MARCH 2003 - CARIBBEAN CRUISE
PLANNED FOR MY BROTHER.

Almost two years had passed since the death of my sister-in-law, and for my brother, it was like yesterday. I wanted to do something special that would give him the chance to alleviate his lonely life, at least temporarily. Therefore, at the beginning of the year, I told Andrew that I wanted to invite Vincenzo to the USA for four weeks, and that would also include a cruise. Andrew took care of the arrangements, and then we sent my brother the surprise invitation with the tickets. I knew in advance that the cruise would make Vincenzo very happy because this would be his first sea voyage and also the realization of an old dream of his.

As soon as Vincenzo got the invitation, he phoned me and happily told me that he would be ready by the scheduled time for the trip to America; I noticed great excitement in his voice. For his arrival, we went to the Atlanta airport to welcome Vincenzo to America. At the airport, we were pleasantly surprised in realizing how well my brother had managed in getting out of that huge complex without the knowledge of the English language. The following day, we left Atlanta for our home in South Carolina.

On the early morning of March 7, we drove to the port of Charleston for the nine-day cruise. The embarkation on the *Galaxy* of the Celebrity Cruise Line began around 11a.m., and the five ports of call were in Charleston, Nassau, Belize, Cozumel, and Georgetown.

On the ship, Vincenzo was very pleased when he saw his cabin. After settling in our places, we started strolling everywhere. My brother was astonished when he saw the grandiosity inside the ship and the many amenities available. He never thought that a cruise ship would be like a luxurious hotel floating in the ocean.

In Nassau, We visited the Fort Charlotte. It had costumed guides leading informative tours through the complex. Here, what my brother enjoyed most were the stories of the pirates that

I was explaining in Italian. "Nassau is also historically considered to be a stronghold of the pirates."

In Georgetown, we visited the Turtle Farm, and the Ironshore landscape of Hell, which is a large area of black rock formations weathered over a long period of time. It is a very spectacular and diabolic-looking place. There we stopped at the post office and sent a few "postcards from hell."

Anyway, in all ports of call, my brother had a great time.

The cruise ended in Charleston, It was early morning when we arrived at the port so that after the disembarkation, we decided to remain there for a few hours to show Vincenzo the city of Charleston. Towards evening we drove back to Myrtle Trace.

At home, we did our best to make Vincenzo feel as comfortable as possible. I also started thinking what to do next to entertain him. With a lot of enthusiasm, one day, we took Vincenzo to see a musical show at the Palace Theatre in Myrtle Beach, but we were disappointed when we realized that Vincenzo didn't care about the show.

The first time he came was with his wife, and that made a big difference because, besides us, they were in each other's company. Anyway, we often took Vincenzo to Myrtle Beach where he enjoyed walking on the beach, and also brought him to other places.

When the time to return to Italy arrived, we drove Vincenzo to the Atlanta Airport for the flight to Rome. The good-bye was sad. He was much moved, and I was touched too, especially knowing that he was going back to an empty, gloomy home. To be brief, we were glad for having invited my brother to the USA and for having given him a memorable cruise.

2004 – OUR CHRISTMAS HOLIDAYS AT SEA

This was a fourteen-day cruise in the Caribbean Sea aboard the Holland America *MS Noordam* ship. In the early morning of December 19, we left Conway and reached the port of Tampa for the boarding, and the sailing began at 5 p.m. Subsequently, almost in every port of call we took the guided tours.

For the Christmas celebration on December 25, the restaurant and the ballroom on the ship were fabulously decorated, and the atmosphere was festive everywhere. Christmas was also my birthday, so in my cabin, I found a birthday card signed by the ship captain, and in the dining room, a waiter brought a cake to my table along with other personnel, singing "Happy Birthday." I didn't anticipate that. It was really a nice surprise. I never dreamed that I would spend a Christmas at sea with the man that I loved! What a happy time it was for me and for Andrew too!

For the New Year 2005 celebration, the restaurant was elegantly decorated in black and white. Everything looked fantastic, and the variety of food served was exceptional. All the passengers received a tiara with the inscription "Happy New Year" to wear for the entire evening. After dinner, there was a comedy show, then a dance, and at midnight, they served special sweets and champagne.

The cruise ended on January 2 in Tampa. What a wonderful voyage it had been. It was an unusual and happy experience to remember for the rest of my life.

I never thought this would be my last happy cruise with Andrew!

1994 – Our new Myrtle Trace home in Conway, South Carolina

1994 - From right: Jean Johnson from Myrtle Trace, Andrew and me.
On the table is a fifty-dollar-tree I made for
the Rodgers' wedding anniversary.

May 1995 –With my brother and his wife
at our home in Myrtle Trace.
In the photos there are also Louis and Rosalie
Giordano, and Frank and Vinnie Petrucelli.

1995 - In St. Louis with the Fantauzzo-
Pona cousins and the Italian relatives

Andrew loved this photo of both of us
taken at a restaurant in St. Louis

September 1995 – Andrew with his relatives from Czechoslovakia in our living room

1996 – Andrew with the French Club group at Barnes
and Noble Book Store in Myrtle Beach

Livorno 2001 - With Giuseppina, Giovanni
and Irene leaving the cruise ship

Rome 2001, with my nephew Vincenzo Arnone

Pompei 2001, Andrew and I

Palermo 2001, with my nephew Giuseppe Giudice

THE GREATEST LOSS
OF MY LIFE

With the deterioration of Andrew's health, everything started to fade away. Up to now, he had been in good physical condition even though Andrew had been taking a medication for his high blood pressure for years.

Then at the start of 2005, after returning from our Christmas holiday cruise, he felt unusually weak and went to see his doctor. Andrew's blood pressure was very high, and Dr. Wilson, at first, increased the dose of the drug he was taking, and then he prescribed new ones for the blood pressure. Therefore, for a while, it seemed that everything was under control, except new problems arose. During the night, Andrew started to have abnormal palpitations and was unable to fall asleep. Subsequently, the doctor sent him to Conway Hospital where they performed some tests and found nothing wrong. But at the end of January, Andrew's blood pressure increased alarmingly, and Dr. Wilson sent him back to Conway Hospital again where they performed a renal MRI, which showed a small mass in the right kidney. Consequently, my husband was sent to Dr. Quillen, an urologist, who ordered a CAT scan, and the result was identical to that of the MRI. At that time, the urologist told him not to worry about the mass as he would check for any growth every six months. Six months later, Dr. Quillen ordered another CAT scan and a biopsy of the renal lymph nodes, and the results were negative. Therefore, for the following three years, Andrew had CAT scans and blood tests every six months. Fortunately, the size of the mass in the kidney never changed.

During the month of September in 2005, one morning, Andrew experienced some unsteadiness. I first checked his blood pressure with the device that we had just bought and could not believe how high his blood pressure was. We went to see Dr. Wilson, but he was on vacation. We decided to go see Dr. Balachandran, a nephrologist who had an excellent reputation. Dr. Balachandran had never seen Andrew; nevertheless, he received him with kindness and right away ordered a comprehensive metabolic panel. The results showed that the potassium level in his blood was extremely low. Then more tests showed that the loss of potassium was caused by an adrenal gland abnormality. Anyway, with the right prescriptions, Andrew's health improved significantly.

With great appreciation, I want to mention Dr. Balachandran because, besides being an excellent doctor, he was and is a very good and compassionate person. I remember when we went to see this doctor for the problems that Andrew was having; with or without appointments, he always welcomed us with a pleasant smile and said, "Come in, Mr. Janovitz, and how can I help you today?" I could see in Andrew's face how pleased he was in seeing the doctor! In the years that followed, Dr. Balachandran remained Andrew's most trusted and favorite doctor.

MAY 2006 – LAST EUROPEAN TRIP WITH MY HUSBAND

At this time, Andrew was feeling much better so that I was able to convince him that a change of scenery would be good for both of us. He agreed, and soon after, I planned a three-week vacation. For a long time, Andrew wanted to do something with his art stamps collection; however, it was just now that he decided to go forward with his project. While I was busy planning the trip,

Andrew put together two art stamp books to bring to Italy—one for Giuseppe Giudice and the other for Vincenzo Arnone. He really did an impressive job, and frankly, I didn't expect that. How pleased and proud I was of him!

We flew from Myrtle Beach to Charlotte, North Carolina, then to Rome, and finally to Pisa. Knowing that there was a stop of four hours in Rome, I had already contacted my nephew Vincenzo Arnone to meet us at the airport in order to give him the art stamp book. Because of the confusion between international and national airports, we missed each other in Rome. Therefore, the art stamp book remained with us for the duration of the trip and back to the USA.

We stayed in Pisa for three days with relatives. At home, we learned that in a few days Irene, Giuseppina's girl, would receive her first communion, and the family wanted us to stay for the celebration. Unfortunately, we had to miss it due to our traveling schedules. Next, from Pisa, we flew to Palermo.

At the airport in Palermo, we found Giuseppe Giudice with his son Lorenzo waiting for us. Before this time, every time we came to Palermo, my Giudice cousins, Giuseppe's parents, would wait at the airport to take us to their home where we would stay for the duration of the trip. This time was different because both cousins were seriously ill. Knowing of the sad circumstances in advance, we tried to make hotel reservations, but Giuseppe insisted that we go to his place instead, so we gladly accepted his invitation.

We stayed in Palermo with Giuseppe's family for five days. At home, we met his wife Pinella, and the rest of their children—Marco and Giuliana—who were pleased to have us with them. I remember the first day there. It was after supper when Lorenzo asked me if I needed euros. It was the most thoughtful and cutest thing the boy could have said to me, and during our trip, he didn't know what he could do to please us. He was wonderful. When Andrew gave Giuseppe the art stamp book,

I cannot describe Giuseppe's reaction and also the reaction of everybody. It was an unexpected beautiful gift, and Andrew was delighted. Subsequently, my nephew brought us to visit his parents every day. I found cousin Rosetta a little relaxed from her cancer ordeal, while cousin Agostino was in very poor health. I was very glad to have spent some time with them and talk about the old days. One day, Rosetta gave me an embroidered cushion that I had made for her in my younger years in Casteltermini. In giving me the cushion, she said to me, "I know that you don't have any of your embroidered work, so take this as a reminder of your first expertise." It was Agostino's birthday on May 23, and his family organized a big party for the occasion. That evening, I met Giovanni with his family, Franca with her two sons, and Tony with his fiancée. On this same day, my cousins Franco and Adalgisa Martorana came to visit me, bringing a huge ice cream cake. They didn't know of the birthday party, and when Rosetta asked them to stay, they couldn't because had other engagements. On our last evening in Palermo, Giuseppe and his family took us to a restaurant near the Politeama Theater in the center of the city. It was an elegant but very expensive place. Overall, we spent a wonderful time in Palermo with Giuseppe and his family, and this was the last time I saw cousin Agostino.

My brother and his son-in-law Nino came to Palermo to take us to Casteltermini.

We went to Casteltermini to visit some sick relatives. We first went to see Cousin Memma Martorana; I almost didn't recognize her because of her condition. As a matter of fact, she died four months later. Then we went to see cousin Lina Arnone, whose husband was very ill too. Once in town, we also visited a few other relatives just to say hello, and we also met Dr. Pietro Amorelly, a dear friend of ours. Pietro wanted us to stay at his home for dinner, and because our time was limited, he insisted and took us with his family to a coffee house for ice cream. I was glad to see his children Chiara and Francesco, his wife, and his mother Nena who was my dear friend. Next, after a long, sad, and exhausting day, the four of us—Andrew, Vincenzo, Nino, and I—finally went to the hotel on the outskirts of the town where we retired for the night. The following morning, we left Casteltermini for Condofuri Marina.

We stayed in Condofuri Marina for one week. It was at the beginning of June, and here we found my niece Alida busy with the preparations for her son's first communion. This was new to us too, but we were glad to be in town and attend the celebration, which was as big as a wedding. Next, Alida knew that Andrew liked the crostata, and I, the pignulata, so she prepared a lot of both sweets to take with us to America. Because her mother was no longer alive, she was doing things that her mother used to do for us. After a pleasant trip there, we flew to Rome from Reggio, and then to Budapest.

We stayed at the hotel in Budapest for three days. From the airport, Aunt Maria first took us to her apartment, and in the evening, she took us to the hotel. For the first time, I was able to convince Andrew that we would stay in a hotel in Budapest and Prague, so before the trip, he wrote to his relatives for the hotel reservations. In the past, I didn't insist on staying in a hotel because I knew how much he wanted to stay with his family despite the fact that I never liked that idea, so to please him, I never complained. During our visit, Maria came to our hotel every morning where we had breakfast together, then went to her place and decided what to do afterward. At the end, we left Budapest for Prague.

In Prague, we settled at the hotel for three days. Upon our arrival at the airport, Lila and Joska brought us to their home to meet the rest of the family, and then they accompanied us to the hotel. I liked very much to be on our own. To my surprise, Andrew was also glad about our decision. While in the city, one day, Joska brought us to his new country house where we found his wife working in the garden. His house, which was far from

Prague, was huge and had many amenities to accommodate their two children's future families. Then Joska took us and his family to the nearby restaurant for lunch. The selection of the Czech foods ordered in advance was great. We all enjoyed the big and delicious meal very much. Another day, Lila, Irene, Honza, and Andrea took us to a nice restaurant in the center of Prague; I don't remember its name, but it was a very elegant place, and the food was good too. From Prague, we flew back to the USA.

The return trip from Europe, including the six hours of waiting at the Cincinnati Airport before taking the flight for Myrtle Beach, was very stressful. Anyway, altogether it was fine, but I started to notice how frail Andrew had become! He was not the same person anymore. To see how his health was deteriorating was silently breaking my heart, and I had the premonition that this was our last trip together.

OCTOBER 2006 – DRIVING THE CAR FOR THE FIRST TIME

In one of the daily walks in Myrtle Trace, Andrew momentarily lost his balance. Thank God that he recuperated quickly and we were able to walk back home where he took the car and drove himself to Dr. Wilson. I soon realized that it was time for me to take over the wheels with no delay as Andrew was too frail to continue driving. Then when I told him that I wanted to get some driving practice, he understood his situation, and with a faint smile, he didn't object. I had a driver license, but I never really drove. Andrew was the only driver, and I enjoyed sitting on the passenger seat and giving him some directions. Therefore, at the age of seventy-three, I started driving our car, and I did fine. Subsequently, while my husband remained satisfied with my driving, unquestionably at the beginning, there was a lot of uneasiness, but I could not show that to him, so I pretended to be fine.

2007 – YEAR FULL OF ANXIETIES

After my husband lost his balance, Dr. Wilson ordered some tests at the Conway Medical Center. The MRA (magnetic resonance angiogram) of the head showed a blockage in the basilar artery and stenosis greater than 80 percent in the bilateral carotid stenosis. Next, Andrew went to see several specialized doctors for consultations and they didn't have any good answer for his problem.

Dr. Elliot was a vascular surgeon at Rutledge Tower in Charleston, South Carolina. When I took Andrew to Charleston, it was the first time that I drove a long distance, a little more than one hundred miles. I felt very uneasy, but when Andrew asked me how I was feeling, I responded, "Better than ever." In Charleston, the doctor ordered more tests. After seeing the results, he told Andrew that he could have a carotid endarterectomy. But a doctor, he had seen for consultation, thought that with the basilar artery problem, any surgery would be fatal. However, after a few months of contemplation, Andrew decided to go through with the operation. For some strange reason, he trusted Dr. Elliot and was ready to take the risk.

On February 6, 2007, I drove Andrew to the hospital in Charleston where he had more tests. The following morning, we were back at the hospital where Dr. Elliot performed the carotid endarterectomy. Subsequently, it took some time to bring the blood pressure to a certain level for it was extremely low and Andrew was at a high risk. Throughout the surgery, I was anxiously waiting until I finally got the news that he had made it. The operation was successful, and that night, I stayed in the hospital with Andrew. With all the medications the hospital staff gave him, he was awake all night and very uncomfortable, and he was also very anxious to leave the hospital. Anyway, it was just a one-day stay in the hospital, but we stayed in Charleston for four days at a hotel near the Hospital.

Several weeks had passed since the carotid surgery, and Andrew thought that by now he would feel much better and stronger than before, but he didn't see any improvement in his health. Instead, he had new problems. He could not turn his neck, and he had pain in his left shoulder—the same side as the operation. I took him to our new doctor, Dr. Camille Mills, a very good doctor and a pleasant person, who ordered some tests and, afterward, sent him to Dr. Presler, an orthopedic specialist. Andrew started physical therapy, and every time I brought him there, I noticed how weak he was, but he didn't want to give up. Seeing no improvement, Dr. Presler stopped the treatment and, luckily, a few months later, the problems with the neck and shoulder disappeared.

In September, Andrew was having problems with his eyes, so I took him to Dr. Riley, our eyes specialist who, after the examination, told him that he needed surgery to remove the cataracts. For some time, he knew that sooner or later he had to have that surgery. Even so, he was doubtful. I also had cataracts; and though my case was not urgent, to encourage him to go through the procedure, I decided to get my surgery first, and the end result was very good. Andrew went ahead with his surgery, and the end result was successful for him too.

For years, Andrew was having problem with his sleep, but now it had gone from bad to worse. He couldn't fall or stay asleep. It was really painful to see him going to bed and staying awake all night long! We visited a few doctors who always prescribed the latest sleeping drugs, but nothing was really effective. They were just good for a short while. Sleeping in the same bed was a problem for me too, so with his encouragement, I often went to a different room to get some sleep, and next I saw him coming to see if I was okay. Then due to the sleeping pills, Andrew started to have hallucinations at night. At this point, I didn't feel I could leave him in the master bedroom alone anymore, so we decided to replace our king bed with two twin beds.

2008 AND 2009 – VERY DIFFICULT YEARS

In January, Andrew went to Dr. Quillen for the follow-up on the mass in one of his kidneys, and everything seemed fine, and the next appointment was scheduled for June.

From time to time, Andrew was having a small pain on his right lower side, and it usually occurred when he was making a turn in bed; but one night, in early February, he told me that the pain on his right lower side was stronger than usual. Knowing that he was not a complaining man, I became very alarmed and was sure that something seriously wrong was going on. The following morning, without any appointment, I took him to Dr. Quillen who performed a CAT scan of the abdomen in his office, and from the result, he became concerned about a lymphoma, so he sent my husband to Dr. Cody, an oncologist, for a second opinion. In March, Dr. Cody ordered CAT scans of the neck and chest, and from the results, she was also concerned about a lymphoma, but she wanted to wait and see if any changes would occur, so she ordered more tests to be performed in three months.

In April 2008, I took Andrew to Dr. Balachandran because, besides the sleeping disorder, he could not walk. The doctor suggested seeing a psychiatrist. Fortunately, we found one in our area, Dr. Van Horne, a neuropsychiatrist who, after a long evaluation, prescribed some drugs. The most effective drug was Pristiq, an antidepressant. In a very short time, Andrew started to sleep and also to walk normally again. How happy he was to be able to sleep once again!

In the middle of June 2008, I took Andrew back to Dr. Cody for the CAT scans, and the results showed lymphadenopathy in the abdomen and chest. When the doctor told us that it was cancer, we remained apathetic, though we knew that cancer was a bad disease. We didn't think it was something very serious due to the medical progress, but how naïve we both were! In the past few months, Andrew had completely lost his appetite. I tried to prepare his favorite meals, but he was telling me that he could not eat; he was not hungry. At first, I thought that it was due to his dental work, but when I told Dr. Cody about his lack of appetite, she knew that the problem was the cancer. She prescribed Megestrol for the appetite and ordered a complete body PET/CT (positron emission tomography/computerized tomography) fusion image, and the result was adenocarcinoma of unknown origin. Then Dr. Cody sent Andrew to various specialists who performed other tests, such as laryngoscopy, colonoscopy, endoscopy, and an MRI of the brain, and the results of these tests were negative; no cancer found. But there was one more crucial test to be performed.

On June 30, I took Andrew to Dr. Huggins, a pulmonary specialist. After a consultation in his office, on the same day, the doctor performed a bronchoscopy and took a biopsy at Conway Hospital. While Andrew was recovering from the bronchial procedure, Dr. Huggins came to see me in the hospital lobby and gave me the terrible news. The result was that the cancer had already metastasized in the lungs so that my husband's prognosis was terminal and the origin of the cancer was unknown. Then he said to me that, in his opinion, Andrew had approximately three months to live. This was the biggest devastating news ever in my life. The dearest person who was also the only one I had on this earth was soon going to leave me. What terrifying news it was for me! In my entire life, I had always fought and worked hard for everything with success, but this time, I was helpless. I couldn't do anything, and the only thing left was to pray to God for strength and guidance. Being completely alone in facing this dreadful reality was horrible, and at the same time, I had to be strong to meet Andrew with a smile as if everything was going to be all right. The days, weeks, and months that followed were very difficult and painful for me. I could not look Andrew in the eyes and remain indifferent, but I tried very hard to keep my composure as calm as possible, though there were times when we were watching TV in the living room or sitting at dinner table, and

I had to go to another room because I could not hold my tears. Andrew didn't know the severity of the cancer. He was hoping for better days ahead.

Subsequently, Dr. Cody suggested chemotherapy if Andrew wanted to go through with it. Andrew didn't know that his cancer was terminal, so he hoped, and I too, that the chemo would help him. In order to select the drug for the chemotherapy, it was necessary to know the origin of the cancer, so after consultations among doctors, they reached the conclusion that the cancer had originated in the kidney. How strange that was because, for over three years since the discovery, the mass in the kidney never changed in size and the functioning of the kidneys was normal! Anyway, there were four types of medications for the renal cell carcinoma therapy, and it was up to us to choose one. We selected the Torisel, which had the fewer side effects. Andrew soon started the weekly chemotherapy treatment at the Coastal Cancer Center. Additionally, every two weeks, there was the infusion of a drug to increase the red blood cells and once a month, the infusion of a drug for the bones.

The Coastal Cancer Center was a small private clinic where many tests were performed on the premises. The therapy was done in a large and bright room with big windows, which had views of the beautiful trees. The room was furnished with many comfortable armchairs, and each chair was facing a television. In my opinion, the clinic made the place as attractive as possible for the patients to feel comfortable. The nurses were very kind, and, for the infusion of the drugs, they were doing their best to search for the veins in the arm of the patient. At the beginning, it was easy to find Andrew's vein, but after a while, it became very painful. Every time I took him for the chemo treatment, I stayed there sitting next to him, spending my time doing Sudoku.

After a few months of chemotherapy and the Megestrol intake for the appetite, Andrew started to feel much better. As a matter of fact, he often wanted to go out to a restaurant for lunch or to the movies, and also he enjoyed taking short walks. I couldn't believe how great he was doing! At the end of September, I took him to Dr. Cody's office for the follow-up. There they performed a CT scan on his chest, abdomen, and pelvic area. The images of the lymph nodes had decreased, and the doctor stopped the chemo for two weeks, then when I told the doctor how well Andrew was doing, she said to me, "But who knows for how long he will be feeling this way."

For the Christmas holidays, as in the previous years, we spent the 2008 Christmas day at our friends', the Giordanos. The dinner and the company were great, and we all had a good time.

Then the 2009 New Year's Day celebration was at our house, and we invited the Giordanos, the Letchs, and the Thompsons. I had ordered some food from the Omaha Steak Company in advance so that I had less cooking to do, and I tried my best to entertain our guests. For me, this year was a very difficult one. Andrew seemed to be restless. He was following me wherever I went and asking me if he could be of any help. I cannot describe how greatly tormented I was inside, thinking that, with all the probabilities, this was my last holiday with him! Anyway, all the guests enjoyed everything.

At the beginning of January 2009, I took Andrew to Dr. Cody's office for the follow-up, and all the results were unchanged.

Then on the evening of January 21, Andrew had the first excruciating symptom with his respiration. He went to a closet to take a small box with a few picture frames that he had recently bought, and when he tried to lift the box, he felt very weak and could not breathe. Subsequently, I helped him to lie down in bed, and soon after, he felt fine, but the following morning, I took him to Dr. Cody's office where they performed some tests. The red blood cells were too low. Therefore, Andrew received a drug to increase the red blood cells. Next, on the evening of January

24, Andrew had a second attack when he tried to get up from the armchair. He felt very weak and could not breathe. I immediately called 911, and when they arrived, Andrew was resting in bed and seemed fine, but I told the medics that this was his second occurrence. They took him by ambulance to Conway Hospital where he received his first blood transfusion and some oxygen that same night. Andrew remained hospitalized for five days, and I stayed with him every night. While in the hospital, Dr. Mills ordered more tests, and the conclusion was that Andrew's red blood cells and hemoglobin were very low. Andrew had more chemo treatments, an infusion of hydration fluid, an iron transfusion, and more CAT scans. The tests started to show some increase in the lymph nodes.

In March, Dr. Cody told Andrew that he could not continue to receive the chemo treatment anymore but that as soon as he was feeling stronger, she would prescribe medications for the cancer. The drug for the cancer, Torisel, had affected Andrew's kidneys. At this point, he asked the doctor what his prognosis was. It was sad to look at Andrew when the doctor answered that the prognosis was not good. He now became fully aware that there was no hope. What horrible news! I tried my best to give him some moral support by saying that nobody knows what the future holds for us and also mentioning my cousin Rosetta who was fighting her cancer battle for more than six years. My Myrtle Trace neighbor and friends knew about Andrew's illness, but I was the only one who was aware of the fatal prognosis. It was a huge burden for me not being able to share my concerns with anybody. The only family member I had in America was Andrew.

In April, even though he was weak, Andrew insisted to come with me to the Rooms To Go store to buy two chairs for our living room because the ones we had were not comfortable for him. At the store, he tried some, and we bought those that were comfortable for him. From the store, we went to the Red Lobster Restaurant for lunch where we both ate with great appetite. A few days later, we got the new chairs and, unfortunately, my husband was able to sit on the new chair only once.

At the end of April, Andrew received the second blood transfusion. On May 8, very worried and with some physical difficulty, I brought Andrew to his preferred Dr. Balachandran, who, as soon as he saw him, ordered me to take him to the hospital immediately. Besides the weakness, his breathing had become painful, and Dr. Balachandran ordered steroids and some other drugs. Subsequently, the breathing improved, but the weakness increased, and Andrew received the third blood transfusion and remained in the hospital until May 16. A day before leaving the hospital, two doctors suggested I place him in a nursing home because of the fact that I was alone at home and Andrew's health had deteriorated tremendously to the point that he needed twenty-four-hour assistance. For me, the idea of the nursing home was unacceptable. I told Andrew that I would get some help at home. At first, he didn't like the idea of having strangers around, but he then realized that there was no other choice. Afterward, Dr. Balachandran prepared some papers to obtain a health care group, and we went back home.

From May 18 to June 16, Andrew received the Amedisys health care at home. The group provided all the equipment necessary for him, and twice a week, a nurse, an aide, a therapist, and an occupational therapist came to visit him. I took care of the rest. After leaving the hospital, the first few days, Andrew felt much better at home. As matter of fact, during the day, he spent very little time in bed. Regarding the weekly therapy, Andrew did his best to go through with it, but it was hard to watch him struggle! The month with the Amedisys Health Care Group was coming to an end, and I was going to be left on my own. Knowing that my husband had a short time to live, I wanted to do the best I could for whatever time was left, but I needed some professional help because it was impossible to handle the situation by myself.

Therefore, I asked the nurse of the Amedisys for a recommendation, and she contacted Heartland Care.

From June 17 to July 17, the Heartland Hospice Care group came to see Andrew twice a week, and for extra help, I hired extra help from an agency in Conway. Janette, a nurse, Virginia, an aid, and Donna and Lydia, two social workers, were great and compassionate individuals. The nurse always asked Andrew if he had any pain or discomfort. It was unbelievable. He never complained of anything, except when he was doing the least movement, which caused him painful breathing that seemed to kill him.

On June 26, Andrew was complaining about his eyes, so I called Dr. Riley's office to see if I could bring him there. Fortunately, the doctor who knew the circumstances was able to see him without any appointment, but to bring him to the doctor was a big risk that I took just to please him. It was very difficult to help Andrew in and out of the car. When we arrived at the doctor's office, the nurses there were very helpful before and after the visit. Thank God, I brought him back home with no problem.

For a few weeks, Andrew's heath seemed unchanged; in fact, with my support, he was able to get up from bed and then went to eat at the kitchen table or went to his study, which was always his favorite place. All the rooms in the house were carpeted, so it was hard for me to push the wheelchair around. Using whatever strength he had left, Andrew tried to help and asked me if it was easier for me to push the wheelchair. He knew well that I was doing my best for him, and he attempted very hard to help me in any way he could.

One evening, lightning hit the neighbor's tree and did damage to our electric utilities. Some were completely destroyed; others had to be fixed, including the alarm system, which went on, indicating that there was a fire inside the house. Consequently, I looked throughout the house, and everything seemed fine. I tried to reset the alarm system but in vain. At this point, not knowing what was wrong, I called 911. In no time, the police and the firefighters arrived. They checked every room, went to the attic, and they found nothing wrong. Therefore, before leaving, they told me to call the alarm service. Close to midnight, I called the ADT, the alarm service. They started giving me instructions on what to do, and I was following their advice; but when I saw that it was taking too long to resolve the problem, I asked them to tell me how to disconnect the alarm. That was the only solution to stop the buzzing. What an eventful evening! Though there was so much commotion in the house, I was able to keep my cool and everything under control. Andrew, who was in bed, seeing the police, firefighters, and so forth, was telling me that he was sorry that he couldn't be of any help! It was too anguishing for me to watch him helpless and worry about me. The following day, I had a few things fixed, and the replacements were left for later.

During Andrew's illness, some neighbors often asked me if they could be of any help. Thank God for the strength he gave me for I was able to manage well all by myself. In addition, when I went out for some reason, I left someone with Andrew. Occasionally, I asked neighbors for some favor, such as doing a little shopping, which they gladly did. I remember the Fourth of July when Kitty Kenney Thompson came to our home with food and a beautiful plant of yellow roses. I planted the roses in front of the house, visible from the kitchen window for Andrew to see. Around July 10, I reached the point that I didn't want to go out and leave Andrew with strangers any longer because, the last few times I did, I found him very excited and disoriented when I came back home.

* * *

July 16 was filled with nice memories and sad happenings. That day, my husband didn't eat at all; he looked serene and was very thirsty. In fact, he continuously asked me for the red drink, which was cranberry juice. Then, when for a while he didn't, I asked him if he wanted a drink. I remember that warm smile and lovely look at me while gently touching my hands, and he would answer me yes. With all his discomfort, his concern for me was indescribable, and how can I forget that extraordinary behavior of exceptional tenderness and love. Certainly, it will remain impressed in my mind forever. The fact that I was alone in this difficult time and everything was proceeding very peacefully, I am sure that God was watching over both of us. That morning, I called Brenda, my hairdresser, to see if she could come to my house to give me a haircut. She said yes, and the scheduled day was for July 18. Next, when the nurse came to see my husband around 6 p.m., I told her that lately my husband had been very restless during the night and I thought that he had restless leg syndrome. She didn't say anything, and I learned much later that those were symptoms of the end of life. This evening, the nurse didn't see anything unusual with Andrew. She asked him a few questions and gave me some instructions. Before she left, I asked her if I could get some daily help, and she said yes, starting the following day.

The evening of July 16, it looked as if a bad sign was written in the sky. A strong storm burst out. From the windows, the lightning was brightening the rooms, and thunders were terribly loud. With my help, Andrew tried very hard to get out of bed, but it was in vain. His breathing was leaving him completely helpless, but he was not giving up. A little later, he tried again, and it was, again, pointless. It was the first time that he didn't succeed, and I sadly saw in his face a sign of agitation not seen before. While the storm was going on, I hoped that the lady I was waiting for to help me get Andrew comfortable for the night would show up. I alone couldn't manage it. However, thank God, she arrived around 10:30 p.m. and did what she had to do and left after 11:30 p.m. Afterward, as I was instructed by the nurse, I put a little morphine under my husband tongue, and he asked me what it was. I answered, "This is morphine to help your sleep." That was the last time we spoke. Attached to Andrew's bed was an alarm that, in case he was moving or something else, I could hear it. I went to sleep around midnight.

JULY 17, 2009 – THE MOST TRAGIC DAY OF MY LIFE

It was almost 6 a.m. when I woke up, and I immediately turned around to look at Andrew. During the night, I didn't hear any alarm going off, and I now noticed that he was motionless; his eyes were closed, and his breathing was abnormal. Without wasting any time, I called the Heartland Hospice office, asking if I had to call the 911. They said that they were on the way to my place. Just twelve hours had passed since the nurse had come to visit Andrew, and she didn't see any sign that his end was near.

It was during the night when Andrew's health suddenly deteriorated so drastically that by noon, he peacefully passed away, surrounded by me, Janette, and Lydia from the Heartland Hospice Care.

It is impossible to understand how I felt throughout Andrew's final hours and after his death. I acted and felt as though nothing was happening around me. In fact, it was like assisting a stranger on a dying bed, and after Andrew was gone, I went to the kitchen, ate breakfast, and, afterward, returned to the bedroom where his cold body was lying.

On this day, the Heartland Hospice people made all the necessary arrangements that normally family members do when a close relative dies. They stayed with me until the people from the Goldfinch Funeral Home came to take Andrew's body away, and they also notified Chaplain Mary Ann Braham to come and see me. Thank God for having sent these wonderful people who helped me before and after Andrew passed away!

Approximately two hours after Andrew's death, I received a phone call from Rome, Italy. It was from my niece Enza Arnone. The first thing Enza said to me was, "Zia Lina, in these last few days, Uncle Andrew has constantly been in my mind. How he is doing?" It looked like she had, had the premonition of what was happening. Anyway, after I gave her the sad news, she notified the Italian family members, and subsequently, my telephone started ringing without stop. My closest relatives were concerned and didn't know what to do; traveling to South Carolina from Italy was too complicated, and in addition, nobody spoke English. I told them not to worry about me. I had many good people around me, and I was doing fine, so we kept in touch by phone.

On July 18, Kitty Thompson put herself at my disposal. She drove me wherever I needed to go while her husband, George, was taking care of little Victoria who was less than two years old. Kitty also accompanied me to the Goldfinch Funeral Home for Andrew's funeral arrangements, which included the selection of the casket, the memorial service, the cremation, and the urn for the ashes. On that day, I notified Andrew's relatives in the Czech Republic of his death. Some of them wanted to come to South Carolina to be with me, but I convinced them that I was doing just fine. It was a nice gesture on their part, but for the time being, I didn't feel like having any company, especially knowing that there was the language barrier between us.

On July 19, Rosalie Giordano took me to the Goldfinch Chapel in Conway for the memorial service, which was led by Rev. Mary Ann Braham from the Heartland Hospice. There, Bob Ridgeway and Kitty Thompson, both from Myrtle Trace, gave a brief eulogy, which I appreciated enormously. Besides my immediate neighbors, some residents of Myrtle Trace community also attended the service. After the brief memorial service, some of the guests came to my place where Kitty, together with Helen and Christine Ridgeway, served food and drinks that they had provided.

On July 20, Andrew's body laid at the Goldfinch's chapel for the entire day. As expected, I didn't want to leave the embalmed body alone there and neither did I want to disturb my neighbors, so I went to the chapel by myself, but when kitty heard my car

start, she immediately came to the garage, and then with insistence, she took me to the chapel where I remained alone all day
long. How difficult it was to look at or touch the strange preserved body. I could not believe it was my husband there. How
suddenly it had all happened! Some personnel from Goldfinch
often came to the chapel to see that I was doing okay and asked
me if I needed anything. At closing time, Kitty returned to the
chapel and brought me back home. On July 21, Andrew was cremated, and a day later, Bob and Helen Ridgeway took me back to
the Goldfinch to pick up the urn with the ashes.

Each in their own way, my neighbors were wonderful, and they
certainly did a lot for me. Anyway, I can only say how lucky I was
that, in this difficult time, I had such good people around me.

COPING WITH MY GREAT LOSS

FOLLOWING MY HUSBAND'S DEATH

At first, I was too occupied with matters that kept me mentally and physically exhausted, but when the realization of the great loss started to sink into my mind, I felt that my entire world had collapsed; I was full of anguish. Days and weeks went by without a soul around me. My grief was my sole companion. All of a sudden, my life had no purpose; I had lost my husband and also the task of taking care of him. Although I knew that this day was coming, I still was not prepared for it, and when it happened, I could not believe how everything happened so rapidly!

When I retired from my job fourteen years earlier; at first, it took a little effort to become accustomed to each other on a daily basis, but afterward, we enjoyed each other's company. We did everything together, and we had become, I would say, inseparable. Maybe that happened because we didn't have any family in America. One of the few things that we didn't like was watching certain programs on television; Andrew liked sports, such as tennis, hokey, but I didn't care about these sports, so I watched something else, and many times during the commercial breaks, we had a drink or a snack together.

The sense of belonging to somebody very close to the heart is the most wonderful thing that a person can have in life, and because my case was particular, due to the fact that I had grown up without parents, this was a unique and beautiful experience. I had spent many satisfying and serene years with my husband and had enjoyed life in full. Practically, I had it all, and how fortunate I was! Now with Andrew gone, a part of me was gone too.

After his death, at the beginning, it was impossible to fall asleep, and the long sobbing nights were endless. During the day, sitting alone in the empty house was agonizing and how many times I hoped that someone would knock on the door or the telephone would ring! Nobody really knew what I was going through. The loneliness was unbearable, and my torment seemed to have no ending. When I was going through the house trying to do something, it was worse because the image of Andrew was everywhere. My thoughts were constantly on his kindness in my regard, especially during the last few months of his life. Taking into consideration how ill he was, I could only say that he was an unusually brave man who made my loss more heartbreaking.

The closest neighbors often called me to find out how I was doing and to let them know if I needed something. I didn't call anybody because I didn't want to trouble them with my sorrow and especially knowing that each one of them had their own problems. However, I remember the Ridgeways. The first evening without Andrew, Helen wanted to stay with me for the night, and I convinced her that I was just fine, and then she brought me food that lasted for a few days. Then there was Kitty Thompson whose kindness and warmth was really special. For more than a month, Kitty came to my place every evening and spent a few hours with me, while her husband George took care of their little granddaughter Victoria. There were also the Giordanos who showed plenty of thoughtfulness. Last, but not least, I had my friend Dina Horowitz who called me every night after 9 p.m.

After more than two months from his death, I started to be realistic; being left on my own, I had to force myself to take care of my personal affairs, whether I liked it or not. I had nobody to do that for me. At the beginning, it was really difficult to make calls, and it was worse when I had to say that my husband had passed away. That was too much of an effort for me to continue the conversation, and consequently, many times, I had to excuse myself by telling the people on the other end that I would call them back. Going out for the basic food shopping or for some business was very stressful, and I couldn't wait to get back home.

To keep my mind occupied, I started working feverishly at home, from morning until late in the evening, going through the many books on various subjects and in several languages that Andrew had collected over the years. This was one of his hobbies. I began with the big bookcase. Little by little, I separated the books and decided what to do with them. I brought those that were in good conditions to the Myrtle Beach library, and the others that I thought were worthless went to the Conway dump for recycling. Therefore, in no time, ten shelves were completely emptied. Before getting seriously sick, Andrew tried to give away some of the books, magazines, and more to people that he knew. Some of them came and took whatever they wanted, and now that he was gone, the task to get rid of the remainder was mine.

Next, I went through the file cabinets and the desk drawers. There were documents of several categories, and some were more than fifty years old as Andrew never threw away anything that he liked. Anyway, this undertaking kept me busy for quite some time. I found some notes that I had written to Andrew before we got married. Believe me, it was very touching to see my writings so well kept that, at a certain point, I had to stop working for the day. Going through his files and drawers, I didn't find anything unusual, proving that there were no secrets between us until the end. Our relationship was really profound and sincere, and the appreciation of what I had and what I just lost was now multiplied.

I also destroyed a big bundle of sheets with notations pertaining to telephone numbers, dates, and times, which Andrew had written over time. For many years, he was suspicious of the many unknown telephone calls or when taking the telephone receiver, people on the other end, were not speaking. I tried to convince him to ignore those anonymous calls, but he could not help himself. He was telling me that I was too naïve for not understanding that there were many wicked people in the world who want to hurt some individuals. I remember when coming home with him, many times, I ran to the telephone and deleted any recorded messages to avoid Andrew's apprehension and my uneasiness. He didn't know that I understood him completely. In my opinion, it all had to do with the trauma experienced in his younger years.

Subsequently, in our garage, there were fourteen big boxes full of paper, such as drafts on banking procedures, newspapers, magazines, and so forth. The drafts on banking, which were written in English, German, and French, had been written by Andrew several years back for his books, which he never finished, and later, he learned that all his work had become obsolete. I went through every piece of paper just to make sure that there was nothing worthwhile. Many of the newspapers in foreign languages dated back to 1964. Over the years, Andrew saved all with the intention that someday he would review them again. Among the magazines were old *Playboys* and banking materials. It was a huge job, but I had plenty of time on my hands, and the work distracted me from my purposeless life.

After a while, I went to my lawyer to take care of our estate. It was my first unpleasant trip to his office, and that seemed an eternity because, just a year earlier, I was there with Andrew to update our wills. The lawyer told me to compile the assets and bring the list together with the last five years of tax returns. Although everything was in both our names, everything had to go to the probate because there were some changes to be made and tax implications too.

This period of my life was demanding in two ways as I had no husband and no family to turn to, and being completely lonesome, I had to put extra effort to help myself overcome my sorrow. Up to now, at home, I needed absolute silence to be immersed in my own thoughts, and every slight noise was very wearisome. Then little by little, I came to realize that though I hated to turn the radio or television on, I needed to hear human voices and see people's faces to bring some distraction to my lonely existence. I was spending most of the time in Andrew's beloved study. The television there had been destroyed by the storm, so I went to a store in Myrtle Beach with Helen and Bob Ridgeway, my good neighbors, and bought a TV, and afterward, Bob installed it.

* * *

At the beginning of October 2009, I decided to invite Donna Dowell, Lydia Jennings, and Chaplain Marian Braham from the Heartland Hospice Care for lunch at my place. I want to mention some particular episodes regarding Donna, the blond, and Lydia, the brunette, who had brought so much joy to Andrew in his final days. Every time they came to visit him, he was always more than glad to see them, but the last time was different for it looked like he had forgotten his illness. In fact, while the ladies were holding his hands and carefully listening to him with amazement, he was talking with a great nostalgia about our world voyages and about the Hungarian and Czech cuisines. It was wonderful to see him so happy with them and, at the same time, looking at me with a sweet smile! Mentally, he was in full control, and until the end, he really enjoyed being surrounded by beautiful women. I promised Andrew and the ladies that on their next visit, I would serve them a poppy seed cake, a Hungarian sweet that was also Andrew's favorite cake. Unfortunately, it didn't happen due to his sudden death. However, I didn't forget my promise. Anyway, the ladies gladly accepted my invitation. I served Italian food for lunch, and for dessert, I served the poppy seed cake. We ate in the kitchen and not in the dining room for it was too much for me to see Andrew's empty seat. When the ladies had finished their meal, I gave each of them a crystal gift from the Czech Republic as a remembrance from Andrew. They were all pleasantly surprised in receiving the nice gift, and I was certain that Andrew would have liked that! For a while, Donna and Marian came to visit me quite often.

*　*　*

There were days when the loneliness was making me very miserable, and I didn't feel like doing anything. However, when my mind was clear, I knew that I could not continue going on with my life in this way. I had to do my best to make it easier, and in my desolation, I prayed to God and the Virgin Mary for guidance and strength.

I was sure that I was not the only person in the world going through grief, and I was looking for people who fully understood my situation, so I went on the internet looking for a support group and found many of them. The Mercy Hospice support group was the closest to my home, so I wrote down the address and went there by myself. However, when I arrived there, I could not enter the premises because I was deeply moved; my tears were uncontrollable, and so I returned home. The next day, I sent an e-mail to the Mercy Hospice for information. I immediately got their answer, inviting me to go there. I went for the interview, but I was unable to talk; I just wrote down my answers. The lady who interviewed me told me that it was too early for me to attend the support group, then she added, "But if you want to come, you are welcome." Normally, people joined the support group after six months from the death of their loved ones, and in my case, it was less than three months since Andrew had passed way.

The grief support group offered by the Mercy Hospice Care had six sessions, having it done once a week. The next available session was starting on October 10, 2009. The leader, Rev. Loran Bulla, a former military chaplain, was a wonderful and caring person, and in my opinion, it seemed that he had gone through some loss himself. The group consisted of three grievers. Before starting the first session, the attendees introduced themselves. James Lannoo had lost his wife one month after Andrew had passed away. Debby had lost her girlfriend three years earlier and still had a hard time coping with her loss, and the third griever was me. James lived in Myrtle Trace, in my community, so when the days became short, he came to pick me up, and we went to the sessions together. Most of the time, I was unable to talk so that I passed when it was my turn. I also preferred to listen to the others who were telling their stories and expressing their feelings with a depth of despair. I was not alone. We were all more or less in the same situation. When I arrived at the session earlier, a few times, Rev. Bulla did his best to help me to open up and express myself. He was a great man and very understanding. I was looking forward to go to the meetings, and in a certain way, it was helping me.

Every week, there was a new subject for the group; for instance, "Care of the Body, Mind, and Spirit," "Memory and Moving Forward," "Comfort and Growing with Poetry," and "Comfort and Growing with Music."

Rev. Bulla told us to write down a poem related to our loved one and bring it to the last session. Even though I was not a poet, I did my best in putting down a few lines. On our last session, a beautiful young lady by the name of Lea Mack Compton came to the meeting with a guitar. After she introduced herself and explained why she had come, she gave us a sheet with musical rhythms on which we had to mark down the rhythm of our choice and return the paper, together with our poem, to her. Then Ms. Lea started to sing by using our poetry with the selected rhythm. She began with the information provided by Debby, then by James, and last by me. Listening to Ms. Lea's beautiful angelic voice and her way of singing the poetry was wonderful. My poem, which was not flowing as such, was as follows:

> I remember the day when I met Him,
> It was during transportation strike in New York City.
> I was at the 84th street corner waiting for a taxi cab,
> A car stopped there
> The man next to the driver asked me where I want to go.
> Wall Street, I said.
> So do I, the man replied,
> Then with a smile he said
> My name is Andrew Janovitz; can I give you a lift?
> Yes, I answered.
> Thus it happened on that day
> When I got a ride and met my future husband too!

Ms. Lea liked my poem so much that she sang it twice. I couldn't stop crying. It was magic in the way she delivered it, and I also vividly remembered that day in January of 1966.

We were all pleasantly surprised that Mercy Hospice Care offered so much for free! At the end, we thanked Rev. Bulla and Ms. Lea for everything and said good-bye. One week later, I got an invitation from the Mercy Hospice to attend "Managing Grief during the Christmas Holidays," which was lead by Rev. Bulla. I went with James Lannoo to the Coastal Grand Mall where the meeting was taking place. There I found other attendees of all ages who were coping with the loss of their loved ones, and as usual, Rev. Bulla gave a great speech with words of comfort. Afterward, there were cookies, drinks, and little mementos for everybody.

It is unbelievable how many dedicated and generous people and organizations there are in America!

Next, I decided to start going to church. I was never a churchgoer, although I never stopped believing in God and praying to him in my own way. At the end of October, I asked my friend Rosalie Giordano from Myrtle Trace if I could go to Saint James Church with her on Sunday, and she was delighted. I went once and then stopped because I was not ready yet. Three weeks later, I tried again to go to the house of worship, and to this day, I continue going there with Rosalie every Sunday.

Then I wanted to have a nice portrait of Andrew to hang on the wall, but that was not as easy as it seems because, all his life, Andrew hated to be photographed alone so that I didn't have anything of him to get my wish. Anyway, I gave an old passport photo to a friend of mine from Myrtle Trace, Thea Letch, who painted a nice portrait of Andrew. Taking into consideration how worn the old photo was, she did a wonderful job. After I had the portrait framed, I could not hang it on the wall for several months because, looking at Andrew's image, it was just too painful!

THE BIBLE STUDY

It was already the end of November; no more support group to go to. The church was only on Sundays, and the rest of the week, I was left with my loneliness and inner turmoil. I physically felt tired of doing nothing, and I was now looking for something to keep my sanity. I knew of the Bible study that was taking place every Monday morning at the Myrtle Trace clubhouse, but I didn't know any of the participants. One Monday, I went there by myself and asked the group if I could join them. A very attractive lady by the name Alta Fox warmly welcomed me with a big hug and offered me a chair to sit next to her. She was the leader of the study group. Then the rest of the people introduced themselves, and among them, I met Phoebe Lee. That day, I could not talk, and in a certain way, they all understood my situation, and the Bible study went on while I did my best to keep my emotions under control. I had never attended any Bible study, but as the weeks passed, I started to be more relaxed and began to participate in the reading. As the weeks went by, Phoebe called me and came to pick me up, and together, we went to the Bible study where Alta, to this day, welcomes me with a nice smile and a hug, while Phoebe became one of my best friends. About the Bible class's participants, they are too many to mention their names, but I can say they are all wonderful people who make me feel quite comfortable.

Once a week, I also joined the volunteer group at the Kingston Nursing Home. My purpose for joining the activity was to visit some lonesome and disabled residents and, occasionally, on a small scale, to give a hand to the employees there. This home is associated with the Conway Medical Center; it has very dedicated employees who really try to do their best to give a family atmosphere to the residents.

Nevertheless, like any nursing home, it is a sad place to be. Because of my foreign accent, very often, some of the residents want to know where I came from, and when I tell them I came from Italy, they smile, and soon after, they start to speak their minds. For me, it is rewarding to see the people smiling and wanting me to come back to visit them!

DINA HOROWITZ

Throughout the gloomiest period of my life, Dina was the person who tremendously helped me morally. I was feeling terribly lonesome, and she was there for me. I had never imagined that she would be so sympathetic in my regards. It is during the most distressing times that we discover who our real friends are!

I met Dina in the late 1970s at TIAA-CREF in New York City. In that period, TIAA-CREF was in great need of good computer programmers and system analysts and reached out to the New York University to get the best and brightest students. Dina was one of the chosen pupils. Her intelligence and analytical mind was incredible, and that I know for a fact because from the first day on which she was hired, we worked on the same projects. I was an old employee with years of experience in the computer field, and she was just out of school, but her thinking and quick grasp of the issues seemed that she already had some experience. Equally reserved by nature, we felt at ease working on the same projects. Every day, we had lunch together, and soon after, we became friends. More than once, Dina and Dr. Horowitz, her husband, invited my husband and me to their house in New Jersey for lunch. The meals were great, but what impressed us most was the beautiful way the fruit was arranged on a nice big platter. We reciprocated the invitation at our place in Queens just once and precisely in 1983. They came with their beautiful daughter Yael, who was about three years old. Subsequently, instead of eating at my place, we went to a kosher restaurant.

In the late eighties, Dina resigned from TIAA-CREF to pursue her wish. She already had two children and wanted to dedicate more time to her family, which was the most important thing in her life. When she left, I was really sad because she was the only good friend I had there. A little later, for personal reasons, she started working again but not at TIAA-CREF, and while I was still working in the city, from time to time, we got together for lunch until I retired and moved to South Carolina. Afterward, Dina and I kept in touch with each other through phone calls, post cards from trips, and holiday wishes. During the happy traveling years, on our return from Europe, many times, we stayed in New York City for a few days, and almost always, we met Dina who insisted on taking us to a restaurant in Manhattan for lunch. She was a warm, kind, and generous person, but she never talked about herself, her job, or her family. Of her three children, I only knew her firstborn, Yael. There was a period in which we didn't have much contact until the month of June 2009 when Dina called me and I told her that Andrew was terminally ill. I was very glad to hear from her, but I had to cut the conversation short because Andrew needed me. The days that followed, Dina often called to inquire about Andrew and how I was coping, and I told her that everything was proceeding as expected.

Then a few days after Andrew's sudden death, Dina just called me to inquire. There was a lump in my throat; I only gave her the terrible news and cut the phone call short. Dina was much occupied with her office managerial job and her family of four, but after Andrew's death, she found the time to call me every night after 9 p.m. She was often on the phone for more than an hour, and many times, she was waiting on the other end quietly. She understood that I was too emotional to be able to talk. I was really down with an unimaginable loneliness, and Dina was the only one who sincerely cared about me, and her enormous patience in my regards was incredible! I had never known a person with so much kindness.

At the end of August 2009, Dina took a day off from her job and flew from New Jersey to Myrtle Beach just to visit me. I cannot describe how pleased I was in meeting her when I went to the airport to pick her up and also could not stop thinking that she was the only person who came from far away to see me. At home, after lunch, I introduced Dina to some of my friendly neighbors—the Thompsons, the Giordanos, the Ridgeways and the Letchs and afterward, I took her for a long walk on the beach in Myrtle Beach. Then I was disappointed when Dina informed me that she was not staying at my place for the night for she had already reserved the hotel room, and so that evening, I stayed with her at the hotel. After supper, I asked Dina how her children were doing and if she had any photos of them. After a short pause, she showed me a photo of her youngest daughter, Keren, and told me that the girl was disabled. I looked at the photo, and I just saw a lovely girl! Anyway, even though Dina's sojourn was for only one day, her coming brought a lot of relief and the knowledge that somebody really cared about me; this day was indeed special for me. I never expected so much from a friend, and as long as I live, I will always remember Dina's goodness with an enormous appreciation. Her behavior was more than family to me! Dina's evening phone calls continued and carry on to this day. I had to be thankful not just to her but to her husband too for his patience and understanding by letting his wife spend time with me on the phone.

Remaining completely alone and without any family members in America, I started to be concerned about my new situation. In fact, it had become a problem that I had to resolve. When Andrew was sick, I made all the decisions for him. Now that he was gone, if something should happen to me, I didn't have anybody to make the choices for me. I mentioned my concern to Dina, and she told me not to worry and that she could help me. Subsequently, when I went to my lawyer to file the changes of my new status, Dina, with her husband's consent, became my power of attorney.

On January 10, 2010, Dina, again, came to visit me for one day; this time, she stayed at my place, and that made me very happy. Nothing could compensate for her generosity and kindness. She is an exceptional human being! Sometime later, Dina and her husband went to Israel for two weeks, and to make sure that I was doing okay, she entrusted her daughter Elana with the phone calls. Elana telephoned me every evening, and like her mother, she was great too. To come to the point, Dina is my best and unique friend who I will treasure forever.

SEARCHING FOR AND FINDING PEACE

MAY 2010 – THE FIRST VOYAGE TO ITALY WITHOUT ANDREW

Approximately ten months had passed since Andrew's death, and I felt an enormous need to go to some place for a while, but I wanted to wait until his first anniversary to take any action. However, because I was feeling terribly depressed and the loneliness was alarming to the point that it was affecting my mind, at least I thought it was, on instinct, I decided to go to Italy. In my heart, I knew that Andrew understood and wanted me to be with my family. Of course, I envisioned the trip to be very stressful, long, and lonely too.

My friend Rosalie took me to Myrtle Beach's airport from where I flew to Charlotte. In Charlotte, I waited for eight hours before taking the flight for Rome where I waited for another six hours. Luckily, my nephew Vincenzo came with his wife to the Rome Airport to meet me and stayed with me until I left for Reggio. When I boarded the plane, I felt a little ill and asked the passenger sitting next to me to get me some water. The flight attendant brought me the water and then asked me if the plane could leave. It was awful to be alone, but thank God, after a few sips, I felt much better. It had been twenty-five long hours since I had left my house in South Carolina. The trip had been very stressful, and I had not reached the destination yet. Finally, the plane landed at Reggio Airport where I found my niece Alida with her family, waiting to take me to their home.

In Condofuri Marina, upon entering the apartment, I immediately noticed how bad my brother's health condition was. His Parkinson's disease was very noticeable. I left Condofuri Marina two days later and planned to come back before returning to the USA. I went to Reggio for the flight to Rome, and then to Pisa.

In Pisa, the meeting with my niece Giuseppina and her husband was emotional as I was alone. At the airport, they took me to the bar for a cappuccino first, and then we went to their home where I met their daughter Irene. Last time I saw Irene was four years before, and now, at the age of thirteen, she was a fully developed young teenager. The following weekend, I met their son, Giovanni, who came home from his military station in Grosseto for two days. Just one week earlier, the Bartolomeos went to Fossano, Italy, to participate in the solemn occasion of their son's oath to the Italian Republic. Therefore, this was the first time I saw Giovanni in military uniform, and he looked very attractive.

It was nice to witness how the entire family seemed to enjoy each other! Giuseppina and Pino were wonderful to me. Their warmth and kindness in a pleasant home environment made me feel really good, and that gave me a much-needed boost to my life. They told me if I decided to move back to Italy, they would be more than happy to have me living close to them. I liked their concern in my regard very much.

After eleven peaceful days, I flew from Pisa to Palermo where I was greeted by my nephew Giovanni Giudice, Cousin Rosetta's son, who was waiting at the airport to take me to his mother's home. During the ride to Palermo, Giovanni and I had a very pleasant conversation; I remembered how well-mannered and quiet he was as a young boy! Giuseppe, Giovanni's brother, also came to the airport, but we missed each other, and we met later at his mother's home.

I stayed in Palermo for five days with my cousin Rosetta. This was our first meeting since she had lost her husband one year before I lost Andrew so that without words, we understood each other. In addition to the big loss, Rosetta had been fighting her terminal cancer for almost seven years, and for the moment, it seemed that she was feeling a little better. For the occasion of my visit, Rosetta's four children—Franca, Giovanni, Giuseppe, and Tony—with their families, organized a family gathering at their mother's home. Thomas, Giovanni's youngest son, didn't want to be at the gathering, but I was able to convince him, and so he came with his father. The evening reunion was very pleasant, especially for my cousin Rosetta.

During my stay in Palermo, as usual, Giuseppe did his best to be available to take me wherever I needed to be. To drive around Palermo is not an easy task as the congestion is unreal, the discipline of the drivers is near zero, and the parking is a huge problem.

It had been more than ten years since I saw my aunt Marietta Butticé Ricotta, then ninety-seven years of age, and before returning to the USA, I wanted to visit her. My cousin Rosetta also wished to see her. They were not related but knew each other from our hometown. Giuseppe took us to my aunt's entrance door where Marietta's son was waiting for us. The reunion of the four of us, Marietta, Rosetta, cousin Gino, and me, was touching and warm, and in no time we started recalling the old days with great nostalgia—Rosetta in particular, because she knew my aunt better than me. Meanwhile, Gino offered us express coffee and Sicilian sweets. Then two hours later, Giuseppe came back to Aunt Marietta's to take his mother and me to his home where Pinella was waiting to serve supper. Here, too, we spent a lovely evening with Giuseppe's family, and at the end, everybody accompanied us home in Via Lombardia, which was very familiar to me since my last residence in Palermo was also on this two-block street.

At home, Rosetta and I had many fond memories to talk about, especially when we went through some of the photo albums. Together, we also went to the nearby open market, visited some relatives, and so forth. Altogether the time spent with my cousin and her family was wonderful, what impressed me most was Rosetta's strong willpower. It was terrific! Next, Giuseppe accompanied me to my other cousins' home.

Franco and Adalgisa Martorana's home, where I stayed for three days, was unfamiliar to me. It was a big and beautiful apartment located in an exclusive area near the Politeama Theatre in the center of Palermo. Here I met their son Ferdinando, whom I hadn't seen for several years, and that same evening, the cousins took me to their daughter Maria Gabriella's home to meet her family—Gabriella's husband Goffredo Naselli, and their two children, Marta and Francesco. Marta had just received her first communion, so they showed me the pictures taken in the church and in other places for the occasion. The photos were gorgeous, and Marta looked like an angel, and I also got a silver memento.

The following day, the Martoranas invited Rosetta Giudice to their home for lunch, and I was very pleased for that. The Martoranas and the Giudices were not related, but Franco and Rosetta knew each other from their childhood, so their acquaintance and friendship was an old one. When Franco called Rosetta, she didn't feel like accepting the invitation, but then knowing that I was there, she convinced herself to come. Franco and I went to pick her up. Returning to the Martoranas' home, Adalgisa had already done her best. The dinner table was elegantly prepared with embroidered tablecloths and silverware, and the food was ready to be served. Entering the residence, Rosetta received a very warm welcome. It was really fantastic, and I felt very happy for her. Once seated at dinner table, the animated conversation between Franco and Rosetta began. There was so much nostalgia in both my cousins' voice when talking about the old times, people, and places, and what a tremendous lift it was for her! In conclusion, this was a really special day, very pleasant and memorable for all of us. In the middle of the afternoon, Franco and I brought Rosetta back home, and then in saying good-bye, I had a lump in my throat, knowing of the ordeal she was going through in her life. She had also told me that she didn't like to go out because coming back to an empty house was worse than before leaving. I understood well how she felt; the "used to be happy" home was now without a soul!

Toward evening, I went with Franco and Adalgisa for a ride to Mondello where my cousins have a villa with a beautiful view of the sea and the mountains. While staying with the Martorana, Franco and I enjoyed taking strolls in the center and in the historic district of Palermo every day, and the walks were accompanied by pleasant and warm conversations. Across the street from my cousins' home, other cousins of mine, Elio and Graziella Ricotta, had a nice boutique, so I went there to meet them, and at the same time, I bought some fashionable clothing. At the end of my trip in Palermo, my niece Alida, her husband, and their son came at the Martoranas' home to take me back to Reggio Calabria. It had been a long time since Franco had seen Alida, and I don't know why, in meeting her and her family, he became so overwhelmed to the point that I could not believe my eyes, and that pleased me a lot. Franco wanted the guests to stay for lunch, but there was no time.

I returned to Condofuri Marine to spend the last ten days in Italy with my brother and was glad I did so. I remembered Vincenzo as an energetic man, but now he was a different person due to the Parkinson's disease. What a terrible syndrome! Thank heavens that his daughter Alida was taking care of him even though she had her own family to think about. During my stay there, I slept at Alida's home for the first time, and she made sure that her place was as pleasant and peaceful as possible. She also expressed her desire to have me living close to her instead of living alone in America.

At the end, Nino accompanied me to Reggio's airport from where I flew to Rome and then to the USA. Arriving in South Carolina, my good neighbor friend George was at the Myrtle Beach airport to take me home.

The accomplishment of my compulsory trip to Italy was incredibly beneficial. The time spent with the family and their encouragement and love were a great boost to my morale, and despite the fact that my life without Andrew would never be the same, I returned home, to some extent, more relaxed and at peace with myself. Soon after, I restarted my old daily routine—taking long walks alone or with my friend Phoebe, meeting a few friends from time to time, and so forth—and when my frame of mind permitted, I continued working on the memoir that I had begun before my trip.

Later in 2010, I went to New Jersey to attend Dina's daughter's wedding. That was a nice break and a good opportunity for me to spend a few days with Dina and her family.

Unfortunately, my peace of mind didn't last for long as I was very sad and lonely. The ups and downs began, and my loneliness was again worrisome. After a lot of thought, I came up with the idea of going back to Italy and finding out if I would like to move there permanently in order to be close to my relatives, and so I did.

SPRING OF 2011 – THE THREE-MONTH TRIAL IN ITALY

Obviously, prior to any decision, I wanted to experience living in the places that I was considering moving to.

San Giovanni alla Vena, Pisa, was the first stop. After spending a few days with my niece Giuseppina and her family, I flew to Reggio to get to Condofuri Marina.

In Condofuri Marina, I spent ten days with my brother, his daughter Alida, and her family. I felt okay at home with the relatives, but outside life was really oppressive. Definitively, this town was not the right place for me. While here, I went to Palermo with Alida's husband to visit my cousin Rosetta who was seriously ill. It was just a one-day round trip, and the distance was quite long. After ten days, I flew from Reggio to Pisa, and then my nephew, Pino Bartolomeo, drove me to Vicopisano.

In Vicopisano, I stayed for twenty days at a bed and breakfast to experience living on my own. I kept myself busy by going around in this part of Tuscany and learning the area. Afterward, I went to the Pisa railroad where I took the train for Rome. Here, at the railroad station, I met Vincenzo and Enza Arnone who were waiting to take me to their home.

While in Rome, I stayed at a bed and breakfast for five days. That was my wish, and every day, I went to my nephew Vincenzo's place, which was just two blocks away from the B and B. The entire Arnone's family, comprised of Vincenzo, Enza, Adriano, Rita, and Daniela, didn't know what to do first to make me happy. Among the historic places, with Vincenzo we visited the interior of the coliseum. For me, it was the first time inside, and I found it very impressive. Then we went to Tivoli, which is an ancient Italian town roughly thirty kilometers from Rome. It has many beautiful attractions such as the Esta Villa, the theater, the castles, and much more. I spent lovely evenings all over Roma, and it was amazing for me to stay out until after 1 a.m. At the Arnones' place, I also met some other relatives, Maria Pia Fantauzzo and her husband Ninni Panneri, who just happened to be in Rome. On my last day in Rome, the family took me to a restaurant near the Vatican, and afterward, we went to Parco Adriano for a stroll. From here, we could marvel at the majestic towering cylindrical building of Castel Sant'Angelo, which was originally a mausoleum, then fortress and is now a museum.

To conclude, I never anticipated spending such delightful time in Rome with my relatives whose behavior was extraordinary. For me, it was like being on a wonderful Roman holiday!

The Arnones then drove me back to Vicopisano where they stayed at the same bed and breakfast for two days since they wished to visit the city of Pisa. On the way to Vicopisano, my nephew, Pino Bartolomeo, came to meet us on the outskirts of the town, and then he lead the way to his home in San Giovanni Alla Vena where his wife had already prepared a superb supper for everybody. Giuseppina, my brother's daughter, and Vincenzo, my cousin Lina's son, were second cousins, and it had been a long time since they had seen each other, so their reunion was very interesting. After a nice evening at the Bartolomeos', Pino accompanied the guests and me to the bed and breakfast for the night. The following day, we all went to Pisa where we had a marvelous time.

The second time in Vicopisano, I stayed at the bed and breakfast for five weeks. I wanted to be by myself and, at the same time, be close to Giuseppina and Pino Bartolomeo's family. The B and B was a nice residential house in a beautiful green environment and had many good amenities at the guests' disposal, and practically, I was free to do whatever I wanted. Being by myself, I had plenty of time to go around and observe the real Italian life, but after three weeks, I got bored and had no more interest in learning the way people were coping with their daily living. Therefore, during the last two weeks at the B and B, I went to the Bartolomeos' every day and stayed there until later in the evening when my nephew drove me back to the B and B.

Toward the end of my trip in Italy, I moved from the bed and breakfast to the Bartolomeos' house where I stayed for ten more days. I felt much better to be with the family. The following weekend, the family took me to Volterra where we spent an interesting day. Volterra is an ancient town well known all over the world for its historic happenings and Etruscan remains. These are the places that I enjoy seeing.

Next, I decided to revisit my ailing cousin Rosetta before returning to the USA. I flew to Palermo with my nephew Pino, and there, we stayed at the police headquarter's guesthouse for two nights; being part of the police force, my nephew had that advantage. In Palermo, Giuseppe, Rosetta's son, insisted and took us to a nice restaurant in Montello where we were joined by his family, and after lunch, he drove us to his mother. There I met the entire Giudice family and found Rosetta in an awful condition, and notwithstanding her situation, she was very happy to see me. In fact, after I left her place, she was calling for me. I also met my niece Serena, her husband Maurizio Biondolillo, and their two daughters, Martina and Samdra, who had come from Casteltermini to Palermo. I was glad to have returned to Palermo as this was the last time I saw Rosetta. Then I flew back to Pisa where I spent my last day in Italy.

* * *

After I returned home, I was overjoyed to receive relatives from Italy. The first group to come to the United States was my niece Giuseppina Bartolomeo and her family, and later, the second group was my nephew Giuseppe Giudice and his family.

Subsequently, my neighbor friend Kitty Kenney Thompson asked me to be the godmother to her granddaughter Victoria. I did not expect that at my age. I was really surprised and honored at the same time. I happily accepted the request, and so, for the first time, I became a godmother.

Regarding my move to Italy, the three months tryout there made me realize that, anywhere I go, nothing could change my innermost feeling. I came back home in South Carolina convinced more than ever that I am better off staying where I currently live.

In spite of being lonesome, I will never find a place like Myrtle Trace where I have almost everything I need. Thus, I conclude by putting my future in God's hands.

AUGUST 27, 2013 – THE BURIAL AT SEA

Suddenly I decided to give my husband's ashes a final resting place. Until now, I had kept Andrew's ashes in an elegant wooden box in my living room, with the intention that someday I would do something special with them. Because my husband and I had no family members in America, both of us thought that the best burial would be to have our ashes scattered at sea.

The Burial at Sea for my husband's ashes took place aboard the Scuba Express Boat off the coast of Myrtle Beach. The boat departed from Snug Harbor in Murrells Inlet, South Carolina, and traveled through the scenic Murrells Inlet to the predetermined latitude and longitude in the Atlantic Ocean. Once we reached the destination, the vessel motor stopped. My friend Dina Horowitz, who had flown from New Jersey to Myrtle Beach for the occasion, conducted a Jewish invocation first, and then my friend Phoebe Lee recited a Christian prayer, during which everybody joined in. Next, as I was opening the bag with Andrew's ashes, a yellow butterfly appeared, and it stayed there until all the guests finished tossing flowers in the sea. What a beautiful symbol to appear at that moment! Three miles out in the ocean…

Then, as the vessel circled the dispersal site as a final tribute, we saw three dolphins jumping in the ocean, and that was another beautiful scene! Present at the memorial were twenty-four guests, all friends of ours.

It was a very sad day for me but, at the same time, I felt very satisfied because everything went better than I had planned. The weather was fantastic. The sky was blue, the sea was calm, and the temperature was mild. It was just a perfect day to finally give rest to my husband's remains. Thank God that my friend Dina expressly came for the memorial. What she did for me was more than a close family member could have done in such an occurrence.

From above I am sure that Andrew enjoyed every moment of the ceremony in his honor. For me he was present in a butterfly form and looking on me with a pleasant smile!

Rome 2011, inside the Colisseum with Vincenzo Arnone

In the outskirts of Rome with Vincenzo's family, Enza, Rita and Daniela

Volterra 2011, With Giuseppina and Irene

August 2011 – The Italian relatives at my home in Myrtle Trace
In the photo are Giuseppina, Pino and Irene
Bartolomeo and my friend Phoebe Lee

This is a lovely photo of my niece Irene who
had a certain attraction to my mailbox

June 2012 in New York City - At the Statue
of Liberty with my Italian relatives.
From left: Lorenzo, Giuseppe, Giuliana, Pinella and Marco Giudice.

2012, Giuseppe rowing the boat, while Pinella, Dina, and
I were enjoying the surrounding in Central Park

In New York City - With Dina Horowitz

The 4th of July, 2012 – The Giudice's Family
and friends at my home in Myrtle Trace

With the wonderful bible study group of Myrtle Trace

April 7, 2012, Victoria J. Black, my godchild

With Victoria and her grandmother, my good
friend Kitty, in front of my home

Andrew Janovitz
born on the 24th of April, 1924
died on the 17th of July, 2009
buried at sea on the 27th of August, 2013

Four years have passed since your soul departed this world.
You left me alone here for a better place up there with God.
You went away without saying goodbye to me.
I kept your cremated body with me until now.
Today your ashes finally find a resting place in the Atlantic Sea,
As it was your wish.
Goodbye, my dearest Andrew, until we meet again **"Al di là"**.
Lina Janovitz

The boat for the burial

Dina and I listening to the boat instructor explaining the procedures for the memorial service.

With Phoebe Lee

Scattering my husband's ashes in the Atlantic Ocean

Tossing flowers at the burial site

With Kitty Kenney-Thompson

Dina and I with Alta Fox.

From far, Liz Maass, Barbara and Paul DiAngelantonio,
Jim Lannoo, me, and Lynn Peachy

With George and Kitty Thompson

On the left Alice Tingler, in the center Tina Notorangelo,
on the right Rosalie and Luis Giordano.

From left, Emily and Stan Kaplan, Helen and Christine Ridgeway.

EPILOGUE

It has not been easy to put my personal history in writing. In fact, I have often been so overwhelmed with emotions that several times, I was compelled to stop my work for weeks and sometimes for months. Going back to certain periods of my life, it was like reliving the past all over again, and my eyes were unable to control the tears.

The best time for my recollections was in the early morning hours and during the long solitary walks in the Myrtle Trace community. It was amazing how clear my mind was in remembering the old times so well to the point that I could not believe myself and what had happened to me in the course of so many years. Occasionally, when I had blurred memories, I searched out pictures in my photo album for help. Of course, there were times when I considered stopping my writing indefinitely, but then again, in my life, I have never been a quitter. Once I started something, I have to finish it.

At this point, I am wondering about my long life's journey, and I cannot explain how it all happened—from a destitute Sicilian child to a very accomplished and happy woman in America. That is really an unbelievable story, although I consider myself fortunate because in the darkest times, many events were gradually falling into place, and each event played a big part in my life. In my opinion, without a doubt, the invisible power of God and the Virgin Mary was inspiring and protecting me all the way.

After the death of Andrew, difficult as it was, writing down my life story was like a prodigious therapy for me. Furthermore, all of a sudden, the urge to go to Italy to be with family members had certainly been God's plan because the outcome of the trips, especially of the second one, had magical effect on me. I returned to the USA as a different person, relaxed, more at peace with myself, and ready to face life as part of my natural journey.

Certainly, my life without my beloved Andrew will never be the same as grief will be part of my living, and even so, I can say: "better to have loved and lost, than never to have loved at all".

FAMILY TREE CHART

My Family Tree

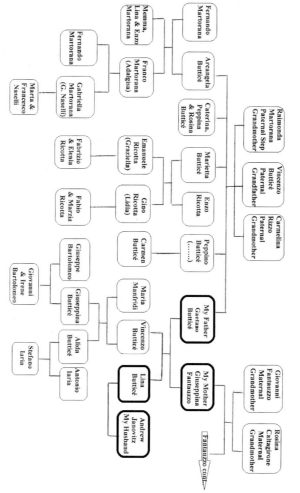

In parenthesis are the spouses

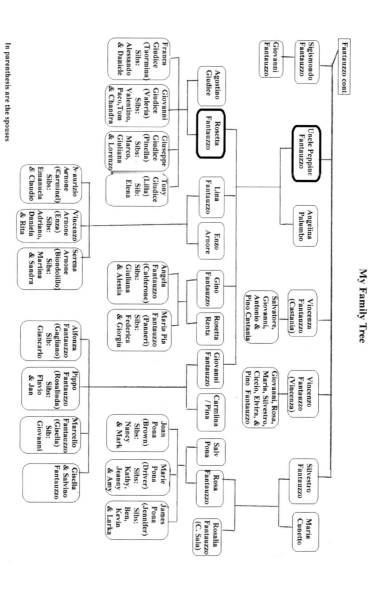

My Family Tree

In parenthesis are the spouses

Fantauzzo coni

Giovanni Fantauzzo

Sigismondo Fantauzzo

Agostino Giudice

Rosetta Fantauzzo

Franca Giudice (Taormina) Sibs: Alessando & Daniele

Giovanni Giudice ('Valeria) Sibs: Valentino, Paco, Tom & Chandra

Giuseppe Giudice (Pinella) Sibs: Marco, Giuliana & Lorenzo

Tony Giudice (Lilla) Sib: Elena

Uncle Peppine Fantauzzo

Angelina Palumbo

Vincenza Fantauzzo (Castania)

Salvatore, Giovanni, Antonio & Pino Castania

Lina Fantauzzo

Enzo Arnore

Maurizio Arnone (Carmine) Sibs: Emanuela & Claudio

Vincenzo Arnone (Enza) Sibs: Adriano, Daniela & Rita

Serena Arnone (Biondolillo) Sibs: Martina & Sandra

Gino Fantauzzo

Rosetta Renta

Angela Fantauzzo (Calderone) Sibs: Giuliana & Alessia

Maria Pia Fantauzzo (Panneri) Sibs: Federica & Giorgia

Giovanni Fantauzzo

Carmlina / Pina

Alfonza Fantauzzo (Gagliano) Sib: Giancarlo

Pippo Fantauzzo (Rosalinda) Sibs: Flavio & Jan

Marcello Fantauzzo (Gisella) Sib: Giovanni

Gisella & Salvino Fantauzzo

Vincenzo Fantauzzo (Vincenza)

Giovanni, Rosa, Maria, Silvestro, Ciccio, Elvira, & Pino Fantauzzo

Joan Pona (Brown) Sibs: Nancy & Mark

Marie Pona (Driver) Sibs: Kathy, Jeanny & Amy

James Pona (Jennifer) Sibs: Ben, Kevin & Larka

Salv Pona

Rosa Fantauzzo

Silvestro Fantauzzo

Maria Cunetto

Rosalia Fantauzzo (C. Sala)

338